This collection of essays on Vaughan Williams, the first major body of new research on the composer to appear for many years, brings together leading British and American scholars and covers a wide range of topics and approaches, exploring musical language, cultural context, biography, manuscript sources, and reception history. Despite Vaughan Williams's seminal importance in British music, international stature as a symphonist, and wider significance as an icon of Englishness, very little new research on his life or music has been published since the mid-1960s. The ten essays presented here, some of which draw on sources that are either newly discovered or have never been discussed before, examine diverse subjects such as the place of Vaughan Williams in the construction of English national identity this century, the role of rhythm in his symphonies, music for propaganda films, and his unpublished early orchestral pieces; major works such as the Tallis Fantasia and the Fifth Symphony are analysed in depth.

VAUGHAN WILLIAMS STUDIES

Vaughan Williams Studies

EDITED BY ALAIN FROGLEY

 CAMBRIDGE
UNIVERSITY PRESS

CAMBRIDGE UNIVERSITY PRESS
Cambridge, New York, Melbourne, Madrid, Cape Town, Singapore, São Paulo, Delhi

Cambridge University Press
The Edinburgh Building, Cambridge CB2 8RU, UK

Published in the United States of America by Cambridge University Press, New York

www.cambridge.org
Information on this title: www.cambridge.org/9780521480314

© Cambridge University Press 1996

First published 1996
This digitally printed version 2008

A catalogue record for this publication is available from the British Library

ISBN 978-0-521-48031-4 hardback
ISBN 978-0-521-08864-0 paperback

Contents

Plates

Bibliographic abbreviations
and score references

Throughout this book the core literature on Vaughan Williams is referred to using abbreviations as follow:

Kennedy, *Works*: Michael Kennedy, *The Works of Ralph Vaughan Williams*, 2nd rev. edn (London: Oxford University Press, 1980)

Kennedy, *Catalogue*: Michael Kennedy, *Catalogue of the Works of Ralph Vaughan Williams*, 2nd rev. edn (London: Oxford University Press, 1982)

R. Vaughan Williams, *National Music*: Ralph Vaughan Williams, *National Music and Other Essays*, 2nd rev. edn (Oxford: Oxford University Press, 1987)

R. Vaughan Williams and G. Holst, *Heirs*: Ralph Vaughan Williams and Gustav Holst, *Heirs and Rebels: Letters Written to Each Other and Occasional Writings on Music by Ralph Vaughan Williams and Gustav Holst*, ed. Ursula Vaughan Williams and Imogen Holst (London: Oxford University Press, 1959)

U. Vaughan Williams, *R.V.W.*: Ursula Vaughan Williams, *R.V.W.: A Biography of Ralph Vaughan Williams* (London: Oxford University Press, 1964)

The two volumes by Michael Kennedy represent a subdivision and revision of the author's original one-volume study *The Works of Ralph Vaughan Williams* (London: Oxford University Press, 1964). *National Music and Other Essays* remains the most accessible source of writings by the composer; citing it poses several problems of chronology, however, as the collection constitutes a volume of selected (certainly not complete) writings spanning some fifty years, some of which have been reprinted a number of times, some of which appear, in the 1987 edition, for the first time outside the organs that originally published them. References to individual essays will include the original date and other details of publication where specifically relevant to the matter at hand; this information can also be found in Peter Starbuck's 'Bibliography of the Literary Writings of Ralph Vaughan Williams' that appears in Kennedy's 1964 volume, and, in slightly expanded form, in Kennedy, *Catalogue.*

Dates of composition and first performance are taken from Kennedy, *Catalogue,* unless otherwise stated. References to specific passages in Vaughan Williams scores use bar numbers for shorter pieces such as songs, and subdivided rehearsal numbers or letters for longer works such as the symphonies, e.g. '4.1' is equivalent to 'the bar at Figure 4', '4.2' two bars after Figure 4, 'C.7' seven bars after Letter C and so on; note, however, that the bars *before the first rehearsal number/letter* are referred to by bar numbers alone, e.g. 'bars 1-6'. References to works by earlier composers such as Mozart and Brahms use bar numbers.

Preface

Vaughan Williams is universally acknowledged as a seminal figure in the development of British music and in the history of musical nationalism. He is recognized as an orchestral composer of international stature. His music has a wide appeal; in this corner of the USA, hardly a day goes by without the local public radio station broadcasting one or more of his works. In broad terms of cultural identity, his music and person have played a significant role in defining one particularly influential version of what it means to be English. Yet when I first began Vaughan Williams research some ten years ago, the possibility of bringing together a book of this kind seemed to belong strictly to the realms of futuristic fantasy. With barely a handful of exceptions,[1] no substantial writing on Vaughan Williams had appeared in print since the authorized life and works volumes were published in the mid-1960s,[2] a few years after the composer's death. In the academic sector there was a clutch of American masters' dissertations, and a few British counterparts, but not a single Ph.D. on either side of the Atlantic. Precious little work seemed to be in progress. Remarkably, what research there was

---

[1] Most notably Hugh Ottaway's brief but perceptive *Vaughan Williams Symphonies*, BBC Music Guides (London: British Broadcasting Corporation, 1972), and the same author's entry on Vaughan Williams for the *New Grove* (*The New Grove Dictionary of Music and Musicians*, 20 vols. (London and New York: Macmillan, 1980), vol. XIX, pp. 569–80). The only substantial monograph to appear during this period was, somewhat ironically, in German – Lutz-Werner Hesse's *Studien zum Schaffen des Komponisten Ralph Vaughan Williams*, Kölner Beiträge zur Musikforschung 134 (Regensburg: Gustav Bosse Verlag, 1983). Despite their critical acumen, none of these writings involved significant new research into musical or biographical sources or background. The only major contributions of this kind dealt with the composer's folksong collecting; see Roy Palmer, ed., *Folksongs Collected By Ralph Vaughan Williams* (London: J. M. Dent and sons, 1983), and Rosamund Strode's cataloguing work discussed in Chapter 6, n. 7 of the present volume.

[2] Ursula Vaughan Williams, *R. V. W.: A Biography of Ralph Vaughan Williams* (London: Oxford University Press, 1964); and Michael Kennedy, *The Works of Ralph Vaughan Williams* (London: Oxford University Press, 1964).

had left the enormous autograph manuscript collection in the British Library virtually untouched. Even the record catalogue was dominated by material from the 1960s and early 1970s. I received much encouragement in my work, and many clearly felt that it was time for a reappraisal of Vaughan Williams – but the harvest was potentially huge and the workers very few.

A decade on, the landscape looks markedly different. With that curious synchronicity that seems so often to characterize cultural phenomena, around the mid-1980s a fresh interest in Vaughan Williams research and performance began to emerge independently from a variety of different directions, a movement which gathered pace in the first half of the 1990s. One important practical stimulus was the establishment in 1985 of a fellowship, offered by the Carthusian Trust and Charterhouse School, which enables American and Canadian scholars to spend time in Britain working on Vaughan Williams projects. Two contributors to this volume, Byron Adams and Julian Onderdonk, are former holders of the award (Byron Adams was the very first), and it continues to facilitate a steady flow of new research. The boom in the recording industry that followed the advent of the compact disc, which has made accessible so many neglected areas of repertory, has paid handsome dividends for Vaughan Williams (although much remains to be done in this area). Works such as *Hugh the Drover* and *The Pilgrim's Progress* have re-entered the catalogue with both old and new recordings, several new cycles of the symphonies have been recorded, and examples of traditionally ephemeral genres such as film scores and radio incidental music have found a home on disc.[3] Several new books have appeared, including Wilfrid Mellers's major study and a Garland Research Guide devoted to Vaughan Williams, and more are set to appear.[4]

[3] Naxos have recently begun a large-scale recording project involving Vaughan Williams's film music. In the realm of orchestral works, the advocacy of conductors from outside Britain, particularly Leonard Slatkin, Bernard Haitink, and Gennadi Rozhdestvensky, has been a particularly significant development.

[4] Wilfrid Mellers, *Vaughan Williams and the Vision of Albion* (London: Barrie & Jenkins, 1989); Neil Butterworth, *Ralph Vaughan Williams: A Guide to Research* (New York: Garland, 1990). Butterworth's guide is useful in many respects but has severe shortcomings: see my review in *Music and Letters*, 72 (1991), pp. 308–10. At the time of writing, a similar guide, by Alison McFarland, is shortly to be published by Scolar Press; also in preparation are a new book on the symphonies by Lionel Pike and a monograph on the sketches for the Ninth Symphony by the present author.

Significantly, important work relating to primary sources is in progress or at the planning stage, including Hugh Cobbe's edition of the composer's correspondence, and a critical edition of selected works, some previously unpublished.

But it would be premature to interpret such positive signs as a fully fledged revival, and important questions remain; above all, why the long neglect, and why the current thaw? While the full answers to such questions, if recoverable at all, are bound to be complex, I believe that certain elements in the equation can now be identified with relative confidence, and that they are symptomatic of forces that go well beyond the reception of this particular composer. One central factor in the rise and fall of Vaughan Williams's critical fortunes has been his co-option to the narrow image of English national identity – parochial, pastoral, and emotionally reticent, if not repressed – that predominated for so much of this century (I shall have more to say on this in my chapter below). But international trends have also been influential, and here recent developments have proved particularly favourable to Vaughan Williams. The last decade has seen an extraordinary breakdown of musical and musicological hegemonies, paralleled, of course, by a comparable fragmentation of established models of authority in society at large. In the area of 'serious' music, one of the most striking developments has been the final dethroning of the idea (already much weakened by the rise of minimalism and neo-romanticism in the 1970s), that avant-garde modernism is ultimately the highest path to which new music can aspire, and of the historical scaffolding that went with that, namely, a master-narrative of musical evolution centred on the Stravinsky – Schoenberg axis. This narrative marginalized a whole host of composers and national traditions, especially those maintaining an explicit allegiance to a traditional conception of tonality, however broadly conceived: its erosion has led to a reassessment of many different composers, both living and dead, whose work was deemed unacceptably reactionary in the 1960s and 70s, ranging from Franz Schreker and Erich Korngold to Howard Hanson and Jonathan Lloyd. And as younger figures such as John Adams and John Tavener have begun to exploit tonal harmony, memorable melodic materials, and opulent orchestral sounds with fresh confidence, and even Pierre Boulez, the doyen of post-war modernism, begins to re-admit tonal elements into his music,[5] so the map of earlier twentieth-century music has begun to take on different perspectives. Furthermore, as the boundaries of serious and popular music have become more and more blurred, and the label of 'accessible' has ceased necessarily to be a stigma for the contemporary composer, so the stars of figures such as Copland and Vaughan Williams have begun to rise again. As with the break-up of the Soviet bloc, not all the results of this fragmented pluralism have been welcome, and the driving forces have sometimes seemed more commercial than artistic, not least in the crude stylistic pigeon-holing so beloved of marketing executives. Nevertheless, we have surely been hearing in the last few years a far wider range of composers than ever before, and of musical styles and philosophies.

The world of musical scholarship has both reflected and helped to shape these trends, not least by reflexively examining the biases enshrined in its own apparently disinterested narratives of music history. But perhaps the most important development has been a widespread re-engagement with a theme on which Vaughan Williams preached throughout his long life: the impossibility of separating music from people, the necessity of relating music to the social conditions in which it arises.[6] True, he would no doubt have been out of sympathy with some of the directions research of this kind has recently taken. Yet current preoccupations with the idea of music as a language of social signification, with cultural history, issues of reception, and the roles of gender, race, and nationality in shaping discourse about music, have set the stage for a reappraisal of Vaughan Williams that goes well beyond a simple revival of scholarly interest and an increase in the number of performances and CDs. Simply put, there now exists the right climate in which to grapple head-on with the neglect of recent decades, and to attempt to understand this in a wider cultural context:

[5] See, for instance, Gavin Thomas's discussion of the apparent softening of Boulez's attitudes in 'Work Not in Progress', *The Musical Times*, 136, no. 1827 (May 1995), pp. 225–9. It is worth noting also that a conception of rhythm more traditionalist than Boulez had previously allowed himself to embrace surfaced earlier in the decade at important points of *Répons*.

[6] For a useful introduction to recent thinking in this area see Philip V. Bohlman, 'Viewpoint: On the Unremarkable in Music', *19th-Century Music*, 16 (1992), pp. 203–16; Bohlman's essay was part of a special issue of this journal entitled 'Music in its Social Contexts'.

however complex the phenomenon may be, it is no accident. As I shall argue in the opening chapter of this volume, Vaughan Williams's reputation has been distorted – at times blighted – not only by the international musical politics of this century, but to an even greater degree by the special ideological tensions of Britain's long decline as a world power; developments both in musicology and in the humanities as a whole place us in a better position than ever before to understand this phenomenon. And the central issues involved remain with us still, both in responses to Vaughan Williams and well beyond, as Britain agonizes over its relationship to the rest of Europe, and across the globe questions of cultural identity become ever more explosive. Indeed, Vaughan Williams offers an unusually rich field of study for anyone interested in the place of art in the politics of national identity, and the complex interplay between the individual artist and the community in which he or she works.

In planning the present volume, then, it seemed important that the nationalism 'problem' be analysed rather than merely set aside, and that questions of social and cultural context be given detailed attention. In addition to my own contribution, four other chapters deal in one way or another with such issues, but all from very different angles. Jeffrey Richards brings his expertise in film history and the shaping of a British national self-image to bear on Vaughan Williams's contribution to wartime propaganda films. Drawing on the composer's letters, Hugh Cobbe examines Vaughan Williams's attitudes to the German musical tradition, the benchmark against which every composer of his generation had to define him- or herself. Julian Onderdonk examines the assumptions underlying Vaughan Williams's folksong collecting, a crucial element in the composer's vision of his own musical heritage, and reveals how these informed the most minute issues of transcription. Byron Adams traces the development of Vaughan Williams's spiritual outlook, and the manner in which this intertwined with his nationalist concerns, from the perspective of the intellectual milieu in which the composer grew up.

Yet giving due weight to reception history and contemporary contexts should not divert us from advancing our understanding of Vaughan Williams's works in terms of more intra-musical concerns. One may well argue that detailed musical analysis should ultimately be grounded in historical and social context; but the argument can also be turned around the other way, that context is of scant use without a sophisticated understanding of text. Vaughan Williams's music has received little close analysis of any sort. This has undoubtedly fuelled the dogged persistence of fundamental misconceptions: indeed, some of the critical clichés that have grown up around the composer cannot stand the test of even a rudimentary examination of his scores. Here again the time is opportune. The methodologies that came to dominate music analysis in the 1960s and 70s, in particular the strict application of Schenkerian methods and of set theory, were ill suited to music that diverged from the norms of tonal practice up to Brahms, but which did not espouse full-blown atonality. The more pluralistic climate that has characterized music theory during the last few years has brought an interest in extending existing methods, and in developing new ones, to embrace the large amount of music from Debussy to Reich that treats tonal materials in non-traditional ways; and also in paying close attention to parameters other than pitch relations. Such developments are reflected in the three analytical contributions to *Vaughan Williams Studies*, all of which break important ground for future work in this area. Anthony Pople adopts a variety of different approaches, as well as evidence from the autograph manuscript, in his study of Vaughan Williams's first undoubted masterpiece, the *Fantasia on a Theme by Thomas Tallis*. Lionel Pike concentrates on the composer's use of rhythm, that Cinderella of the musical elements, as a structural force in three of the symphonies. Tonality is back centre-stage in Arnold Whittall's essay on the Fifth Symphony, but as a problematic element whose instability seems inevitably to throw open the extra-musical dimension, and the question of meaning in instrumental music.

This last topic stands at the centre of Oliver Neighbour's panoramic essay, in which Vaughan Williams's far-reaching growth as a symphonist, and with it his philosophy of musical expression, is reassessed as a backdrop to the specific case of the Eighth, the composer's penultimate work in the genre. At the other end of the composer's career, Michael Vaillancourt examines Vaughan Williams's early formation as a composer of orchestral music, surveying the important legacy of substantial and largely unpublished orchestral works that preceded the composer's first symphony. This is one of a number of essays that draws heavily on the collection of the composer's autograph scores and sketches now in the British Library, and it serves as a vivid reminder of just how much basic research remains to be done on many areas of the composer's life and music, and on the surviving sources of his work – this despite the pioneering and invaluable efforts of Michael Kennedy and Ursula Vaughan Williams. And, along with Jeffrey Richards's account of the film music and with a number of other essays here, Vaillancourt's study underlines both the size and variety of Vaughan Williams's extraordinary output. In many ways, the work of Vaughan Williams research has only just begun.

Many people have helped to make this book possible. My thanks go in particular to Penny Souster, Oliver Neighbour, and Stephen Banfield for encouragement and advice, especially in the initial planning stages; to colleagues at Lancaster University and latterly the University of Connecticut; to the staff of the British Library; to the University of Connecticut Research Foundation, which awarded me a summer fellowship to work on the project and funded a research assistant; and to Sean Flanagan, who assisted so ably on many fronts, and well beyond the call of duty. Thanks are due also to Oxford University Press for allowing quotation from Vaughan Williams's published music and writings; and to Ursula Vaughan Williams for permission to quote and reproduce extracts from the composer's manuscripts – a gesture entirely characteristic of the generosity that Mrs Vaughan Williams has shown over many years to countless admirers of her husband's music, from specialist scholar to enthusiastic amateur.

Alain Frogley

Storrs, Connecticut, September 1995

xvii

1 Constructing Englishness in music: national character and the reception of Ralph Vaughan Williams

ALAIN FROGLEY

Mention the name Ralph Vaughan Williams and into most people's minds come immediately three words: English, pastoral, and folksong. Few composers produce quite such a strong reflex action. Musicologists for a long time deemed such phenomena as lying beyond the scholarly pale; now, taking a Freudian lead from colleagues in other disciplines, we have begun to realize that unreflective reactions of this kind can be analysed in a respectable intellectual framework, and that they can often tell us a great deal about the ideological substrata on which our view of the musical world is built. Of course, the popular image of nearly every composer involves distortion and over-simplification. Yet when the image arouses reflex reactions that almost invariably carry an aura of adverse criticism,[1] as is the case with Vaughan Williams, we should feel under a degree of obligation to examine them more closely. And where they also run counter to some very salient evidence, available to most informed listeners on just one moment's reflection beyond the knee-jerk response – in the case of Vaughan Williams, how can the composer of the Fourth and Sixth symphonies, say, or the favourite pupil of Ravel, possibly be summed up with those three words? – that obligation hardens to duty.

It is common enough for advocates of Vaughan Williams to

---

[1] So well established are the pejorative critical traditions that surround Vaughan Williams that Michael Oliver felt it natural to make them the backbone of a programme on the composer in Oliver's BBC Radio 3 series 'Soundings', first broadcast 8 March 1992. The programme countered effectively such notions as Vaughan Williams's supposed amateurishness of technique and the lack of interest in his music outside England; perhaps inevitably in a feature of this kind, however, there was no attempt to analyse the wider context of the composer's distorted reception.

1

bemoan the crudely simplistic terms in which this complex and multi-faceted composer is often viewed. Yet the roots of this problem have traditionally been attributed to causes either widely general or narrowly personal in scope – the slump in reputation that so often follows a composer's death, for instance, or an inevitable reaction against the enormous acclaim that Vaughan Williams enjoyed during his lifetime. These factors have undoubtedly played their part. Yet we need to look further; for example, what was the basis of the composer's great popularity that made a reaction likely, if not inevitable? And, why did much of the mythology surrounding Vaughan Williams first develop while the composer was alive and prominently in the public eye, rather than in the years after his death?

The obvious place to start, of course, is with the issue of nationalism. And here the historical ground has recently been well fertilized, not so much by musicologists as by scholars in cognate disciplines.[2] During the last decade or so historians, literary critics, and others have published a wealth of important new work on nationalism, particularly in its more covert manifestations, and this has profound implications for music. Some of the most interesting work has been on British history between about 1880 and 1945, a period that covers the zenith of Great Britain's world dominance as an imperial power.[3] Yet while music has not been ignored in this research, it has still to be treated in any depth, and there has

----

[2] The role of discourses of gender in music and musicology has rightly been receiving a good deal of attention of late. Constructions of national identity – which, if less fundamental than those of gender, are nevertheless crucial to the definition of self and other – have yet to be given sustained emphasis by the 'new musicology', although there have been some striking individual contributions; perhaps to some extent, ironically, because explicit nationalism, however loosely conceived, has always loomed large even in traditional narratives of music history and historiography.

[3] Of central importance to the present discussion is *Englishness: Politics and Culture 1880–1920*, ed. Robert Colls and Philip Dodd (London: Croom Helm, 1986). See also *Patriotism: The Making and Unmaking of British National Identity*, ed. Raphael Samuel, 3 vols. (London and New York: Routledge, 1989), especially vol. III, *National Fictions*; and *Myths of the English*, ed. Roy Porter (Cambridge: Blackwell, 1992). A landmark volume for this whole area of research is *The Invention of Tradition*, ed. Eric Hobsbawm and Terence Ranger (Cambridge: Cambridge University Press, 1983); see in particular Chaps. 1 and 7, both by Hobsbawm.

been little detailed reference to Vaughan Williams.[4] Furthermore, musicologists concerned with the British scene have so far paid almost no attention to such new thinking; the writings that exist have emanated largely from scholars trained in other disciplines, and the results have been very mixed.[5] This history is still being lived and musicologists' neglect of such questions is part of the wider paucity until late of serious scholarly investigation into British twentieth-century music, a deficiency

[4] The most extended discussion of a musical topic in the above volumes is Jeremy Crump, 'The Identity of English Music: The Reception of Elgar 1898–1935', in *Englishness: Politics and Culture 1880–1920*, pp. 164–90. Alun Howkins refers to musical developments in his contribution to the same volume, 'The Discovery of Rural England', pp. 62–88; a number of points arising from this form the starting point for the same author's brief essay 'Greensleeves and the Idea of National Music', in *Patriotism: The Making and Unmaking of British National Identity*, III, pp. 89–98, which includes some useful remarks about Vaughan Williams's orchestral fantasia on the 'Greensleeves' tune. See also Robert Stradling, 'On Shearing the Black Sheep in Spring: The Repatriation of Frederick Delius', in *Music and the Politics of Culture*, ed. Christopher Norris (London: Lawrence and Wishart, 1989), pp. 69–105.

[5] The most substantial example of the latter has appeared recently, in the form of a book by historians Robert Stradling and Meirion Hughes, entitled *The English Musical Renaissance 1860–1940: Construction and Deconstruction* (London and New York: Routledge, 1993). Although the authors independently arrive at a number of the same broader observations offered in the present essay, their treatment of Vaughan Williams is tendentious and misguided; and while portions of their study represent a significant contribution to the field, much of it is profoundly flawed, merely skating the surface of many of the more important issues, peppering its argument with half-truths, and inexplicably failing to take account of some of the most pertinent recent research on British nationalism. More successful, although in musical terms much narrower in focus, is Georgina Boyes, *The Imagined Village: Culture, Ideology and the English Folk Revival* (Manchester: Manchester University Press, 1993), which appeared at almost exactly the same time as the Stradling and Hughes book; Boyes makes no attempt to deal with art music, concentrating instead on the social context and impact of the folk-music revival up to the present day. It must be said, though, that Boyes too is unsatisfactory on Vaughan Williams: she fails to appreciate the complexity of his attitude to folksong, treating his views as simply an extension of those of Cecil Sharp (which they were not, as I shall suggest below). For a perceptive review of both these books see Calum Macdonald, 'The Chauvinistic Lark', *Times Literary Supplement*, 5 November 1993, pp. 3–4. Julian Onderdonk explores current attitudes to the folksong revival and Vaughan Williams's place within that in his contribution to the present volume.

3

which, as I shall suggest later, is at least partly due to the confused ideological legacy of earlier nationalistic debates. This affects British musicologists especially deeply, but its influence is also strong outside the native shores; and there neglect is reinforced by the bias of most writing on twentieth-century music history towards the modernistic Stravinsky – Schoenberg axis, a bias which has left most major British composers, along with many others, out in the cold.

Yet if scholars of Western music decide to devote sustained attention to the cultural politics of nationalism and imperialism, they will need to give close consideration to the British scene around the turn of the century: here is a case-history of music situated at an unusually crucial position in the ideological fault-lines of an imperial power *par excellence*. And the composer nearest to the epicentre was and is Ralph Vaughan Williams. Not only must Vaughan Williams occupy an important place in any discussion of English national identity in music; to turn the equation around, I believe that the reception of Vaughan Williams's music has been blighted by broader cultural forces, in particular by tensions in the national self-image, and that an understanding of these is essential if we are to achieve a more accurate assessment of his overall achievement, and a less prejudiced response to his music.[6] It must be borne in mind, however, that distortions of this kind are common enough in matters nationalistic: to quote an aphoristic translation of the words of the French historian Ernest Renan, 'Getting its history wrong is part of being a nation'.[7]

As a preliminary step towards understanding the process of distortion affecting Vaughan Williams, I shall address here three related issues: (1) the nature and limitations of the current associations of the label 'nationalist' as applied to Vaughan Williams; (2) how this label has evolved over the years; and (3) its links with broader constructions of English

---

[6] That Elgar's reputation has also suffered such a blight, but for different reasons, has long been accepted; see, for instance, Crump, 'The Identity of English Music'.

[7] E. J. Hobsbawm, *Nations and Nationalism since 1780: Programme, Myth, Reality* (Cambridge: Cambridge University Press, 1990), p. 12. Renan's original statement, dating from 1882 and given by Hobsbawm in a footnote, was less pithy: 'L'oubli et je dirai même l'erreur historique, sont un facteur essentiel de la formation d'une nation et c'est ainsi que le progrès des études historiques est souvent pour la nationalité un danger'.

national identity in the twentieth century.[8] Given the complexity of the issues involved, the discussion will, inevitably, often take the form of notes to future research.

*

At its simplest level, Vaughan Williams's reputation as a nationalist composer is based on four overlapping elements: his published writings arguing the importance of national roots for musical styles; work as a collector, arranger, and editor of native folksongs and hymn-tunes; educational and administrative activity as a teacher, competition adjudicator etc.; and the manifold influence on his music of a variety of English musical, literary, and other kinds of sources, above all folksong, Tudor and Jacobean music, and English literature of the sixteenth and seventeenth centuries, most notably the King James Bible and Shakespeare. But other, more shadowy, identifications have arguably played an even greater role in shaping the composer's image, especially in filtering the more straightforward elements of his nationalism, and in determining the emphasis given to different parts of his output. Almost invariably, Vaughan Williams's music has been deemed to reflect essential features of the English national character, of the English landscape, and of the English language. And Vaughan Williams the man, not least his commitment to society at large, and the practical nature of much of his activity, has also tended to acquire emblematic status. The power of such

[8] I shall make no attempt here to trace what Carl Dahlhaus has described as the 'immutable ethnomusical component' which investigations of musical nationalism have often sought to identify (*Nineteenth-Century Music*, trans. J. Bradford Robinson, California Studies in Nineteenth Century Music no. 4 (Berkeley and Los Angeles: University of California Press, 1989), p. 40). Whether or not such components exist, they are notoriously hard to pin down, and, as Dahlhaus suggests, the historian is better advised to concentrate instead on functional aspects of musical nationalism (in this context see also Dahlhaus's essay on nationalism in *Between Romanticism and Modernism: Four Studies in the Music of the Later Nineteenth Century*, trans. Mary Whittall (Berkeley and Los Angeles: University of California Press, 1980)). I should also add that I am not seeking to reconstruct a kind of 'Ur-Vaughan-Williams', free of all ideological additives: such a figure never existed. But there are, of course, many different degrees of ideological distortion and of awareness of one's involvement in such processes.

identifications derives from the way in which they tap into wider currents of the national self-image. But the current flows in both directions. Facets of Vaughan Williams's character and music have helped to focus and, in turn, to mould some of the most influential perceptions of what it means to be English.[9]

The most enduring example of this process, and of its potentially negative consequences, has been the association of Vaughan Williams's music with the English landscape, and with the genre of the pastoral. Television, film, and radio, such crucial media in modern image-making, offer frequent reinforcement of the link; a special favourite is *The Lark Ascending*, composed in 1914, to which a whole documentary programme was devoted recently on BBC Radio 4.[10] A work such as this is considered by many to epitomize a particularly English experience of the natural world, by extension a species of national spiritual experience, that had never before been expressed with such immediacy. For others, the picture is rather different: the 'cowpat school' sobriquet sometimes applied to Vaughan Williams and his disciples is rarely used more positively than as an expression of indulgent affection, as if for a senile elderly relative or a half-witted country cousin; more often it is a term of derision. Not that this is a denial of the 'Englishness' of such music. On the contrary: it represents, I believe, a profound uneasiness, more often implicit than explicit, with specific aspects of the English national self-image of this century, an uneasiness which takes us to the heart of the cultural forces acting on the reception of Vaughan Williams, the origins of which we must now explore.

The period *c.* 1880–1950 is generally seen by historians as the high summer – or perhaps darkest winter, in view of its belligerent consequences – of nationalism; the term itself did not emerge until the end of the nineteenth century (although the roots of many national movements

---

[9] Except in the case of folksong I shall not attempt here to disentangle the complex and problematic issues surrounding distinctions between English and British national identity, the apparently casual blurring of which has important political implications.

[10] First broadcast 18 May 1992, as a special edition of the arts programme *Kaleidoscope*.

that came to prominence around this time go back much further, of course).[11] Despite the dramatic proliferation of new nation-states in the aftermath of World War I, and the ensuing ascendancy of right-wing national movements, the pre-war period was if anything more momentous, as it saw the profound transformation in the concept of nationalism that made post-war developments possible. Crucial to this transformation was that for the first time ethnicity and language became the core elements of identification for existing nations, and, in like manner, that ethnic minorities within established nations increasingly came to see independence in new nation-states as the only honourable aspiration for them to entertain. Similarly, although musical nationalism is an important force throughout the nineteenth century, it becomes most colourful towards the end of this period, with a proliferation of distinctive national schools, of which one of the latest to emerge is the English. Leon Plantinga expresses the traditional understanding of the roots of nineteenth-century nationalism in the arts, and of the reasons for which England did not fit the general mould, when he writes:

> The usual factors in the growth of cultural nationalism – status as a developing nation, struggle against a foreign oppressor, feelings of cultural inferiority – were of course lacking in England. It was mainly in a quickening of interest in the 'Celtic fringes' that certain nationalist traits appeared in music, and this occurred only late in the century.[12]

And when commentators discuss the English musical nationalism that finally emerged in the twentieth century, it is seen as a sort of cultural icing-on-the-cake: a pre-eminently powerful and confident nation belatedly

---

[11] The literature on nationalism is vast. Hobsbawm's *Nations and Nationalism since 1780* is an excellent introduction to the phenomenon for the period under discussion; see also the same author's *The Age of Empire 1875–1914* (New York: Pantheon Books, 1987), Chap. 6. Most books on nationalism, including Hobsbawm's, make no more than passing reference to music. It is interesting to note, however, that, whereas the *New Grove Dictionary* has no entry at all for nationalism (this situation will be remedied in the revised version currently in preparation), the *Encyclopaedia Britannica* considers musical nationalism worthy of its own entry, with all other subdivisions of the topic grouped under a single heading.

[12] *Romantic Music* (New York: Norton, 1984), p. 400.

7

adds distinctive musical creativity to its undoubted excellence in other areas of artistic endeavour.[13]

In fact, although in the last quarter of the nineteenth century Britain was still enormously powerful, and continuing to assert its cultural values, grave doubts about the future were beginning to set in. One manifestation of this was the search for reassurance and inspiration in previous golden ages of the nation's history, the Elizabethan era in particular. Although such concerns obviously had a passive and inward-looking side, they could also be turned to active and positive effect, as recent scholarship has shown.[14] With the growth of military and economic competition abroad (most notably from Germany and the United States), the need to hold together an expanding empire, and social and political unrest at home, a perception began to develop amongst the ruling classes that, for British pre-eminence to be maintained, there would need to be a deliberate fostering of national identity and solidarity, and an associated promotion of certain moral and social qualities. These qualities were for the most part considered to be those of the countryside, particularly in so far as this embodied an idealized English past, as against the corrupting influences of the modern city: both Tudor and rural England offered an antidote to the ills of urbanization and industrialization, which threatened to undermine nation and empire.[15]

[13] The idea of 'lateness' figures prominently in much writing on English twentieth-century music. Donald Mitchell puts the point forcefully when he writes, 'For English music, such was its curious historical predicament, had to relive its past if it were ever to secure a future. It had, as it were, to start all over again' (*The Language of Modern Music* (London: Faber, 1963), pp. 109–10, n. 2). Elsewhere in the same book Mitchell asserts, 'It is a strange but undeniable fact that a time-lag seems to operate, whereby English composers often come late – and fresh – to a language that elsewhere may already have grown tired' (p. 132).

[14] See the volumes cited in n. 3, especially *Englishness: Politics and Culture 1880–1920, passim.*

[15] See Howkins, 'The Discovery of Rural England', pp. 70–1; and Brian Doyle, 'The Invention of English', in *Englishness: Politics and Culture 1880–1920*, pp. 89–115, especially 89–91. Howkins makes a point with important ramifications for music, namely that, 'Tudor England was not the period in which England was ruled by the Tudor dynasty, 1485–1603, rather it was a construction based on the later years of the reign of Elizabeth, lasting until the 1680s but with gaps, especially the 1650s'. This definition of 'Tudor' embraces the whole period from Tallis to Purcell, and thus all the older English music that was to exert such a powerful influence on the twentieth-century renaissance. The roots of an idealized vision of the country go back a long way: see Raymond Williams's

It was against this background that English musical nationalism emerged. It became essential to have music that not only could hold its head up against that of competitor nations, but which could do so in a way that was overtly English, which clearly projected aspects of the national character; links with rural folksong and with Tudor music were the ideal purveyors of Englishness in such a context.[16] At one level this is obviously a simplistic formulation. Yet it is remarkable just how closely parallel, in both dates and dialectic, musical and broader cultural and political trends can be seen to run, as is suggested by a reading of cultural historian Alun Howkins's essay 'The Discovery of Rural England'. To take but one example: the period *c.* 1890–1914 saw a number of landmarks in the revival of interest in Tudor music, such as the first appearance in print of the Fitzwilliam Virginal Book, and the establishment of the Cobbett composition prize, which stipulated the use of Tudor models in newly composed chamber music; in architecture of the same period, to quote Howkins, 'English taste, whether for domestic building or for show, had become all but synonymous with the "Tudor"'.[17] Howkins makes significant reference to music in his wide-ranging discussion, but all his points bear amplification. One is struck, for instance, by the fact that English folksong should be 'discovered' at this precise historical moment, it having been long assumed that, unlike their Scottish or Welsh neighbours, the English had no native folk music. The standard literature generally sees this as a sign of a wider musical inferiority complex, and of the low status accorded to music in Victorian society; conversely, the discovery of folk music is taken to be an early symptom of the English musical renaissance. There is no doubt a good deal of truth to this interpretation, and many factors must have played their part, including an English Romantic tradition going back to Wordsworth and nurtured by such influential figures as John Ruskin and William Morris (one thinks, for instance, of Ruskin's concern for the use of natural materials in building, which offers an analogy,

classic study *The Country and the City* (London: Oxford University Press, 1973); W. J. Keith, *The Rural Tradition: A Study of the Non-Fiction Prose Writers of the English Countryside* (Toronto and Buffalo: University of Toronto Press, 1974); and Martin J. Weiner, *English Culture and the Decline of the Industrial Spirit, 1850–1980* (Cambridge: Cambridge University Press, 1981).

[16] This is no doubt one of the reasons for which Elgar's largely European musical language did not go on to form the basis of a national school.

[17] Howkins, 'The Discovery of Rural England', p. 73.

albeit not exact, to the use of folksong in original composition). And the folksong movement was part of a widespread contemporary interest in preserving and reviving folklore. Yet this was itself a reflection of the nationalist preoccupations of the age, and for these the discovery of folksong was especially timely: here was potentially powerful new support for a national identity whose need had not been felt so acutely, say, in the first half of the nineteenth century, a time when serious folksong collecting could equally well have been undertaken. This may account to a large degree for the extraordinary alacrity with which folksong was taken up in the school curriculum.[18] English folksong was also helpful on another front. A feature of the period was that cultural Englishness had to be defined not only against the threat of the continental 'foreigner', but also against the 'Celticness' of Scotland, Wales, and Ireland (for this reason I have been careful here not automatically to equate England with Great Britain). To return to the earlier quotation from Plantinga, if a 'British' musical nationalism was all that was required, there was plenty of folk material already available, and English composers of the nineteenth century had already turned to this on occasion (although so had continental composers, most strikingly in the case of Scottish music). The idea that the folksongs discovered in England in the early twentieth century were distinctively and demonstrably English in origin has now been largely discredited.[19] What matters here, though, is the perceptions of the actors. Cecil Sharp and Vaughan Williams, for instance, were in no doubt that the songs they collected contained the essence of a national, racial identity. In 1907 Sharp wrote:

> We may look therefore to the introduction of folk-songs in the elementary
> schools to effect an improvement in the musical taste of the people, and to

---

[18] See Vic Gammon, 'Music in the Primary School: Aspects of History and Ideology', unpub. P.G.C.E. Special Study, University of Sussex, 1982; cited in Howkins, 'The Discovery of Rural England', pp. 77–8.

[19] See, for instance, A. L. Lloyd's landmark study *Folk Song in England* (London: Lawrence & Wishart, 1967), pp. 46–7, where he remarks that many of the characteristics Cecil Sharp identified as being peculiar to English folksong are in fact 'shared by many other peoples' (the wording of Lloyd's title is significant, avoiding as it does the equation of country of domicile with country of origin). This passage is quoted in Ian Kemp, *Tippett: The Composer and his Music*, rev. pbk edn. (London: Oxford University Press, 1987), p. 69, where some of these problems are discussed in the context of English music of the 1930s.

refine and strengthen the national character. The study of the folk-song will also stimulate the growth of the feeling of patriotism.[20]

Vaughan Williams used similar terms many years later in the lectures that went on to be published as *National Music*:

> Can we not truly say of these [English folk-songs] as Gilbert Murray says of that great national literature of the Bible and Homer, 'They have behind them not the imagination of one great poet, but the accumulated emotion, one may almost say, of the many successive generations who have read and learned and themselves afresh re-created the old majesty and loveliness. . . . There is in them, as it were, the spiritual life-blood of a people.'[21]

This strongly echoes, of course, the rhetoric of 'national spirit', stemming from Herder and Hegel, that informed so much nineteenth-century historical thought, including that on music. It is somewhat ironic that German influence should have played such a large part in shaping an English nationalist movement that, particularly in music, was very much concerned with a 'German threat'.

It is interesting to note, though, that Vaughan Williams was in general more circumspect than Sharp in his attitude to folksong. Indeed, in an article published in April 1902 he questioned how folksong could become the basis of an English school of art music, when none of the art-music composers came from the peasant class and could not therefore claim folksong as their own.[22] It is true that by the autumn of 1902, when Vaughan Williams lectured on folksong in Bournemouth, he was claiming for it a more comprehensive significance, as a 'sure index to national tempera-

---

[20] *English Folk-Song; Some Conclusions* (London: Simpkin, 1907), p. 135. It is interesting to note that the final sentence of this quotation survived as far as the third edition of the book, published in 1954, but was removed for the fourth, which appeared in 1965, a time when the concept of patriotism was in Britain reaching its nadir. Sharp died in 1924 and these later editions of his book were prepared by his acolyte Maud Karpeles.

[21] *National Music*, p. 23. For a more detailed discussion of the intellectual background to such thinking see Byron Adams's essay in the present volume.

[22] 'A School of English Music', *The Vocalist*, 1/1 (April 1902), p. 8. It is worth stressing in this connection that however deeply Vaughan Williams may later have assimilated aspects of English folksong into his melodic language, only a handful of his major works, and those dating mostly from before the First World War, quote directly from folksong. The popular view that his mature music is 'based on folksong' is therefore misleading at best.

11

ment'.[23] Yet before the First World War his views on both nationalism and folksong remained more flexible and judicious than they were to appear in parts of *National Music*. In an essay of 1912, 'Who Wants the English Composer?',[24] he exhorts English composers to take as their inspiration all kinds of music from their immediate environment – football chants and the songs of factory girls, for instance – as well as folksong, which he seems anxious to go beyond. The emphasis on urban rather than rural music is noteworthy, and it reflects Vaughan Williams's major compositional project of the time, *A London Symphony*, which was first performed in 1914. This was the work, it seems, that in many people's minds first established Vaughan Williams as a musical spokesman of the nation, and as the leading composer of his generation. Once again one can note a certain irony, the supposed high priest of the pastoral coming to prominence with a tribute to what was then the largest city in the world. As I have argued elsewhere,[25] the tribute is shot through with dark pessimism about the future of both London and the nation and empire which it governs; but this pessimism stems from a socialist critique of capitalism run riot, rather than from any rejection of the urban experience as such, which Vaughan Williams seems to have relished.

Mention of socialism may raise an eyebrow. In the wake of the Fascism of the inter-war years, we tend to associate expressions of nationalism as full-blooded as those of Sharp and Vaughan Williams with right-wing ideology. In fact, throughout Europe nationalism took on different political hues according to local conditions; it 'formed a sort of general substratum of politics'.[26] In England, ruralist nationalism was attractive all across the political spectrum, and even imperialism was by no means exclusively the preserve of the Right. Although Elgar was a Tory, Vaughan Williams and Cecil Sharp, along with Gustav Holst, were socialists. Part of

[23] See Kennedy, *Works*, p. 34.

[24] First published in *The R.C.M. Magazine*, 9/1 (Christmas Term 1912), pp. 12–15: reprinted in Hubert Foss, *Ralph Vaughan Williams: A Study* (London: Harrap, 1950), pp. 197–201.

[25] 'H. G. Wells and Vaughan Williams's London Symphony: Politics and Culture in Fin-de-Siècle England', in *Sundry Sorts of Music Books: Essays on the British Library Collections. Presented to O. W. Neighbour on his 70th Birthday*, ed. C. Banks, A. Searle, and M. Turner (London: British Library, 1993), pp. 299–308.

[26] Hobsbawm, *The Age of Empire*, p. 144.

the reason for which English socialists could express such ideas with a clear conscience was that, for all the home country's faults, it was more democratic than most of its European competitors, including Germany (the main oppressor in things musical), and Englishness and socialism were seen to be linked by powerful historical bonds.[27] These went back to the Puritan revolution of the seventeenth century, when the reformers, taking the Old Testament as their model, developed the idea that the English were a chosen people in world history, and made England the first overtly nationalistic country in Europe. Implicitly at times, explicitly at others, the folksong movement championed the music of the rural working class against the decadent tastes and products of the upper and upper-middle classes – and drew some hostility on that account. The broader message, however, was one of social regeneration and cohesion, not class struggle – the leading lights were, after all, members of the ruling classes themselves. It is no doubt true, as a number of writers have argued, that such socialism actually bolstered the existing power structures of which it was critical. Yet the socialist aspirations of important strands in the folksong movement, and of Vaughan Williams in particular, have often been obscured completely. This has made it possible for Vaughan Williams to be cast at times as a cosy Establishment figure playing opposite the left-wing young bloods of Tippett and Britten in the 1930s, and then of a younger generation of composers, such as those of the 'Manchester School', in the 1950s.[28]

[27] See, for instance, George Orwell, *The Lion and the Unicorn: Socialism and the English Genius* (London: Secker and Warburg, 1941); and Stephen Yeo, 'Socialism, the State, and Some Oppositional Englishness', in *Englishness: Politics and Culture 1880–1920*, pp. 308–69. A work such as Bunyan's *The Pilgrim's Progress*, which became enormously popular in the early part of this century, and was so important to Vaughan Williams, is a crucial link in this tradition. On Vaughan Williams's political beliefs see Paul Harrington, 'Holst and Vaughan Williams: Radical Pastoral', in *Music and the Politics of Culture*, pp. 106–27.

[28] Just how far Vaughan Williams's left-wing beliefs have been obscured by the accumulated associations of his music, and by changes in the British political landscape, is suggested by a trenchant remark in the left-wing historian Tom Nairn's book *The Break-Up of Britain: Crisis and Neo-Nationalism* (London: NLB, 1977). In a chapter on ruralist elements in the extreme right-wing nationalism of politician Enoch Powell, Nairn writes, 'He still partially inhabits this Disney-like English world where the Saxon ploughs his fields and the sun sets to strains by Vaughan Williams' (p. 262). It must be said that many British socialists of the 1960s and 70s were deeply critical of their nineteenth- and early

That the dark side of *A London Symphony* was largely overlooked by contemporary critics (as it has been, indeed, by most subsequent commentators) may be related to the extraordinary consensus that obtained across much of English society in the 1920s, a consensus which promoted loyalty and social cohesion as signs of respect for those killed in the recent conflict and the bereaved they left behind (the symphony had only one pre-war performance, and became widely known after the war in the revised versions of 1918 and then 1920). But there were, in any case, other trends in the 1920s that were helping to shape an attitude to Vaughan Williams which would make *A London Symphony* appear somewhat eccentric; these trends may also account for the apparent narrowing of the composer's views on folksong and nationalism that can be discerned in *National Music*. Many problems of Vaughan Williams reception go back to the 1920s and early 1930s, and to the manner in which the pre-war cultural tendencies discussed above were reinforced by the cataclysm of the Great War. Although the phenomenon has sometimes been exaggerated, the inter-war years did undoubtedly see a strong vein of insularity, and a tendency towards nostalgia and escapism, in British attitudes: there was a turn away from the global scene, where British influence was waning, to domestic concerns (this was

twentieth-century forebears, to a large extent because they had espoused gradualist rather than more revolutionary political change; nevertheless, one wonders if Nairn would without qualification have linked Vaughan Williams to a right-wing figure like Powell if he had known something of the composer's political background. Although it contains no further references to Vaughan Williams, Nairn's book, and in particular the chapter from which the quotation is drawn, provides a useful additional perspective on a number of themes addressed in the volumes cited in n. 3. For broader discussions of the political background to the folksong revival and its historiography see Boyes, *The Imagined Village*; James Porter, 'Muddying the Crystal Spring: From Idealism and Realism to Marxism in the Study of English and American Folk Song', in *Comparative Musicology and Anthropology of Music*, ed. Bruno Nettl and Philip V. Bohlman (Chicago: University of Chicago Press, 1991), pp. 113–30; and Julian Onderdonk's chapter in the present volume (I am grateful to Ron Woodley for drawing my attention to the Porter essay). Well before the recent wave of interest, some of the class politics of the folksong revival were touched upon in David Josephson, 'The Case for Percy Grainger, Edwardian Musician, on his Centenary', in *Music and Civilization: Essays in Honor of Paul Henry Lang*, ed. Edmond Strainchamps and Maria Rika Maniates, in collaboration with Christopher Hatch (New York and London: Norton, 1984), pp. 350–62.

to some degree a worldwide trend, at least when one looks at the economic protectionism of the period).[29] The ruralist ideas of the pre-war years had taken on tremendous emblematic importance in the trenches, even for the urban working classes,[30] and they became enshrined in the national self-image during the post-war period, given additional support through the new mass media of radio and cinema. In music, as in poetry, pastoralism and the influence of folk models were at their height. Vaughan Williams produced a number of pastoral works in the years just after the war, including his most explicit and extended work in this genre, A Pastoral Symphony, first performed in 1922. In the early reception of this symphony we can already see, both amongst supporters and detractors, how one facet of the composer's art was starting to be magnified and refracted in a distortive manner: a mythology was being born. Responses to the work have been related at some length by Michael Kennedy,[31] and I shall not dwell on them here. One point stands out, however. Those who had reservations, or stronger negative feelings, about the work tended to express these in terms of a perceived monotony and naïvety in its rural associations, and of an exclusive Englishness: this is the beginning of the 'cowpat' idea, showing the influence of a reaction in some circles against the rural cult and against insularity. The young Michael Tippett, for instance, reacted against what he seems to have viewed as the 'inane heartiness' of the scherzos of both this symphony and its predecessor, the 'London'.[32] Writing in the mid-1930s in Music Ho!, Constant Lambert advanced the view that the appeal of the 'Pastoral', and of Vaughan Williams's music in general, was so dependent on its distillation of Englishness that if foreigners did not like it, there was

---

29 For a synoptic view of these tendencies and some of their manifestations in music, see Stephen Banfield, *Sensibility and English Song: Critical Studies of the Early 20th Century*, 2 vols. (Cambridge: Cambridge University Press, 1985), vol. I, pp. 159–60 (although I cannot subscribe to the author's implied association of Vaughan Williams's folksong arrangements for military band with 'mindless gregariousness', given the genuine high spirits and gentle poetry of this music, and its place in the context of the composer's other work of the period).

30 See Howkins, 'The Discovery of Rural England', pp. 81–2; also Peter Brooker and Peter Widdowson, 'A Literature for England', in *Englishness: Politics and Culture 1880–1920*, pp. 116–63.   31 *Works*, pp. 155–7.

32 See Kemp, *Tippett*, p. 70. Although Tippett's disapproval is clear, it is difficult to determine from the context whether the particular phrase 'inane heartiness' stems from the composer or from Kemp.

15

nothing to be said; one could not point, as one could with Elgar, to the more neutral matter of its technical accomplishment, which, Lambert implies, is negligible.[33] Yet even close friends of the composer were capable of talking in terms which encouraged such a view: take, for instance, Sir Hugh Allen's famous remark that the symphony suggested 'V. W. rolling over and over in a ploughed field on a wet day'.[34] It is difficult to believe that such comments could have been made about this symphony. The orchestration is masterly; the earlier sections of the work make it clear that the heavy sound in parts of the Scherzo is quite intentional; and I defy anyone who is seriously listening to this music to hear in it 'inane heartiness' (an equally absurd description in the case of A London Symphony). And why it should be incomprehensible to a foreign audience is by no means clear. While English influences have obviously played a vital part in its genesis, both A Pastoral Symphony and its predecessor would equally be unthinkable without the influence of Debussy and Ravel. Yet the 'Pastoral' is also remarkably original. It does not occur to Lambert that the sheer novelty of the work, particularly in its use of uniformly slow or slowish tempi, and of an individual technique of melodic and rhythmic development, may well have accounted for the relative incomprehension shown by foreign audiences, and that its readier acceptance – if not actually comprehension – in England was probably due in large part to the esteem in which Vaughan Williams was already held, and to the way in which aspects of the symphony appeared to feed existing national appetites.

All this is particularly ironic in the light of the composer's revelation, not made until the late 1930s, and then only in a private communication, that the symphony was inspired originally by the landscape of wartime France, not, as everyone had assumed, that of peacetime England;[35] Michael Kennedy has made the persuasive suggestion that the work is, in fact, Vaughan Williams's 'war requiem'.[36] One can understand why the composer may have wished to conceal such painful associations in the immediate aftermath of the war. Yet one also wonders if he were not to some

[33] Music Ho! A Study of Music in Decline (London: Hogarth Press, 1934), p. 107. For other highly critical – and also wickedly funny – remarks on the vogue for things pastoral and Elizabethan, see pp. 125 ff. and p. 205.
[34] Quoted in Kennedy, Works, p. 156.
[35] See U. Vaughan Williams, R.V.W., p. 121.   [36] Works, p. 155.

degree overwhelmed by the strength of the nationalistic discourses of the time, especially those pertaining to the rural and the Tudor, and the way in which these had become attached to his music. It seems to have been around this time that a number of myths about Vaughan Williams began to develop, including the erroneous idea that he was a true 'countryman' (although born in Gloucestershire he lived for the greater part of his life in the heart of London), and that his music had rejected the immediate past wholesale and was based almost exclusively on folk and Tudor models. The latter idea has become so ingrained that it goes unchallenged even by the revisionist Alun Howkins in his comments on Vaughan Williams. This is hardly surprising, though. As a non-musicologist consulting, say, Hugh Ottaway's otherwise excellent article on Vaughan Williams in the *New Grove*,[37] Howkins would have little cause to suspect that nineteenth- and early twentieth-century continental music had played a central role in the formation of the composer's musical language; this despite the fact that the bulk of Vaughan Williams's work was in genres such as symphony and opera, not mass, motet, or folksong setting. As such misconceptions began to develop in the inter-war years, *National Music* could only have added fuel to the fire. Although it contains some statements that actively discourage an attitude of narrow insularity, others suggest a hardening of the composer's earlier opinions. Take, for instance, the firm assertion, 'I do hold that any school of national music must be fashioned on the basis of the raw material of its own national song'.[38] Another statement that could not help but appear provocative to some younger composers (we know it did to Tippett, for instance):[39] 'If [the artist] consciously tries to express himself in a way which is contrary to his surroundings, and therefore to his own nature, he is evidently being, though perhaps he does not know it, insincere'.[40] Elsewhere he writes somewhat defensively that, 'I was told the other day that some of the English music that appeals to us at home is considered "smug" by foreign critics. I was delighted to hear it, because it suggested to me that our English composers had some secret which is at present for our ears only.'[41]

---

[37] *The New Grove Dictionary of Music and Musicians*, 20 vols. (London and New York: Macmillan, 1980), vol. XIX, pp. 569–80. [38] *National Music*, p. 41
[39] Kemp, *Tippett*, p. 69. [40] *National Music*, p. 3. [41] *Ibid.*, p. 64.

17

By 1932 the international scene was looking increasingly threatening, especially with the re-emergence of Germany as a potential aggressor, and, although Vaughan Williams was never a jingoistic patriot in political terms, it is difficult to escape the impression that he was swayed to some degree by the further heightening of nationalistic sentiment around this time. But in his words, not his music. What is particularly striking is that at just the time when the pastoral and parochial image of Vaughan Williams was taking such a firm hold, perhaps even on occasion confusing the composer himself about where his real strengths lay, he was, in fact, at his most experimental and adventurous. While he was giving the series of *National Music* lectures at Bryn Mawr college, Pennsylvania, in the autumn of 1932, he was also working on the Fourth Symphony.[42] Far from being based on English folk-song, the Fourth is notorious as a violent and convulsive work, dominated by grinding dissonances of an aggressively modernistic and, it might be argued, international kind. Furthermore, it is the culmination of a string of pieces written between the mid-1920s and mid-30s that clearly suggest analogies with, if not the actual influence of, continental movements; the *Concerto Accademico* for Violin and Orchestra (1924–5) has many neo-classical traits, for instance, and the percussive Piano Concerto (1926–31) was 'much admired' by Bartók.[43] Throughout his life Vaughan Williams made a point of keeping up with contemporary developments abroad as well as at home, whether or not he thought them worthwhile, and it is difficult to accuse him of insularity in the inter-war years – or at any other time, for that matter. As for his verbal utterances, in addition to being to

[42] There are no references to work on the Fourth Symphony in accounts of the Bryn Mawr visit in the standard Vaughan Williams literature; it was the composer's major work-in-progress at this time, however, and his Bryn Mawr address appears on f. 2^r of the autograph full score of the symphony now in the British Library (Add. MS 50140). His lectures were timely: by the early 1930s some composers in the United States were beginning to draw in their music on traditions of Anglo-American folksong and hymnody, a movement that would gather pace as the decade progressed. There are a number of parallels to be drawn between the British and American compositional scenes in the first half of the twentieth century, some of which I explored in 'Vaughan Williams and America', a series of programmes broadcast on BBC Radio 3 in March and April 1994. Vaughan Williams's music has long been accorded a warmer welcome in the US than in any other country outside Britain.

[43] See Kennedy, *Works*, p. 237.

some degree trapped by the nationalist discourse of the day, as were most commentators who tried to address such issues, he always liked to be provocative. Ultimately, we would do well to give much more weight to Vaughan Williams's music than to his words. Lest this seem a truism, it is worthwhile remembering just how misleading, and sometimes deliberately deceitful, composers can be when talking about the background to their work. Furthermore, for those who seek to link music and wider cultural trends, it is also a reminder that we should not expect music, as opposed to discourse about music, to act as a simple mirror of its context: indeed, it seems at least as often to function subversively, and to provide an outlet for forces otherwise repressed in the society in which it arises. And, without wishing to deprecate the social dimension, we must also recognize the strong internal logic that often drives developments in musical style.

The simplification of Vaughan Williams's image was to become much more marked during the Second World War. By now he was the established leader of British music (in World War I it had been Elgar). Furthermore, the fight against Nazi Germany was a cause to which a socialist could give himself wholeheartedly, and, as he was too old for military service, Vaughan Williams served in other ways, principally by setting himself to the task of writing a substantial amount of music that was overtly patriotic rather than implicitly nationalistic, including scores for propaganda films. The idea of the island race fighting a lone battle against Fascism reinforced elements in the national self-image that had already become strongly associated with Vaughan Williams, and his music became an important point of emotional focus for many listeners of the time, even to the extent of being credited with a prophetic message.[44] Perhaps the most extreme, and certainly the most thoroughgoing, identification of Vaughan Williams with Englishness is found in the first full-length study of the composer, written by Hubert Foss and published in 1950.[45] For Foss, the composer's publisher and a personal friend, Vaughan Williams is almost literally the personification of England, warts and all. This fascinating book merits an essay in its own right. Not surprisingly, the rural and Tudor themes are developed to the full; the book is saturated with natural and organic metaphors, and in the opera *Sir John in Love* 'the two earlier musics of England meet, the music of

---

[44] *Ibid.*, p. 279.   [45] See n. 24.

the aristocrat and the music of the peasant: they meet in the soul and the score of a living Englishman, who has an innate understanding of Shakespeare, his librettist, and yet lives among us now'.[46] Foss's study is also revealing, however, on specific attributes of national character that I have not had space to address here, but which have had a considerable, and generally harmful, impact on the reception of Vaughan Williams's music. To take just a few of the most glaring examples, Vaughan Williams is 'dogged', 'obstinate', and 'clumsy'; he is an improviser who eschews advance planning. Yet these are presented in the main as strengths not weaknesses, however unattractive they may appear to other nations, whose character types are brought in time after time by Foss for subjection to unfavourable comparison.[47]

Against this kind of background, it is much easier to understand the reaction against Vaughan Williams, and against what he appeared to stand for, that began to gather momentum in the 1950s and continues to dog the composer's reputation even today. The 1950s saw the beginning of a widespread rebellion against the 'Establishment', including many of the dominant images of the English national character. In music, a perceived amateurishness and indifference to continental developments were the

---

[46] See p. 70.

[47] It is illuminating to read Foss alongside a recent essay on nineteenth-century English writing on the Duke of Wellington. Wellington's image was tendentiously fashioned in a remarkably similar way, primarily as a foil to a great foreign enemy, Napoleon, and in a manner that helped articulate emerging stereotypes of Englishness: see Iain Pears, 'The Gentleman and the Hero: Wellington and Napoleon in the Nineteenth Century', in *Myths of the English*, pp. 216–36. Vaughan Williams, it must be said, often described himself as musically clumsy; but how far this did more than simply reproduce an already well-established national habit and vocabulary of self-deprecation – a self-deprecation, however, that often hints that the English value deeper, more important qualities than those at issue – is open to question. Also striking, given that he was a personal friend, is Foss's mistaken belief that Vaughan Williams grew up in Gloucestershire; in fact, although he was born in Gloucestershire, he moved to Surrey at the age of two-and-a-half. Gloucestershire has played an almost talismanic role in the English rural mythology of the twentieth century, having strong associations with a number of Georgian poets, with the Arts and Crafts movement, and with several composers, including Gustav Holst and Ivor Gurney, both of whom had closer ties to the area than Vaughan Williams; given the general tenor of Foss's book, it seems likely that he was carried away by this powerful history.

20

prime targets, and Vaughan Williams came in for attack on both counts. It is sobering to see the rhetoric of national character now turned against him: writing in 1955 about the Christmas cantata *Hodie*, first performed the year before, the influential critic Donald Mitchell asserted that, 'There is a level below which "directness" and "forthrightness" of utterance – qualities for which Vaughan Williams is praised – deteriorate into a downright unacceptable and damaging primitivity';[48] these qualities were seen as typically English virtues in the eyes of the time. Mitchell was one of the principal champions of Benjamin Britten's music, and the reaction against Vaughan Williams is in many ways inextricably intertwined with the rise of Britten. The heated debate surrounding Britten kept returning, either implicitly or explicitly, to matters touching on national character and identity, with the example of Vaughan Williams always looming in the background. Cosmopolitanism versus nationalism, professional technique versus sincere expression, 'cleverness' versus directness – many critics saw Britten's music as somehow 'un-English'.[49] Though such preoccupations militated against a thorough understanding of either Britten or Vaughan Williams, in the long run it is Vaughan Williams who has suffered most in the process.

[48] 'Contemporary Chronicle: Revaluations: Vaughan Williams', *Musical Opinion*, 78, no. 931 (April 1955), p. 411; quoted in Kennedy, *Works*, p. 331. In fact, in the decade prior to his death in 1958, Vaughan Williams produced some of his least direct music, although what is perhaps his most ambiguous work, the Ninth Symphony, was still to come at the time Mitchell was writing.

[49] Britten's pacifism and his homosexuality were often lurking beneath the surface of such judgements. The role of gender-related concepts and vocabulary in the construction of Englishness in music deserves an extended discussion in its own right. It is clear from work in other areas, however, in particular concerning attitudes to English literature and the development of the English language, that concepts such as 'directness' and 'simplicity' formed part of a discourse in which sexual, racial, and national issues were closely intertwined. Language about music and music history had already developed its own veiled inscriptions of cultural norms in these areas, of a variety of oppositions of self and other; for a useful introduction to such issues see Leo Treitler, 'The Politics of Reception: Tailoring the Present as Fulfilment of a Desired Past', *Journal of the Royal Musical Association*, 116 (1991), pp. 280–98; and by the same author, 'Gender and Other Dualities of Music History', in *Musicology and Difference: Gender and Sexuality in Music Scholarship*, ed. Ruth A. Solie (Berkeley and Los Angeles: University of California Press, 1993), pp. 23–45. On the concatenation of forbidden sexuality and orientalism in Britten's music, see Philip Brett, 'Britten's Dream', in Solie, *Musicology and Difference*, pp. 259–80.

The 1950s set the agenda for the critical slump that followed Vaughan Williams's death in 1958. Although his reputation has now recovered to some extent, it is still mired in the confused ideological landscape of Britain's long slide from international power. On the one hand, a terror of insularity runs strong in the intelligentsia; on the other, unchecked xenophobia thrives in the tabloid newspapers. One need look only at recent debates over the Maastricht treaty to see the continuing relevance of many of the issues touched on here; and it hardly needs saying that nationalism has once again become a literally explosive issue in Europe. I have not sought in this essay to deny categorically the existence of national characteristics, in music or in any other area of human activity; I have merely tried to show how, in the case of Vaughan Williams, ideas of national character have, consciously or unconsciously, been selectively manipulated. Scholars can no longer pretend to inhabit lofty heights of 'objectivity', safe from the prejudices of nation or age; we can aspire, however, to a greater awareness of the more shadowy forces that shape our thoughts. Nationalism this century has penetrated deep into the irrational domains of human feeling long associated with music: a detailed study of the reception history of English music this century would, I believe, have implications well beyond the current reputation of Vaughan Williams.

2 Coming of age: the earliest orchestral music of Ralph Vaughan Williams

MICHAEL VAILLANCOURT

Writing in 1964, Michael Kennedy issued a cautionary note concerning the early years of Vaughan Williams's career: 'Because so many early works were suppressed there is a tendency to imagine that the composer suddenly and surprisingly burst forth in about 1907. That certainly was when he emerged as a musician of positive and idiosyncratic character. But the years in the chrysalis were not barren and fruitless.'[1] Writings on Vaughan Williams have largely avoided 'the years in the chrysalis', and in particular the troublesome business of discussing the good number of substantial orchestral and instrumental works from this period that the composer later withdrew. The situation has not changed greatly in the last three decades. Because most of the works written before 1907 are unavailable in score it has been difficult to form a clear picture of the slow but steady development of Vaughan Williams. It has been impossible even to validate the usual contention that the composer 'suddenly burst forth' around the middle of the first decade of the century. Those writers who do at least make some reference to Vaughan Williams's earliest instrumental compositions nevertheless minimize their importance; Kennedy, for instance, calls the *Serenade* and the *Bucolic Suite* 'gauche' with no further explanation.[2] Even *In the Fen Country* (original version 1904), the first of the composer's orchestral works that he allowed to remain in circulation – albeit heavily revised – has fared little better, having been viewed primarily as imitative of continental musicians such as Richard Strauss, revealing little evidence of the mature Vaughan Williams.[3] Many

---

[1] Kennedy, *Works*, p. 22. [2] *Ibid.*, p. 76.

[3] James Day, *Vaughan Williams* (London: J. M. Dent and Sons, 1961), p. 133, dismisses *In the Fen Country* with the following: 'there is little that foreshadows the great composer who was to come; the craftsmanship is competent, the orchestration rather heavy, the form conventional, the harmonic treatment unambitious'. Kennedy, *Works*, p. 83, notes the Strauss connection and also mentions Butterworth.

studies begin discussion of Vaughan Williams's mature music with the Rossetti and Stevenson song-cycles.[4]

Whatever the quality of the early vocal music, its privileging in the literature is in many ways misleading, since the greater part of Vaughan Williams's compositional activities during this period were devoted to orchestral and chamber music; what is more, these pieces were crucial in establishing Vaughan Williams's reputation as a rising young composer.[5] A review of an early performance of the *Two Orchestral Impressions* spoke of their 'power and originality' and emphasized the modernity of the musical style.[6] An important step forward in the career of Vaughan Williams occurred in 1903 when he figured prominently in a pair of articles devoted to the younger generation of British composers. Both articles place special emphasis on the young man's accomplishments in the field of instrumental music. W. Barclay Squire singles out Vaughan Williams along with Cyril Scott and Cecil Forsyth and notes that, 'Good as his vocal music is, it is the remembrance of a very striking orchestral work, which was performed some time ago at a concert at the Royal College of Music, that makes me regret that the undoubted power he exhibited on that occasion has not yet resulted in the production of some instrumental composition of important dimensions'.[7] He refers undoubtedly to the *Heroic Elegy and Triumphal Epilogue*, which received its first performance at the Royal College of Music in March 1901. The second article, by Edwin Evans, is particularly interesting because the author acknowledges that the composer was involved in

---

[4] Frank Howes says of the *Songs of Travel*, 'the authentic Vaughan Williams appears with all the ninetyish atmosphere dispersed and proclaiming...the new era'. (*The Music of Ralph Vaughan Williams* (London: Oxford University Press, 1954), p. 238.) Hubert Foss places the coming of age of the composer slightly earlier, with *The House of Life* (*Ralph Vaughan Williams* (New York: Oxford University Press, 1950), p. 80).

[5] I have chosen to deal exclusively with orchestral music in this study, despite the fact that the large-scale chamber music dating from this period does share many characteristics with the orchestral music. Apart from considerations of available space, the orchestral music allows a somewhat wider scope of discussion, especially regarding texture, instrumentation, and tone colour.

[6] *The Times*, 13 November 1907, p. 14. The review is unsigned. Kennedy, *Works*, p. 89, quotes a portion of the review.

[7] W. Barclay Squire, 'On Some English Music', *The Pilot*, 21 March 1903, p. 280. Kennedy, *Works*, p. 56, quotes from this article.

choosing the works to be discussed. Again, the *Heroic Elegy and Triumphal Epilogue* is singled out for special attention, occupying a greater portion of the discussion than any other work by the composer.[8] Although both articles suggest the young composer had yet to discover his ultimate orientation, neither leaves any doubt that Vaughan Williams had arrived as a distinctive voice on the contemporary scene.

Around the turn of the century Vaughan Williams wrote and lectured on various musical subjects; the topics suggest a concern with large-scale instrumental composition and its problems. A series of short articles appeared in *The Vocalist* during 1902 and 1903, of which 'A School of English Music' is particularly instructive.[9] It reveals an attitude towards the viability of folksong in concert music far different from that suggested by the later and more familiar writings. Describing the activities of the preceding generation of English composers, Vaughan Williams comments: 'Here the pioneers of the English school made a great mistake; they sought a panacea, and sought it abroad. This universal remedy was to be the "Folk-song"; on the continent its exploitation was in full swing.'[10] While we can debate the significance of such statements in light of the composer's later writings, one point is clear: in 1902 Vaughan Williams was in many ways a different man than the composer of *Hugh the Drover* or *A Pastoral Symphony*. The series of *Vocalist* essays also underscores Vaughan Williams's familiarity with the latest continental styles. Among the works discussed are the late music dramas of Wagner, the Fourth Symphonies of both Tchaikovsky and Brahms, and Strauss's *Ein Heldenleben*; the latter, which had just received its first London performance, is analysed in some detail.[11]

---

[8] Edwin Evans, 'Modern British Composers. VI.', *The Musical Standard*, 25 July 1903, p. 52.   [9] 'A School of English Music', *The Vocalist*, 1/1 (April 1902), p. 8.

[10] *Ibid.* Kennedy quotes portions of this article and interprets them as fully in accord with Vaughan Williams's later attitudes towards folksong (see Kennedy, *Works*, pp. 29–30). While it is possible to view these youthful remarks as in some ways foreshadowing the composer's later ideas, the connection remains dubious. A reading of the entire article (especially those parts not cited by Kennedy) gives the impression of diametrically opposed attitudes on the part of the young composer and the mature artist famous as a spokesman for English folksong.

[11] 'Ein Heldenleben', *The Vocalist*, 1/10 (January 1903), p. 295. On Vaughan Williams's views on contemporary German music as expressed in his letters, and his connections with German and Austrian musicians, see Hugh Cobbe's contribution to this volume.

Table 2.1 Vaughan Williams's early orchestral works

Date of composition	Title	First performance
1898 (rev. 1901)	*Serenade*	Bournemouth, 4 April 1901
1900 (rev. 1904)	*Bucolic Suite*	Bournemouth, 10 March 1902
1900–1901?	*Heroic Elegy and Triumphal Epilogue*	RCM, 5 March 1901
1896–1902 (rev. 1904)	*Fantasia*	none
1901–3	*Symphonic Rhapsody*	Bournemouth, 7 March 1904
1902–3?	*In the New Forest* + (*Burley Heath;* ++ *The Solent*)	London, 19 June 1903 (*The Solent* only)
1904–7	*Two Impressions for Orchestra* (*Harnham Down; Boldrewood**)	London, 12 November 1907
1904 (rev. 1907 and 1935)	*In the Fen Country*	London, 22 February 1909

* manuscript lost or destroyed by composer
+ only two of the four movements planned survive
++ incomplete

During the crucial formative years between 1898 and 1904 Vaughan Williams composed ten orchestral pieces. He used a wide range of genres and styles, from multi-movement suite and serenade to Lisztian symphonic poem and single-movement pastoral (see Table 2.1).[12] The *Serenade* for small orchestra may have originated during Vaughan Williams's study in Berlin with Max Bruch in the winter of 1897–8. During

---

[12] The manuscript of the *Heroic Elegy and Triumphal Epilogue* is held by Yale University Library, shelf number OSB Music MS 504; in the same collection, as MS 505, is a copy of the *Serenade* (see Alain Frogley, 'Vaughan Williams and the New World: Manuscript Sources in North American Libraries', *Notes: Quarterly Journal of the Music Library Association,* 48/4 (June 1992), pp. 1175–92). The manuscripts of all other works discussed are found in the British Library Additional Manuscript series with the following shelf numbers: *Serenade,* 57272; *Bucolic Suite,* 57275; *Fantasia,* 57276; *Burley Heath, The Solent,* and *Harnham Down,* 57278.

this period Bruch himself was probably at work on the serenade later published as his Op. 75.[13] It might seem tempting to search for points of influence; however, Bruch wrote what amounts to a three-movement violin concerto, quite different in style and gesture from the Vaughan Williams work. The most obvious point of contact is a certain melodic effusiveness. Vaughan Williams's *Serenade* teems with melodies, most of which are not developed extensively, a common feature of the large-scale instrumental works of Bruch. The appellation *Serenade* was an afterthought: Vaughan Williams originally called the piece 'suite' and only later crossed that out and wrote 'serenade'.[14] More extensive revisions were the addition of a fifth movement and of a coda to the final rondo. The addition of a movement may have prompted the composer to change his mind regarding the title, although the nineteenth-century genres suite and serenade have many characteristics in common.[15] The *Serenade* comprises five character-pieces, none of which employs the sonata-based structures typical of symphonic movements (see Table 2.2).

The Romance is of particular interest because it is dominated almost entirely by the wind instruments; the strings assume a subsidiary role, playing only a few short melodic segments between wind phrases. This procedure is highly reminiscent of the Serenade No. 1, Op. 11, by Brahms, a work for large orchestra that contains one movement for two clarinets, bassoon, and flute, reinforced by a few discreet cello pizzicatos.[16] The Andantino is perhaps the most striking movement of the *Serenade*. By contrasting low-lying, syncopated string figures with a lyrical clarinet solo, the composer generates a musical

---

[13] Wilhelm Lauth, *Max Bruchs Instrumentalmusik* (Cologne: Arno Volk, 1967), p. 131. [14] Kennedy, *Catalogue*, p. 7.

[15] Although nineteenth-century writers disagree regarding the form and content of the serenade, most mention several basic characteristics: a number of movements exceeding the three or four found in most sonatas and symphonies, a preponderance of short character-pieces such as the march, lyric piece, or various dance genres, and a predominantly light character. The most detailed modern discussion, citing nineteenth-century authorities such as Franz Ludwig Schubert and Gustav Schilling, is Christoph von Blumroder, 'Serenade', *Handwörterbuch der Musikalischen Terminologie*, ed. H. H. Eggebrecht (Stuttgart: Franz Stainer, n.d.), IV: S-Z.

[16] The movement in the Brahms work is the Menuet I.

Table 2.2 Movement characteristics in 'Serenade'

Movement	Key	Metre	Tempo	Form	Genre
I	A minor	3/4	Andante sostenuto	variation	fantasia
II	E minor	6/8	Allegro	scherzo	scherzo
III	E major	3/4	Allegretto con moto	ABA	romance
IV	A minor	3/4	Andantino	ABA	lyric piece
V	A minor	2/4	none given	rondo	rondo-finale

tension that drives the entire movement. In doing so he displays an impressive command of long-term rhythmic structure that suggests a mature musical creativity.

The movement also embodies the first appearance of a formal procedure that Vaughan Williams would return to often, especially in the programmatic orchestral pieces composed between 1902 and 1907. The composer begins with an opening section featuring clear-cut groups of themes developed towards a single climax.[17] There then follows a contrasting section that exhibits traits of both a contrasting lyric interlude and a symphonic development section: the former because the composer introduces new thematic material, the latter owing to the fact that the section is tonally unstable, modulating through several key areas. In addition, fragments of themes from the A section are developed together with the new material. Having established expectations for a conventional recapitulation, or at least a symmetrical three-part structure, Vaughan Williams provides only a drastically shortened form of the A section, more in the nature of a coda than of a recapitulation. He would adapt this procedure for many future compositions, among them the

---

[17] My discussion of form in this study will concentrate for the most part on thematic rather than tonal and harmonic issues. This reflects what appear to have been the composer's own priorities at this time; while tonality and harmony would merit a chapter in their own right, Vaughan Williams seems at this stage of his career to have been more concerned with the thematic articulation of structure.

first movement of *A London Symphony*, in which the entire plan is expanded.[18]

Like the *Serenade*, the *Bucolic Suite* is a work of assimilation in which the composer borrows numerous formal and stylistic elements from the serenade-divertimento tradition. Here the formal disposition more closely resembles the standard four-movement symphonic pattern, with a substantial opening movement followed by a short slow movement, an intermezzo, and a quick finale. The first movement displays some traditional symphonic hallmarks, including a large-scale tripartite division and an extensive development. The return of the tonic near the end of the exposition, however, suggests a rondo model. The development introduces several new themes, serving as a second phase of exposition and further deflecting attention from the initial sonata idea. Also notable in the development is the frequent division of the orchestra into discrete rhythmic entities, with the strings in 6/8 and the wind band in 3/4. The resulting rhythmic tension adumbrates Vaughan Williams's procedures in several later works, including the scherzos of the three middle symphonies.

The Intermezzo third movement displays unmistakable affinities with the third movement of Brahms's Second Symphony. Both are marked 'Allegretto' and begin in triple metre; both begin with the oboes presenting a simple symmetrical phrase (see Example 2.1a; throughout this example the top line is by Vaughan Williams, the bottom by Brahms).[19] Brahms restricts his opening paragraph to the woodwind choir and a pizzicato bass line in the cellos; Vaughan Williams employs the full string section but nevertheless emphasizes the woodwinds. Perhaps even more striking is the section that follows, in which Vaughan Williams, like Brahms, suddenly shifts to 2/4 for a staccato theme in running quavers. The melodic contour is similar too: a group of three repeated notes followed by a leap. Vaughan Williams even follows his model by accenting the fourth note in each of the first two bars (see Example 2.1b). Brahms later introduces yet another section, a 3/8 Presto, while Vaughan Williams is content to return to his

---

[18] It is possible to interpret the first movement of *A London Symphony* as a large-scale ternary design with slow introduction and coda. In this scheme, the middle section (especially the episode beginning at BB in the 1920 edition) functions both as development of material heard earlier and as a contrasting lyrical interlude.   [19] The Brahms movement is marked 'Allegretto grazioso'.

Example 2.1 Vaughan Williams, *Bucolic Suite*, III; Brahms, Symphony No. 2, III

first, fashioning an ABA structure. At the close of the movement, Vaughan Williams casts one last glance towards Brahms by imitating in the woodwinds the arpeggiated sighing figure found in the cellos of the Brahms movement.

Even in his earliest works Vaughan Williams rarely imitated directly the musical gestures of an established master. It is tempting, then, to look for some symbolic significance in this act. It may well lie in the fact that Brahms was revered by both Parry and Stanford, Vaughan Williams's principal teachers at the Royal College of Music: the young composer may have intended his Brahmsian references as an act of homage to his mentors, and as an attempt to stake his claim as a composer of orchestral music, inviting comparison with the established canon of musical masterworks.

In the *Fantasia* for piano and orchestra the young composer attempts to master a different musical tradition. Although the virtuoso nature of the piece sets it apart from most of Vaughan Williams's work, the structural element holds the most important ramifications for the development of the composer's musical language. It represents Vaughan Williams's first attempt to compose a large-scale instrumental movement and is his most ambitious purely instrumental work to appear before *A London Symphony*. Whereas the *Serenade* and the *Bucolic Suite* were assembled by combining several short movements, the *Fantasia* is cast as a continuous span of over

30

400 bars. Around this time Vaughan Williams seems to have reassessed the viability of multi-movement instrumental compositions. In particular, the problems posed by the conventional finale may have led him to concentrate on one- or two-movement structures during the years just after the turn of the century. In his April 1902 article entitled 'The Soporific Finale', Vaughan Williams noted this quandary: 'One may almost say that, unless the decorative scheme of the whole work demand it, the conventional "steady run-home" style of Finale is an artistic mistake'.[20] That the *Fantasia* created a daunting challenge to the young composer is borne out by the fact that it took at least six years to complete, and was then later revised.

The *Fantasia* owes little to typical nineteenth-century concerto form other than the highly rhetorical solo introduction.[21] For such a long movement there are relatively few themes; rather, the composer concentrates on rigorous and exhaustive development of the material. He introduces almost all of the principal thematic material in the cadenza-like section that opens the piece and in the orchestral tutti that follows. There are three primary solos; each introduces a new tempo, the first moderato, the second lento, and, finally, poco animato. Thus it is possible to discern the outlines of the composer's favourite tripartite division. A coda introduces a new thematic idea and a change to 12/8 metre, rounding off the movement. Each of the three primary sections is developmental in character, reshaping the principal material or adding figuration to themes played by the orchestra.

Vaughan Williams's overriding compositional problem in the *Fantasia* is one of structural unity. Without recourse to established formal patterns, the composer solves this dilemma by deploying his themes in a coherent network tied together by thematic transformation. The most thoroughgoing example of this technique is the development of the

---

20 'The Soporific Finale', *The Vocalist*, 1/1 (April 1902), p. 31.
21 Although the *Fantasia* displays some outward similarities to the Franck *Symphonic Variations* (1885), it lacks the adherence to classical variation-form found in the latter. Other single-movement concertante works for piano and orchestra, such as those by Schumann or Weber, bear little resemblance to the Vaughan Williams composition. In terms of form it is unlikely (although not impossible) that the composer was influenced at this stage by seventeenth-century English fantasias, as this work predates by some years the widespread revival of interest in such repertory, and Vaughan Williams's own series of fantasias (on the background to the latter see Anthony Pople's chapter in this volume).

Example 2.2 *Fantasia* for Piano and Orchestra, transformation of second theme

a)

b)

c)

d)

e)

opening theme of the orchestral tutti beginning in bar 25. The idea remains associated with the orchestra, but during the piece it undergoes a variety of transformations (see Example 2.2).

Version (b) is closest to the original, involving only a change in melodic direction in its third bar and the transposition of the second phrase up a perfect fourth. Version (c), although heard soon after the primary motif, represents a more thorough transformation. While retaining the basic rhythmic structure, Vaughan Williams inverts the shape; individual intervals are altered as well, so that only through context can it be seen to be related to the original. Version (d) is another example of inversion, at least for its first five bars, with the addition of a chromatic passing note in the second bar so that the opening still outlines a perfect fifth. Only in the coda does the solo part deal extensively with this material, in a 12/8 version of the main idea (version (e), which is closely modelled on version (b)).

Thematic transformation obviously brings to mind Liszt and the symphonic poem, and this connection surfaces fully in the *Heroic Elegy and Triumphal Epilogue*. That Vaughan Williams was not averse to learning from the progressive wing of central European composers is suggested by his article on *Ein Heldenleben*, published in January 1903.[22] Although Vaughan Williams gives the piece a decidedly mixed review, most of his criticisms concern the thematic material. He is far more positive when describing Strauss's techniques of motivic development and his handling of orchestral resources.

From its first performance the *Heroic Elegy and Triumphal Epilogue* occasioned comment regarding its unusual structure. Although the title suggests a two-part outline with a main section followed by a coda or concluding subsection, the piece exhibits a more complex construction. In his 1903 article, Edwin Evans pointed to the introductory nature of the *Heroic Elegy* and stressed both the structural primacy and qualitative superiority of the *Triumphal Epilogue*:

> The two movements of which it is composed vary widely in importance, the first being considerably shorter than its companion. ... The second section of the work is much more important, and is, indeed, subdivided in a manner which would almost suggest an independent work but for the presence, in the course of the development, of much of the material of the elegy. On the whole, I consider it superior to the piece which precedes it, and which, whether the composer intended it or not, I feel rather disposed to regard as introductory. For one thing, the themes are more interesting, particularly that which opens the movement and plays an important part in it.[23]

The opening Elegy is indeed the shorter and simpler of the two movements, comprising a slow march with contrasting trio section and a modified return of the opening. The trio is actually longer than the march section. The latter comprises two statements of the 'heroic' melody, the first played by the trombones, the second by the horns. Vaughan Williams employs several effects traditionally associated with the funeral march, including emphasis on the wind band in order to create an 'outdoor' sound,

---

[22] See n. 11.   [23] Edwin Evans, 'Modern British Composers', p. 52.

a pulsating string accompaniment using a low tessitura, and, near the end of the section, a prominent descending chromatic-scale passage. A marking on the manuscript shows that the original title was to have been 'Heroic Romance'. This suggests a connection with several later symphonic movements such as the third movement of the Fifth Symphony. The composer seems to have employed the title 'Romance' or its derivatives for movements with an especially serious affect. The central section contains some notable colouristic effects; most striking is the ghostly *pianissimo* in the upper registers of the violins that recalls the contemporary works of Gustav Mahler. It is uncertain how much of Mahler's music Vaughan Williams knew at this time, but three movements of the Third Symphony were premièred in Berlin in March 1897, when Vaughan Williams was staying in that city.[24]

The musical structure of the *Triumphal Epilogue* is of particular interest. It is perhaps the most imaginative design to be found in any of the early orchestral works. The movement abounds with structural surprises, employs a sophisticated brand of thematic manipulation, and displays more varied and colourful orchestral writing than any of its predecessors. At the outset we hear an introductory theme played by the strings that is soon juxtaposed with a triple-metre, march-style tune from the winds, another feature reminiscent of Mahler's methods. After working up to a bold climax, the music suddenly subsides and we are presented with distant fanfares marked 'Andante sostenuto – The Tempo of the Elegy'. The fanfares serve as background for a return of the most important themes of the Elegy. The abrupt change of character serves to underline the special importance of this development, as does the detailed working out of the themes. In a section some fifty bars in length thematic elements drawn from the two main themes of the Elegy are recombined and transformed in a variety of ways (see Example 2.3); particularly important are the ascending upbeat figure of Theme A and the three-note chromatic descent of Theme B. Thus the Andante sostenuto serves not only as a unifying device by recapitulating material heard earlier, albeit in altered form, but as a delayed development section for the Elegy as well.

[24] The second, fifth, and sixth movements of the Mahler symphony were performed on this occasion. See Henry-Louis de la Grange, *Mahler*, vol. I (Garden City, New York: Doubleday and Company, 1973), p. 396.

Example 2.3 Transformation of themes between *Heroic Elegy* and *Triumphal Epilogue*

(a) Elegy, main theme (A)

(b) Elegy, second theme (B)

(c) Triumphal Epilogue, transformations

1.

2.

3.

4.

5.

Following the Andante sostenuto Vaughan Williams introduces a faster section, Allegro moderato, that presents new material together with a transformed version of the Elegy's first theme. To these ingredients are added new versions of the fanfares derived from the Andante sostenuto. This segment is, in effect, another long development, and it contains some of Vaughan Williams's most assured orchestral writing in the early works. Yet another transformation of the opening theme of the Elegy serves as the basis for the coda.

The *Heroic Elegy and Triumphal Epilogue* undoubtedly contains weaknesses; most obvious is the highly sectionalized nature of the whole, with abrupt transitions between widely differing themes and even styles. But this should not obscure the real advances made here by the composer. For the first time in an orchestral piece, rather than imitating standard formal models Vaughan Williams allows the content, and what we might term the poetic conception, to determine the structure. His approach to thematic development and orchestral colour easily surpasses his earlier accomplishments. Having begun by absorbing the relatively conservative style of Brahms and other composers in his orbit, Vaughan Williams synthesized in the *Heroic Elegy and Triumphal Epilogue* the more progressive central European manner of Liszt, Wagner, Mahler, and Richard Strauss. He was ready for something new.

Around the beginning of 1902 Vaughan Williams seems to have reassessed his attitude towards orchestral composition. The works he produced for this medium in the years following 1902 give evidence of a new direction in his thought. Of course, many similarities run through the music of the entire period, but a comparison of the pre-1902 pieces with those composed just after reveals substantial changes in scope, style, and technique. Rather than returning to established genres such as the suite, serenade, extended symphonic poem, or concerto, Vaughan Williams now turned his attention to shorter, one-movement programmatic pieces.[25] This was a period of experimentation and he eventually scaled down plans for several

---

[25] It is beyond the scope of the present study to consider the programmatic dimension of these works as such; suffice it to say that this appears to be restricted to evocative titles for whole works, rather than involving detailed scenarios with specific structural implications.

groups of these short movements. He did manage, however, to complete substantial portions of at least four such works.

Even a cursory exploration of post-1902 orchestral pieces reveals some striking changes. Many of the melodic ideas are now clearly based on modal or pentatonic scales, with predominantly conjunct motion and distinctive rhythmic profiles. Most pieces utilize a relatively small amount of basic material. While some earlier compositions contained a profusion of themes, Vaughan Williams now contents himself with less material but more development. Texture is another element in which we can observe a marked change: on the whole, textures are lighter than before, creating a more transparent orchestral sound.

Characteristics familiar from Vaughan Williams's mature music become much more prominent during this period. Having imitated and mastered the basic styles of the recent past, Vaughan Williams seems to have been ready to adopt a more individual idiom. One strand in this is the emergence of folksong-like elements in Vaughan Williams's music. Yet we must be careful as to what precise source of influence we ascribe this development. Although Vaughan Williams's absorption with folksong dates to his student years and we know from his own testimony that he was composing 'modal waltzes' during his period of study with Stanford,[26] it was not until December 1903 that he began collecting songs in the field, and his knowledge of folk music was fairly limited before this. Yet by late 1903 he had already composed *Burley Heath* and *The Solent*, two scores in which folksong-derived melodies play an appreciable role.

There are, in fact, good grounds for believing that before it was shaped by folksong itself, Vaughan Williams's individual manner was influenced by Charles Stanford's treatment of folksong. In 1902 Stanford published his *Irish Rhapsody No. 1*, a work he had written during the previous year.[27] It is the first of a series of pieces that evokes an Irish ethos through quotation of folksong or folksong-like material. Stanford's technique of gradually assembling the folk melodies by initially using only fragments, and then allowing the complete tune to coalesce during the course of the movement, was appropriated by Vaughan Williams on several occa-

---

[26] See U. Vaughan Williams, *R.V.W.*, pp. 44–5.
[27] See Frederick Hudson, 'A Revised and Extended Catalogue of the Works of Charles Villiers Stanford (1852–1924)', *The Music Review*, 37 (1976), p. 116.

sions during the early years of the century. Perhaps the most notable example is the first theme of the *Norfolk Rhapsody No. 1*. The latter work, completed in 1906, shares many features with the Stanford *Irish Rhapsody No. 1*. Both juxtapose quick, dance-like sections with a more lyrical segment based on a folksong. Where Stanford uses the quick dance as his primary section, however, with the slower segment as a contrast, Vaughan Williams reverses the process by giving greater weight to the quiet, reflective material. A similar mode of thematic exposition can be found in the third movement of Stanford's *Irish Symphony*. Vaughan Williams was familiar with the latter through the arrangement for two pianos.[28]

The first pieces to exhibit this new approach were composed in 1902 and early 1903. Vaughan Williams planned a cycle of four impressions to be called *In the New Forest*.[29] *The Solent*, the second piece of the cycle, is the only one of the four to survive complete. 168 bars remain of the first impression, *Burley Heath*. It would appear that approximately two-thirds of the piece are represented, comprising two contrasting sections and the beginning of a recapitulation of the first. The remaining two works have disappeared; the only traces of them consist of the composer's heading 'Four Impressions for Orchestra' on the title page for the two surviving works, and a note that, 'the triangle is silent in nos. 1, 2, and 4'.

Burley Heath is characterized by extremely spare textures, with substantially developed inner parts reserved for climactic moments, where the texture thickens to sonorous effect. The work begins with a sustained open fifth in the bass that accompanies the entire opening segment and establishes a tonal focus on G. Vaughan Williams presents the primary thematic material gradually, by first introducing a static motif played by two horns, then adding a new motif with a wider range and greater rhythmic animation. These motifs are juxtaposed as various instruments join in the contrapuntal interplay, accompanied by the ever-present drone fifth in the bass. The interaction of motivic counterpoint and bass pedal creates a coherent

---

[28] See U. Vaughan Williams, *R.V.W.*, p. 44.

[29] Regarding the first performance of *The Solent* Kennedy gives the date and writes 'This is a diary marking. Where the performance took place is not known. Possibly it was played through privately' (*Catalogue*, p. 22). Kennedy does not indicate the source.

Example 2.4 *Burley Heath*, development of principal motifs

textural – harmonic matrix without the necessity of resorting to traditional harmonic progressions or chord patterns.

Vaughan Williams establishes a clear shape for the first section largely through textural means. As in many of the works from this period, the opening displays an almost hesitant character, with fragmentary initial presentation of the themes. The composer builds tension through an increase in textural complexity, dynamic levels, and thematic density. The opening section seems to contain four distinct thematic ideas. Closer acquaintance, however, reveals that the third and fourth ideas are simply variants of the first two. The transformations are accomplished by presenting an interrelated sequence of similar, but each slightly different, versions of each thematic strand. The opening motif is little more than a reiterated melodic third. Subsequent restatements expand on the basic interval, presenting versions with both major and minor third. Vaughan Williams appropriates a descending fourth from a new motif first heard some twenty-five bars into the piece, and transforms the original melodic shape with a conjunct turn figure in a new rhythmic profile (see Example 2.4).

The Solent achieves structural coherence through the balanced juxtaposition of diverse harmonic elements. Modal and tonal materials are combined to generate symphonic tension in a manner that recalls the tonal dualism employed in traditional symphonic style. In addition, the piece reflects the composer's growing mastery in handling orchestral sonority.

After its initial presentation by a solo clarinet, the primary theme is repeated by the string body in a way that suggests a kinship with the textures

Example 2.5 *The Solent*, harmonization of main theme

of the *Fantasia on a Theme by Thomas Tallis* (see Example 2.5). The melody is present in the uppermost voice throughout the extract, with single phrases or subphrases doubled by various accompanying voices. The range of texture covers four-and-a-half octaves, although most of the material is centred upon the extreme upper and lower regions of the continuum. This generates the particularly luminous sound often associated with the mature string music of Vaughan Williams. The interaction of the voices is clearly derived from polyphonic models; Tudor music is perhaps the most obvious source. The polyphonic matrix produces a highly ambiguous harmonic outline. The six-bar excerpt under consideration contains a shift of a minor third (G major to E major), a device that would become a particular favourite of Vaughan Williams in later years. The shape and range of the melody, encompassing only a minor sixth (B–G) between the pivotal pitches, suggest no clear tonal centre. The passage uses only four simple

Example 2.6 *The Solent*, primary thematic material

chords: G major, D major, C major, and E minor.[30] However, the chords are arranged in a progression that effectively nullifies much of the tension between tonic and dominant. Vaughan Williams weakens the dominant chord by 'hiding' the leading note of G throughout most of the passage.

The three main themes of the work are set out in Example 2.6. The ambiguous harmonic implications present in the first melody and its ensuing harmonization are balanced by the subsequent appearance of the fanfare theme, introduced by the brass. The rising perfect fourths give the music a clear tonal profile even while the bass alternates between E and F. The juxtaposition of this theme with the preceding material produces a harmonic dualism between modal and tonal colouring in the two successive themes. Thus Vaughan Williams generates tension by contrasting two different scales rather than two tonal planes within a single tonal hierarchy. On another level, this contrast obscures the kinship between the two

---

[30] The only exceptions are the final chord of the passage, E major, and its dominant-minor preparation (B minor) on the third beat of bar 5. Interestingly, it is not only the texture and harmony here that adumbrate the mature Vaughan Williams. Themes closely related to the melodic line of Example 2.5 play a prominent role in *A Sea Symphony*, on which Vaughan Williams began work in 1903, and, at the other end of his career, in the film score *The England of Elizabeth* and the slow movement of the Ninth Symphony, both completed shortly before his death in 1958 (see Kennedy, *Catalogue*, pp. 22–3).

melodies, especially the prominent rising fourth. The latter interval links both themes with the main material of the contrasting middle section, an agitated, recitative-like figure given initially to solo oboe (see Example 2.6 (c)).

The character of the oboe recitative calls to mind once again the Tallis Fantasia, and there are a number of parallels between the two works that might be pursued. Well over half a decade separates their composition, yet the earlier work may be viewed as a trial run for a number of the techniques that would later make the Fantasia a breakthrough work in the Vaughan Williams canon. The close affinity between the two pieces suggests that the style of the Tallis Fantasia was not simply an obedient response to the dictates of its source material, but an integral part of the young musician's evolving manner. The spectacular effect achieved at the première of the Fantasia has led many commentators to emphasize its qualities of newness, while overlooking the connections with Vaughan Williams's earlier works.

Harnham Down takes further many tendencies found in earlier works, often pushed to such a degree that the piece takes on an aura of experimentalism. This is especially the case regarding harmonic ambiguity. In *The Solent* and *In the Fen Country* (and in the slightly later *Norfolk Rhapsody No. 1*) Vaughan Williams begins with an unaccompanied tune, only gradually adding more voices. In contrast, *Harnham Down* presents twelve bars of introductory material before we hear the first clear-cut melody. The introduction is based on a string of parallel intervals, undulating between B and C, that suggests a kinship with the opening of *A Pastoral Symphony*; the harmony comes to rest on a diminished-seventh chord built on F♯, suggesting a move towards G, but Vaughan Williams instead begins the main section in A♭ major. The composer also shows a newly intense interest in chromaticism: a contrasting second theme in the opening section is little more than a decorated chromatic scale, and the lone theme of the brief middle section has a strong chromatic colouring. Perhaps the most unusual harmonic effect is reserved for the final sonority, a chord consisting of F♯, C, and E. The 'missing' third, A, can be inferred from the pizzicato bass interpolation four bars before the end; but closing on such a sonority – the notoriously ambiguous 'Tristan' chord – in a work that has primarily emphasized A♭ and E♭ is truly a leap 'toward the unknown region'.

Harnham Down continues the trend towards structural compression observed in *The Solent* and *Burley Heath*. The form is a clear ternary design, but the middle section is a mere twenty-two bars long and contains only five varied statements of a single melody. Its compact dimensions and inconclusive final cadence are appropriate to the work's function as the first of a pair of pieces. It is interesting to note that although the second piece, *Boldrewood*, has disappeared, *The Times*' review of the first performance of the pair hints that *Boldrewood* was the more substantial of the two.[31]

Vaughan Williams's high regard for *In the Fen Country* is suggested by the fact that he revised it on several different occasions, and that it is the only one of his early orchestral works that he did not withdraw. It was composed in April 1904, but according to annotations on the manuscript it was revised in 1905 and 1907, and the orchestration was altered as late as 1935.[32] It is thus difficult to place within the context of Vaughan Williams's development. It represents a more finished product than *Harnham Down*, which was begun in July of 1904 and so at one level postdates it, but the 1905 and 1907 revisions no doubt benefited from work on *Harnham Down*. Certainly the orchestration of *In the Fen Country*, not completed until thirty years after the initial composition, achieves a luminosity of texture and beauty of tonal colour far beyond that found in any of the early orchestral works.

In the Fen Country continues Vaughan Williams's preoccupation with the contemplative tone of *The Solent* and *Burley Heath*. Again, it hints at a vague outline of ternary form, although in this piece the composer ventures further from the framework established in the two earlier efforts. The central section dominates the whole; it is almost twice the length of the opening section and contains several internal subdivisions. It is characterized by a shift from 6/8 to 3/4 and the introduction of a syncopated accompaniment that creates a strong contrast with the more placid rhythms of the opening. Also notable is the ending of the piece: the gradual fading into nothingness would later become a Vaughan Williams trademark. *In the Fen Country* seems to be the first appearance of this technique in his output.

The opening portion is a meditation on an Aeolian tune first heard on cor anglais (see Example 2.7). Vaughan Williams expands on the theme

---

[31] *The Times*, 13 November 1907, p. 14.
[32] The work was not published until 1969 (Oxford University Press).

Example 2.7 *In the Fen Country*, opening Aeolian tune (bb. 1–3)

through a series of imitative entries and a gradual accumulation of textural density. As A. E. F. Dickinson has pointed out, *In the Fen Country* is largely an imitative composition, and this sets it apart from most of Vaughan Williams's music of the period.[33] It is also notable for its modal stability. William Kimell has shown how the composer often introduces variety into his melodic lines by mixing scale types or modulating frequently between various pitch profiles.[34] In this case, however, Vaughan Williams eschews modal modulation, preferring a continuous emphasis on the Aeolian scale established in the opening bars. The pitch centre migrates primarily between G, E, and C, but the piece is essentially monomodal. This monomodality, and the predominance throughout of imitative textures, give the work a strong sense of surface continuity that serves to mask the underlying rhythmic contrasts between sections.

Modal consistency is reinforced by thematic consistency: the opening tune abounds with possibilities for further development, and Vaughan Williams takes this cue to construct a work that is essentially monothematic. The imitative opening centres attention upon the mainly stepwise opening bars of the theme, but it is the distinctive descending third in bar 3 of the theme that serves as the basis for the melodic material heard in the central part of the work. The melodic third emerges as an important element in the passage at E.5 ff., and it becomes dominant in the 'new' theme introduced at letter H, which is almost entirely composed of thirds, both major and minor.

Third relationships are central to the broader harmonic and tonal progressions of *In the Fen Country*, and Vaughan Williams's handling of these displays a new harmonic sophistication, with melodic cells constructed to emphasize harmonic movement on both local level and larger

---

[33] *Vaughan Williams* (London: Faber and Faber, 1963), p. 165.
[34] 'Vaughan Williams's Melodic Style', *The Musical Quarterly*, 27/4 (October 1941), p. 494.

Example 2.8 *In the Fen Country*, recurring chordal motif (bb. B.6–9)

scale; the harmonic curve is employed not only as structural underpinning, but for coloristic effect as well. The piece abounds with tertian harmonic shifts that play a leading role in the unfolding development. The most significant of these recurring harmonic motifs is first heard at B.6 (see Example 2.8). The primary tonal centre at this point, D major, is juxtaposed with both B♭ major and F major triads. This motif functions as a structural unifier, as it is heard at several significant points in the composition: it is used at the climactic point of the first section (bars D.12–E.1), just before E major is established as the new key, and also in a roughly analogous place (O.14–P.3) in the shortened restatement of the opening section. Yet another juxtaposition of thirds forms an integral part of the middle section. The passage at E.5 ff., led by two solo clarinets, begins by suggesting C major but soon veers towards E major, a shift confirmed by the answering phrase of the strings; in this case, the underlying tonal shift is complemented by parallel thirds in the harmony and a melodic shape in which thirds predominate.

In the Fen Country represents the composer in full control of his material. There is a compelling relationship between the various facets of musical expression, with melody, harmony, and orchestration fused to a degree not yet encountered in a large-scale Vaughan Williams composition. He had finally discovered his own musical language and acquired the ability to exploit it.

An important aspect of Vaughan Williams's growth to maturity is reflected in the orchestral pieces written between 1898 and 1904. Compared with that of some of his contemporaries, the development was a slow one, but it proceeded at a steady pace. The period might be said to represent a period of assimilation and exploration; assimilation represented by the *Serenade*,

Bucolic Suite, and portions of both the *Fantasia* and the *Heroic Elegy and Triumphal Epilogue,* exploration by the one-movement programmatic works. In the former group, Vaughan Williams mastered formal models and stylistic gestures of the nineteenth century, and this is reflected in the predominant position given to melodic considerations, most notably thematic development. Only after completing this process of assimilation could the composer begin to experiment with a more personal idiom, one that sounds to us much closer to the mature Vaughan Williams. This experimentation was a lengthy process, with some elements, such as chromaticism and thematic profusion, eventually discarded. By the end of the period, however, several stylistic elements – modal and pentatonic melodic language, harmonic diatonicism, ternary structures, and a dense but widely spaced textural continuum – were already integral parts of the composer's language. Vaughan Williams had acquired a personal style that would, with few modifications, serve him well for more than fifty years.

3 Vaughan Williams, Tallis, and the Phantasy principle

ANTHONY POPLE

I

The *Fantasia on a Theme by Thomas Tallis* is today one of Vaughan Williams's best known and most highly regarded works. Wilfrid Mellers describes it as '[the] work wherein Vaughan Williams first discovered his identity ... his first *great* masterpiece'; Michael Kennedy suggests that 'to apply the adjective "sublime" to this music would not be overstating its wonderful blend of spiritual strength and physical exaltation'.[1] The work was not always so highly thought of, however: it receives scarcely a mention in A. E. F. Dickinson's otherwise appreciative book of 1928,[2] and does not seem to have been commercially recorded before 1936, when Vaughan Williams was in his mid-sixties.[3] Writing in the early 1960s, after the work had become extremely well known, the level-headed Dickinson reminded his readers that 'it would be a mistake ... to regard it as more than one side of the composer's development. ... Its hold over audiences is an incident of promotional history which will find its due level in the future.'[4]

With hindsight, one might indeed feel that the Tallis Fantasia lies outside the sequence of fine works inspired by literary figures – notably Whitman and Housman – that occupied Vaughan Williams between

---

[1] Wilfrid Mellers, *Vaughan Williams and the Vision of Albion* (London: Barrie & Jenkins, 1989), pp. 48–9; Kennedy, *Works*, p. 126.

[2] A. E. F. Dickinson, *An Introduction to the Music of Ralph Vaughan Williams* (London: Oxford University Press, 1928).

[3] The session with the augmented Boyd Neel orchestra was held by Decca on 28 January 1936. Letter from Walter Yeomans to Adrian Boult, in Lewis Foreman, ed., *From Parry to Britten: British Music in Letters 1900–1945* (London: Batsford, 1987), p. 190.

[4] A. E. F. Dickinson, *Vaughan Williams* (London: Faber and Faber, 1963), pp. 175–6.

Toward the Unknown Region and the *Five Mystical Songs*. But any musician of the day who chanced during 1910 to hear the title of Vaughan Williams's new work for the Three Choirs Festival of that year would probably have taken it to signify a piece lying within a familiar orbit, that of a broader run of compositions whose title it almost shares. The many 'Phantasies' submitted for W. W. Cobbett's competitions, or in some cases written to commissions from him, included by that time prize-winning works by such figures as Hurlstone, Bridge, and Ireland – the first two competitions alone (of 1905 and 1907) having occasioned the submission of 134 manuscripts.[5] Vaughan Williams's own Phantasy Quintet – a very different work from the Tallis Fantasia – dates from 1912, yet one can hardly imagine him being unaware two years earlier of the Cobbett competitions or of their ostensible basis in a revival of the Jacobean 'Fancy', 'Fancie', or 'Fantasia'. The year 1910 saw the first performance not only of the Tallis Fantasia but also of the *Fantasia on English Folk Song*; 1912 that of the *Fantasia on Christmas Carols*, as well as the composition of the Quintet which bears Cobbett's 'Ph' spelling.

Exactly what Cobbett meant by a 'Phantasy' was at first only vaguely defined. For the 1905 competition string quartets were solicited, 'the piece to be of short duration and performed without a break, but, if the composer desired, to consist of different sections varying in tempo and metre'.[6] Writing at length of these competitions for his *Cyclopedic Survey* (1929), i.e. some years after the event, Cobbett felt obliged to give a fuller description of the types of work to which his stimulus had given rise. In doing so he was careful to let others speak for him: principally, he took his material from an article published by Ernest Walker in the *Music Student* of 1915, but this itself quotes J. A. Fuller Maitland and Charles Stanford at key moments. Walker (with the evident approval of Cobbett) draws particular attention to the range and diversity of seventeenth-century works labelled 'Fancy',

---

[5] Walter Willson Cobbett, ed., *Cobbett's Cyclopedic Survey of Chamber Music*, 2nd edn [with supplementary material edited by Colin Mason] (London: Oxford University Press, 1963), vol. I, pp. 284–5. The prize money was generous: for example, the first prize won by Hurlstone in 1905 was £50, a considerable sum in Edwardian England.

[6] The original description paraphrased by Cobbett in *Cyclopedic Survey*, vol. I, p. 284.

'Fantasia' (etc.); he also points out that Cobbett's stipulations to composers entering his competitions were minimal, and observes that those Phantasy works successful in the competitions vary considerably in layout: 'its forms are capable of well-nigh unlimited variety, without in any way transgressing the spirit of Mr. Cobbett's own rules'.[7]

In assessing some of the actual works produced, however, Walker has to seek firmer ground and so prefaces his remarks with two rather more substantive descriptions of the Phantasy by other authors. The first is from Fuller Maitland, writing in the second edition of Grove's *Dictionary* (1904–10):

> A piece for concerted instruments in a continuous movement (with occasional changes of tempo and measure), occupying a shorter time than the usual classical works, and free from the structural laws of the 'classical' [sonata] form. In place of these it is ... recommended that the development section ... be replaced by a movement [*sic*] in slow tempo, which may include also a scherzando. ... In any case a logical connexion with the thematic material of the first part is maintained. A return to the characteristics of the first part of the movement is made, but not necessarily a definite repetition; and a developed coda is added as a finale. ... It will be seen that the revival of an old form takes proper cognizance of the tendencies of modern music since Liszt, with his 'transformation of themes'.[8]

The second is taken from Stanford's *Musical Composition* (1911):

> The reason for ... the Phantasies' ... existence may not improbably be a natural rebellion against the excessive length... of many modern works. ... The form which the remedy has taken is to condense all the movements of a work in sonata form into one.[9]

---

[7] Ernest Walker, 'The Modern British Phantasy', *Chamber Music: a Supplement (appearing alternate months) to the 'Music Student'*, 17 (November 1915), pp. 17–27, quoted in Cobbett, *Cyclopedic Survey*, vol. I, p. 287.

[8] J. A. Fuller Maitland, 'Fancy, Fantasy, or Phantasy', in *Grove's Dictionary of Music and Musicians*, 2nd edn, 5 vols. (London: Macmillan, 1904–10), vol. V, p. 638. Quoted in Walker, 'The Modern British Phantasy', p. 18, and thence in Cobbett, *Cyclopedic Survey*, vol. I, pp. 285–6.

[9] Charles V. Stanford, *Musical Composition: a Short Treatise for Students* (London: Macmillan, 1911), p. 162. Quoted in Walker, 'The Modern British Phantasy', p. 19 and thence in Cobbett, *Cyclopedic Survey*, vol. I, p. 286.

As Walker points out, the tone of Stanford's description is essentially dismissive of the Phantasy concept, yet the question of length is one to which we shall return in connection with the Tallis Fantasia. It is Fuller Maitland's discussion which offers the greater scope for comparison with Vaughan Williams's work, though it should be evident that Vaughan Williams needed no Cobbett, Walker, or Fuller Maitland (let alone Stanford) to enlighten him on the subject of Jacobean music or to show its possible implications for him as a composer. The present study does not mean to suggest that Vaughan Williams adhered to, or measured himself against, any set pattern in writing the Tallis Fantasia – the chronology of the sources would make this highly questionable in any case – but rather it seeks to exploit the existence of influential norms in order to construct an interpretation of the Tallis Fantasia that takes into account such matters as the composer's revisions to the score. And while it ought not to be said that Vaughan Williams treated Cobbett's activities with disdain, his own 'Phantasy' (the Quintet) is a slight work, written to commission and quirky in its design – if thereby distantly related to the longer examples among Purcell's string Fantazias and perhaps for this reason meeting with Cobbett's especial approval.[10] Conversely, the Tallis Fantasia may be seen to deal far more profoundly with matters of faith, rediscovery, revival, national roots, and convivial music-making than Cobbett, for all his cultured enthusiasm, might ever have dared to hope.

II

Many of the work's more profound aspects have been explored over the years in critical appreciations. In some cases ideas have been developed out of all proportion, particularly in the last decade or so of the composer's life when one author after another sought to pay fulsome tribute to the Grand Old Man of English Music. Recurring ideas in this literature include:

- a perceived relation of the work to antiquity, ecclesiastical architecture and vocal church music
- anthropomorphic descriptions, frequently concerning the singing voice
- evocation of the rural outdoors
- the music's unitary, evolutionary span

[10] Cobbett, *Cyclopedic Survey*, vol. I, p. 262.

There is a great deal of common ground between the authors involved, some of it reflecting the passing down of interpretative ideas rather than a convergence of entirely independent thoughts. For example, the music's apparent evocation of antiquity through innovative means was identified by Fuller Maitland in his review of the first performance for *The Times* – 'Throughout its course one is never quite sure whether one is listening to something very old or very new'[11] – and this observation, only slightly developed for rhetorical effect, reappeared in the words both of James Day ('Here is something as old as the soil of England itself, yet for ever fresh and original') and of Michael Kennedy, who wrote of 'the strong impression that this music is as old as time itself and yet as new as though it had been written yesterday'.[12]

Other ideas were not simply passed down, but seized upon extravagantly to almost sycophantic effect in the composer's last years, or in immediately posthumous tribute. The association of the work with church architecture again took its cue from the effect of its première in Gloucester Cathedral, as reported by Fuller Maitland in *The Times*:

> We can recall no piece of pure instrumental music produced at a Three Choirs Festival which has seemed to belong to its surroundings so entirely. ... It could never thrive in a modern concert-room, but in the quieter atmosphere of the cathedral the mind falls readily into the reflective attitude necessary for the enjoyment of every unexpected transition from chord to chord ...[13]

Whilst many musicians since Fuller Maitland's time, Mellers and Kennedy included,[14] have been struck by the work's particular effectiveness when performed in the acoustic of a large church, a number of commentators have gone considerably further by ascribing a cathedral-like spaciousness to the music itself: Scott Goddard tells his readers that '[the] chords are of vast proportions', whilst James Day describes the fifteen-minute work as

11 Quoted in Kennedy, *Works*, p. 93.
12 James Day, *Vaughan Williams* (London: J. M. Dent and Sons, 1961), p. 135. Kennedy, *Works*, p. 126.   13 Quoted in Kennedy, *Works*, p. 95.
14 Mellers: 'The ecclesiastical building is part of the music's acoustic' (*Vaughan Williams and the Vision of Albion*, p. 57). Kennedy: 'There are sombre minutes, in which darkness and doom seem to be contemplated; there are others in which sunlight floods through the arches and coloured glass of the cathedrals in which this music is often played' (*Works*, p. 126).

'massive, spacious, powerful and ruminative'.[15] Ursula Vaughan Williams suggests that '[the composer's] early love for architecture and his historical knowledge were so deeply assimilated that they were translated and absorbed into the texture and line of the music', and for Hubert Foss 'The English Cathedral is with us in the freshness of its birth ... the blocks are in truth as rough and heavy as those that pattern the massive pillars of Durham Cathedral'.[16] Percy M. Young's expression of this idea is perhaps the most spectacular:

> Tallis's melody ... is utilitarian music and may be related to the architectural principles of the Normans, to which Tallis was accustomed at Waltham Abbey. By repetition Vaughan Williams builds, as it were, an arcade. ... His habit of altering the basic material by sudden and mystical changes of tonality shows a similar fascination to that which is experienced as the eye catches this arch lit by the high light of the sun, that in one shadow, that in another, a fourth softened by light filtered through *grisaille*. ... The atmosphere of the cathedral is surely felt within the music.[17]

Such ideas have even attached themselves to musical details: Day describes the motion from an F minor triad to a G major triad at bar U.2 as being, in its effect, 'like a shaft of golden sunlight in the aisles of a great cathedral';[18] while Young's architectural metaphor is elaborated with reference to bars 3 ff. ('the illusion of distance first created by the violins'), the *Poco più animato* ('Further analogy may allow relation between the fantasia proper, commencing at letter I, and the involutions of mediæval vaulting'), and to the work's climax between letters R and S ('the whole body of players is exercised in counterpoint of energy and spaciousness').[19]

Once more, J. A. Fuller Maitland had the first say, but by no means the last, in a line of thought that transferred the choral attributes of Tallis's theme to the purely instrumental sounds of Vaughan Williams's *Fantasia*. His suggestion that '[the] voices of the old church musicians ... are around

[15] Scott Goddard, 'Ralph Vaughan Williams, O. M.', in A. L. Bacharach, ed., *British Music of Our Time* (Harmondsworth: Pelican, 1946), p. 87. Day, *Vaughan Williams*, p. 133.

[16] U. Vaughan Williams, *R. V. W.*, p. 88. Hubert Foss, *Ralph Vaughan Williams: A Study* (London: Harrap, 1950), p. 118.

[17] Percy M. Young, *Vaughan Williams* (London: Dobson, 1953), p. 45.

[18] Day, *Vaughan Williams*, p. 134.   [19] Young, *Vaughan Williams*, pp. 45–7.

one'[20] is echoed rather more fantastically by Mellers, who likens the music of Orchestra II at bars E.7 ff. to 'a choir of slightly distraught angels',[21] whilst Young draws attention to 'the responsorial aspect of the harmonic arrangement' at bars 4 ff.:

> [The] unison presentation of the first part of the first line of the melody, strengthened beyond the capacity of the precentor's voice[,] is noticed; to which the choir, in harmony and in gentle variation of the faux bourdon arrangement by Tallis of the phrase conclusion, makes answer.[22]

But it is not only ecclesiastical voices that have been heard in this music. Kennedy writes of bars U.2 ff. that '[the] violin and viola, operatically intertwined, seem almost to assume human and personal significance',[23] and Mellers, who describes the opening of the viola solo at letter I as 'beginning with three "speaking" repeated notes', goes so far as to suggest that in bars E.7 ff. 'the harmonic dislocations of Orchestra I are humanly corporeal and dramatic'.[24] Further dependent on anthropomorphism is the manner in which the work's interaction of sacred and secular aspects has been connected in the minds of several critics with the evocation of the rural outdoors through allusion to folksong. Mellers writes of bars I.1 ff. that 'four soloists ... metamorphose the Tallis hymn into a liberated melody of folk-like cast'; the viola solo at I.1 'flows in flexible rhythm ... transforming ecclesiastical devotion into pastoral lyricism ... the spirit of Bunyan helps Vaughan Williams to carry Tallis's "people's prayer" into the open fields'.[25] Young, for his part, suggests that '[the] final recapitulatory passage ... goes outside the church and embodies something of the pastoral contentment of *The Lark Ascending*'.[26]

If these last two authors seem to have suggested a programmatic aspect to the music, it is interesting that on this issue their points of musical focus should diverge, for any consideration of the work's possible programmatic quality has to reckon with the assertion by most if not all critics that it is exceptionally unified and/or organic in nature. Kennedy is unequivocal

---

[20] Quoted in Kennedy, *Works*, p. 93.
[21] Mellers, *Vaughan Williams and the Vision of Albion*, p. 53.
[22] Young, *Vaughan Williams*, p. 46.   [23] Kennedy, *Works*, pp. 125–6.
[24] Mellers, *Vaughan Williams and the Vision of Albion*, pp. 55, 53.
[25] *Ibid.*, pp. 57, 55.   [26] Young, *Vaughan Williams*, p. 47.

on this point, stating that 'in performance it sounds unified and indivisible'; Mellers balances his identification of ideas with specific passages against a conviction that the music 'is in essence evolutionary'; Young writes that '[the work's] material form grows from contemplation of the nature of the theme'; while Day describes 'a steady growth of relentless pressure'.[27] None the less, to conceive the work as organic does not necessarily conflict with the more general programmatic idea – one might prefer to call this a scenario – which is expressed in strikingly similar terms by Mellers ('in the course of the work some rite of passage occurs'), Young ('the subject, having suffered visionary analysis, is invested with spiritual power'), and Goddard, who saw in this work 'the calm unfolding of a dream of abstract beauty ... it has the force of a revelation'.[28] Mellers articulates this by identifying aspects of synthesis: at letter K or thereabouts, 'Folk song becomes a many-in-oneness like Tudor polyphony in full flight', and when the orchestras join forces, just after letter P, 'Tallis's hymn and Vaughan Williams's pastorally Edenic song become one with the marriage of the divided choirs'.[29]

The concept of this piece as a programmatic work that operates by the re-synthesis of organically derived and evocatively differentiated musical types is, strictly speaking, at some remove from the more abstract concept of the Fantasia or Phantasy. Whilst the opening up of this critical space might not be disconcerting in itself, there lies within it an assumption of authorial intent that needs addressing. The clearest example of this is to be seen in Mellers's discussion of the Fantasia, which explicitly forms part of a larger psychological portrait of its composer as a 'double man'. Seeing the Fantasia's subject as the healing of the breach that arises from a 'Fall from grace to disgrace', Mellers does not hesitate, for example, to liken the double orchestra to the two choir stalls of a Tudor cathedral and beyond this to the idea that 'the Whole has been sundered'.[30] It is entirely typical of Mellers's writings that he does not fear to tread here; in contrast, the earlier authors

27 Kennedy, *Works*, p. 124; Mellers, *Vaughan Williams and the Vision of Albion*, p. 57; Young, *Vaughan Williams*, p. 45; Day, *Vaughan Williams*, p. 133.

28 Mellers, *Vaughan Williams and the Vision of Albion*, p. 51; Young, *Vaughan Williams*, p. 45; Goddard, 'Ralph Vaughan Williams, O. M.', p. 87.

29 Mellers, *Vaughan Williams and the Vision of Albion*, p. 55.

30 *Ibid.*, pp. 50–1.

cited above did not always acknowledge their assumption of authorial intent, though this was transparently an evasive tactic when the credibility of their fantasies – many of them written, in both senses, prior to the 'death of the author' – was dependent, at the very least, on their being understood as plausible developments of the composer's own view, or, perhaps more typically, on their being taken directly to signify and illuminate the composer's thoughts.

It would be idle, however, to pretend that such writing should be straightforwardly dismissed. Better to grapple with the problem – as Vaughan Williams resolutely attempts to do, in relation to Wagner's writings, in the course of his substantial critical essay on Beethoven's Ninth Symphony. Surprisingly, having castigated 'Wagner's attempt to give the whole work a "meaning", as was the fashion in that materialistic age ... of "romanticism"', and though conducting his discussion largely in technical language, Vaughan Williams ultimately resorts to a choice of words that would appear to do what he accuses Wagner of: he writes in quick succession of a 'momentary triumph', of a 'sexless chord of A', of 'sinister, soft barks on the trumpet'.[31] Immediately, however, he sees the difficulty, and proposes a way out of it:

> Music can indeed portray the very depths of the soul, but it does not
> do so on the lines of a story, but rather on those of a building ... the
> 'recapitulation' in a Beethoven symphony is not a mere saying of the same
> thing twice, but a restatement of the initial ideas now seen in a new light
> derived from all the phases the music has been through since it set out on its
> journey. And ... these new lights on old faces are to be found in that part of
> the composition which leads back from the section of contrast to the section
> of restatement, or, to put it architecturally, the curve of an arch back to its
> supporting pillar, and this curve is known as the 'development' section.[32]

For all his good conscience Vaughan Williams, too, is unable to close the critical space: having opened this Pandora's box of fantasy, his insistent architectural/structural metaphor cannot protect him from writing of 'portrayal', of 'restatement', of the music's 'journey', of 'new light on old faces'.

---

[31] The essay 'Some Thoughts on Beethoven's Choral Symphony', dated 1939–40, is reprinted in R. Vaughan Williams, *National Music*, pp. 83–120. The quoted passage on Wagner appears on p. 89 and the brief epithets on p. 97.

[32] Vaughan Williams, *National Music*, pp. 97–8.

III

There are a number of ironies here, not least that one of the recurrent fantastical themes in the critical literature on the Fantasia is that of church architecture, in which arches and pillars predominate. Perhaps most ironic is that Vaughan Williams's discussion should set such store by the development section of a sonata movement in articulating what he is happy to call a musical 'journey' – cf. Mellers's 'rite of passage' – when it is precisely the lack of a development section, or the question of what is substituted for it, that is central to attempts to circumscribe the nature of a Phantasy in the prosaic terminology of musical construction. In all this, it might be observed, the aporia lies between the principals of a fantasy and the Phantasy principle.

The question of the work's form is in any case clouded to some extent by the fact that Vaughan Williams revised the Fantasia after its first performance and again before publication. Whilst the autograph full score contains generally clear evidence of the details of these revisions, they have received comparatively little attention from scholars.[33] The first, dated 12 January 1913, was made shortly before the work's second performance, which took place at one of Balfour Gardiner's London concerts on 11 February 1913;[34] a further revision is dated 7 April 1919. Most of the changes may be likened to the 'nips and tucks' of a tailor or dressmaker. Nineteen bars were cut in this way: four before letter E, eight around letter G, three between letters O and P, and four between letters Y and Z. The most

[33] I am grateful to Rosalind Cyphus of the Royal Academy of Music Library, London, and to Christopher Clarkson and David Dorning of West Dean College, Sussex, for kindly assisting me towards my study of this source and generously providing me with specialist facilities. The RAM library's catalogue entry for the manuscript (MS 7) summarizes the physical evidence of the revisions and draws attention to the loss of the first restatement of the Tallis theme. A similar description is to be found in A. E. F. Dickinson, 'The Vaughan Williams Manuscripts', *Music Review*, 23 (1962), pp. 177–94.

[34] RAM MS 7, p. 38. This would seem to contradict Ursula Vaughan Williams's comment on the 1913 performance that 'after this first hearing in a concert hall [Ralph] knew what revisions he wanted to make' (*R.V.W.*, p. 107), unless these intentions were retained in the composer's memory and implemented in 1919.

far-reaching alteration – probably dating from 1919[35] – accomplished the almost complete excision of a full but highly varied restatement of Tallis's theme after letter U. This further cut of fourteen bars made the work altogether some thirty-three bars shorter, in the version that is generally known, than when it was first heard. Vaughan Williams made jottings in the manuscript to keep track of the total reduction in length and the implication of this for the work's duration in performance – perhaps in response to reactions like that of the anonymous critic who reviewed the first performance for the *Gloucester Journal*: 'We had short phrases repeated with tiresome iteration ... there was a feeling of relief when the *Fantasia* came to an end. ... The piece took nineteen minutes in performance.'[36] Like *A London Symphony*, which was cut by the composer far more severely, the Fantasia evidently met in some quarters with a sense of incomprehension which accused the music of fragmentation, and thereby of failing to sustain its length. To the extent that thematic fragmentation is part and parcel of the Tallis Fantasia's format, such criticism was in this case to some extent perceptive. But subsequent reaction has placed a more positive construction on this aspect of the work, seeing it as the key to its organicism. Mellers, for example, writes of the work's 'discovery of generation and regeneration within techniques basically melodic rather than harmonic'.[37]

It is arguable, however, whether such organicism is a genuinely technical feature or is more properly considered programmatically. In the second part of his essay 'The Evolution of the Folk-song', and in 'The Influence of Folk-song on the Music of the Church', Vaughan Williams seeks to intertwine the history of folksong and church music during medieval and Renaissance times, using English music as his principal example:

---

[35] Circumstantial evidence to support this assertion may be gleaned from a systematic comparison between the various points of revision, on the basis of the physical method of making the cuts (e.g. by pasting new MS pages over the existing, and in such cases the types of paper and adhesive used), the sizes of nib used for the musical notation of replacement material, the shades of blue pencil used to indicate bars to be omitted and the ways in which this is shown, and the musical nature of the revision (e.g. straightforward omission, paraphrase of old material by new, cut with adjustments at the join).

[36] Quoted in Kennedy, *Works*, p. 94.

[37] Mellers, *Vaughan Williams and the Vision of Albion*, p. 58.

> There is no written record of a musical soil which could have produced such
> … flowerings as when the wonderful Tudor school suddenly appeared, as
> [historians of early English music] pathetically complain, 'from nowhere'. Of
> course, these things do not spring from nowhere, of course, the English
> were 'carolling' … all through the Middle Ages, disregarded by the
> Frenchified court and the Italianized church, but coming to their full
> fruition in the age of Elizabeth. … When the great School of Tudor music
> arose, it could go straight to the fountain head for its inspiration …
> inheriting its energy and vitality from the unwritten and unrecorded art of
> its own countryside.[38]

This is the reverse of the sequence of thematic derivation which is normally understood in quasi-organicist accounts of the Tallis Fantasia – according to which the folksong-like viola theme (I.1 ff.) is 'derived' from the third phrase of Tallis's theme – but it accords very well with the order in which musical ideas are presented at the beginning of the work. The five elements which lead to the first statement of the Tallis theme (A.5 ff.) may be enumerated as shown in Example 3.1. Element a is an early Vaughan Williams fingerprint, as has been widely noted;[39] if it is to be associated with either church music or folksong it must be with the latter, through the pentatonic basis of its upper line. (Although the texture as a whole is far from pentatonic, one may substantiate this connection through Vaughan Williams's approving remarks, in his essay 'The Folk-song', on the harmonic practice of Musorgsky and others, who 'evidently preferred to build their [neo-modal] harmony from the melody downwards'.)[40] Taken in this way, it also establishes from the outset – even before the introduction of church music – the principle that this work will transfer vocal music to the textures of the double string orchestra. Following this, the melodic fragments c and c', which do not move outside a pentatonic framework, are not yet identified with Tallis's theme; their monodic presentation and responsorial treatment in conjunction with d and d', noted by Young, is more likely to associate them with plainsong than with polyphonic church music, whilst d and d', on the other hand, clearly evoke organum. Again, Vaughan Williams's comments on these genres are apposite: in 'The Influence of Folk-song on

[38] Vaughan Williams, *National Music*, pp. 50, 52.
[39] For example, in Kennedy, *Works*, p. 124.
[40] Vaughan Williams, *National Music*, p. 26.

Example 3.1 Elements of the 'evolution', bb. 1–A.4 (with original time signatures and metronome markings)

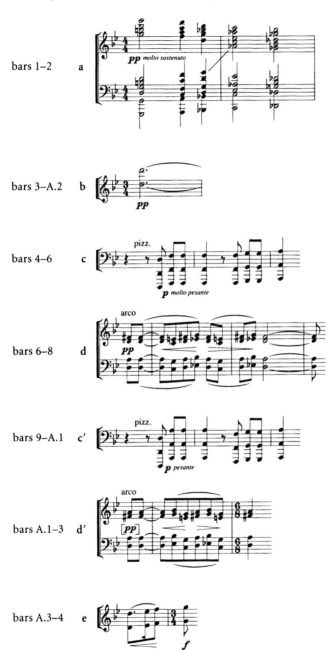

the Music of the Church', he argues at length that 'We have direct evidence of the effect of folk-song on … plainsong … in the history of French song [from the time of Charlemagne]. … in plainsong … we see the muse of the people'; in 'The Folk-song' he observes that 'harmony grew out of the Organum'.[41] Thus from the sequence folksong–plainsong–organum–Tallis we may infer something exactly in line with Vaughan Williams's ideas of musical 'evolution' – there being ample evidence that, in common with others such as his teacher Hubert Parry, he saw musical history in evolutionary terms.[42] And in line with current thought in the psychology of listening, encapsulated in Marvin Minsky's concept of the 'sonata as teaching machine',[43] we may see the presentation of this sequence as didactic, serving to expound to the listener Vaughan Williams's view of the relationship between folksong and Tudor church music, with the clear motivic relationship between c–c'–d–d' and Tallis's theme simply enhancing the evolutionary sense of the passage. Although, since the theme dates back to the sixteenth century, it is indisputable that in terms of compositional process the theme came first and the motivic fragments were derived from it, this is *not* the order of events that Vaughan Williams chooses to present. On the contrary, the listener's likely knowledge that the theme dates from Elizabethan times invests the composer's own material – preceding the theme in an historically projected presentation – with an even greater, and indeterminate, 'antiquity'. All of this happens within the Fantasia's opening moments – less than twenty bars in all.

After the double presentation of the theme, the next thirty-two bars lead from an extension of Tallis's final phrase, through various melodic fragments, and into the folksong-like solo viola theme. In the original version this passage was significantly longer, with four additional bars before E and fourteen (very different) bars where we presently have F.4–G.1, thus making forty-four bars in all. Certainly, Vaughan Williams flexes his harmonic muscles in this part of the work – I shall return to this

---

[41] *Ibid.*, pp. 75, 77, 25.

[42] It should not be overlooked that Charles Darwin was Vaughan Williams's great-uncle. For a more detailed discussion of Darwin and other aspects of Vaughan Williams's intellectual background see Byron Adams's essay in the present volume.

[43] Marvin Minsky, *Music, Mind, and Meaning* [AI memo no. 616] (Cambridge, Mass.: MIT Artificial Intelligence Laboratory, 1981).

below – and the motivic link-back between the opening of the viola melody and the third phrase of Tallis's theme is crystal clear, but the intervening material does not immediately seem to trace, say, an 'evolutionary' path from Tallis's Elizabethan style through to Vaughan Williams's own. The use of motif e near the beginning of the viola theme satisfies Fuller Maitland's criterion (quoted by Walker quoted by Cobbett)[44] that in the middle section of a Phantasy 'a logical connexion with the thematic material of the first part is maintained', but it is arguable whether it does so by taking 'proper cognizance of the tendencies of modern music since Liszt, with his "transformation of themes"'. As Mellers puts it: '[from E.5] the music develops in a technical sense: though one might more accurately call it anti-development, in so far as it functions by fragmenting aspects of Tallis's theme and discovering within them unpredictable cross-references'.[45] Whilst in the context of the Phantasy principle the use of the word 'development' is fraught with difficulties, Mellers's implication that this passage indulges in obfuscation in order to prepare for subsequent clarity would be perhaps not altogether wide of the mark, were one to understand the music merely in thematic terms. In this light, it is interesting to observe that the 'logic' by which motif e emerges at I.2 is a little clearer in the original version of the score. Example 3.2 shows the fourteen bars (1910/F.4–G.7) that were replaced by the present 1919/F.4–G.1, together with a schematic outline showing the emergence of the motif – a process largely powered by the antiphonally scored rocking figure first heard at 1910/G.4. The replacement bars paraphrase some of the earlier material, with a focused presentation of e at 1919/F.7–G.1, but the rocking figure is excised altogether and the revision does not project the same sense of thematic process.

This does not tell the full story, however. Although the thematic material at E.5 is not new, the important idea of antiphonal scoring is here introduced to the music for the first time. After a series of exchanges between the large and small orchestras, this principle of antiphony is reduced – liquidated, in the Schoenbergian sense – to the point at which single chords are exchanged across the orchestras (1910/G.1–4, 1919/F.5–7). It is from this point in the 1910 version that the rising motif e is generated – re-generated

[44] See p. 49 above.
[45] Mellers, *Vaughan Williams and the Vision of Albion*, p. 53.

Example 3.2 bb. 1910/F.4–G.7

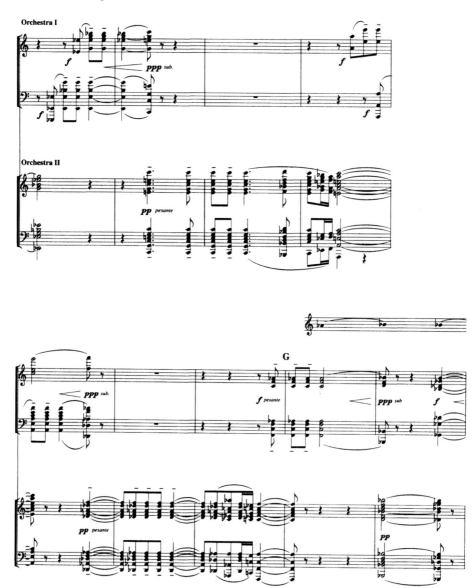

Example 3.2 (*cont.*)

from nothing, as it were – whereas in the definitive version of the score e emerges fully formed (1919/F.7–G.1). What is more, the textural liquidation from E.5 may be understood to reinforce an ongoing thematic liquidation already in progress. In the 1919 version this is set in train at E.1, when the last melodic cadence of Tallis's theme is interrupted in mid-stream and turned into an oscillating figure. In the original version of the score, four additional bars at the outset mean that the process of liquidation from 1910/D.7 is more gradual and perceptible (see Example 3.3).

Without this four-bar link into E.1, the tonal shift at E.3 is thrust even more strongly into relief. Tallis's theme provides the aural context for this continuation, and thus must also do so for a study of the expansion of harmonic and modal resources that Vaughan Williams swiftly embarks upon. The melody of Tallis's theme, as quoted by Vaughan Williams, lies entirely within the Phrygian mode on G (3♭: G–A♭–B♭–C–D–E♭–F),[46] but Tallis's

---

[46] Designations such as '3♭' will be used below to identify the key-signature (in this instance, three flats) which by convention signifies the diatonic collection concerned.

Example 3.3 bb. 1910/D.7–10

harmony adds B♮ (in the frequent *tierce de Picardie* cadences), and briefly A♮ and F♯ (in the solitary triad on D, quoted by Vaughan Williams at A.8 and C.5). This is not out of line with Vaughan Williams's statement that 'When harmony grew out of the Organum, composers found that they could not work in the modes with their new-found harmonic scheme. ... The harmony of Palestrina and his contemporaries is therefore not purely modal'.[47] The most frequent alternative harmonic focus to G in Tallis's theme is C (modal degree iv); the last part of the theme (from the appearance of motif e) concentrates harmonically on uninflected (i.e. diatonic) triads rooted on modal degrees iv, VI, II, and vii, prior to the final i.[48] In the original version, the music continues fully within this framework from 1910/D.7, cadencing on to iv at 1910/D.8. The following two bars expand the harmonic basis through a *tierce de Picardie* cadence on to VII (F major triad) at 1910/D.10. At F.1–2, this F has clearly been taken up as a pitch centre within the same diatonic collection as before, using as i, VII, and III three of the chords that were previously prominent in a G-Phrygian context at the end of the theme. Thus the excision of the four bars 1910/D.7–10 causes the music to jump the gun a little in the definitive version; none the less, the music of E.1–2 functions as a clear continuation of the end of the theme, using the same repertory of chords and the same diatonic basis: only the pitch centre has changed.

At the change of mode into E.3, the extent to which an aspect of continuity balances against the more obvious disjuncture depends in turn upon the extent to which the oscillating upper line has been established as a point of focus in the musical texture prior to the modal change. Arguably, this focus is more strikingly achieved in the revision than in the 1910 version. Either way, the change of mode is, on paper at least, extreme (see Example 3.4a): the pitch centre moves by a tritone (ic6) and the modal diatonic collection moves essentially by the same interval class.[49] Two additional

[47] Vaughan Williams, *National Music*, p. 25.
[48] Upper- and lower-case Roman numerals are employed here to indicate whether the triad in question has a major or a minor third.
[49] The term 'interval class', conventionally abbreviated to ic, is used by music theorists to denote intervals counted in semitone steps, thereby encompassing enharmonically equivalent spellings (e.g. a minor third and an augmented second are both examples of ic3). It is appropriate to employ this terminology when, as in certain aspects of the Fantasia, both diatonic and enharmonically equivalent spellings are found in comparable musical situations and the difference is immaterial. (It will be plain that in other aspects of the work the question of a diatonic, whole-tone, or other similarly constrained basis is of great significance, and terminology will be applied appropriately.) The term ic is more usually employed in discussions of music where pitch class and register are regarded to a great extent as separable phenomena; thus 'ic' will also be used here in connection with passages in which sketches or revisions involve

Example 3.4 bb. E.1–4: (a) change of mode by ic6, with four common pcs; (b) ic3 root progressions across bar-lines

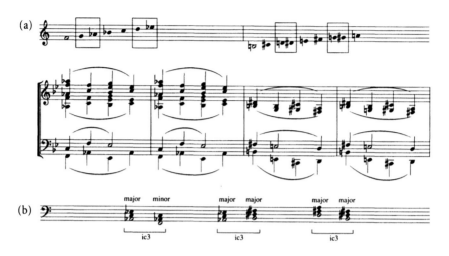

common pcs, however, are retained through the alternate use of both minor and major thirds, and both minor and major sixths; one of these common pcs (E♭/D♯) is employed pivotally in the upper line across the bar-line from E.2 to E.3. Another factor which serves to maintain continuity over moments of potential disruption, and indeed does so more generally in the Fantasia, may be detected in the root progressions across the bar-lines at E.1–2, E.2–3, and E.3–4 (see Example 3.4b). In each case, the root moves up or down by ic3; the first example, being entirely diatonic, involves a major triad followed by a minor, whereas across the change of mode at E.2–3, and also at E.3–4, both triads are major. The last of these progressions places the successive major triads in a context of modal mixture, inflecting the minor third to major at the point of arrival (as in Tallis's *tierce de Picardie*

wholesale transpositions which are more exact with respect to pitch class *per se* than to the totality of the musical texture in its registral layout. The many nuances of latent meaning in such terminological alternatives – fascinatingly compounded in a work such as this by the not-quite-interchangeability of modal and tonal terminologies – is one reason why the technical discussion of early twentieth-century music remains much more of an art than a science.

cadences). This establishes, for the first time in the course of the work, a characteristic harmonic progression – also seen, for example, in the opening of the second song of *On Wenlock Edge*, an emblematic passage in early Vaughan Williams (Example 3.5a) – that will feature at significant moments later on. The same root progression is found at the half-bar within both E.3 and E.4. Thus, by the double bar-line, a series of subtle connections has translated us from Tallis's harmonically inflected Phrygian modality – which, in Vaughan Williams's broader view, and as presented directly at the opening of the work, had 'evolved' from organum – into a musical language encompassing the most dramatic shifts of expanded diatonic resource, the use of common tones and melodic focus to project continuity over such disjunctures, a characteristic root progression of ic3 between triads (in particular, a root progression of ic3 downwards linking two major triads), and, in the 1910 version at least, the principle that pitch centres may change whilst an underlying referential pc collection remains constant.

The root progression into E.5 is by ic4 upwards – another new departure, therefore, but once again counterbalanced by the fact that the chord of arrival would lie within the established mode were its third not inflected from minor to major. The same cannot be said of the progression in E.6–7, though this again involves root progression by ic4: the D minor triad is clearly differentiated from the diatonic collection F♯–G♯–A♯–B–C♯–D♯–E to which bars E.5–10 otherwise adhere. A change of mode, to E♭ Phrygian with major third, is accomplished through the characteristic falling ic3 progression (spelled enharmonically) at F.1; this mode holds sway through to F.4, at which point the two versions of the score diverge.

The 1910 version continues in the manner of the preceding bars: the first orchestra contributes to two further changes of mode through the antiphonal exchanges – the first through the familiar downward ic3 progression, the second through an upward ic4 progression similar to that in bar E.7 – whilst the second orchestra's material develops away from close reminiscences of Tallis's theme, though still continuing broadly in the same vein. (With hindsight, one can understand why Vaughan Williams chose to excise these passages, which have no clear longer-term function thematically.) As noted above, at 1910/G.1 the

Example 3.5 Emblematic progressions from 'From Far, From Eve and Morning' (*On Wenlock Edge*)

(a) bb. 1–3

(b) bb. 8–11

principle of antiphony is liquidated to the point that single chords are exchanged between the orchestras. The initial progression on to a B♭ major triad from F minor is entirely diatonic (with the preceding C minor triad, F Dorian); but the following progressions take up the pattern of E.6–7, F.1, 1910/F.5 and 1910/F.8, with root progressions through ic4 downwards (both triads major), ic6 (major/minor), and ic3 downwards (both triads minor). The ascending upper line of these bars is transmuted into the rocking melodic figure (supported by diatonic harmonic changes) from 1910/G.4, out of which motif e emerges at 1910/G.6–7. In significant contrast to the 1919 version of the score, the final melodic cadence of this motif is supported here by the now familiar descending ic3 root progression.

In the later version of the score, 1919/F.5–7 paraphrases the chordal exchange of 1910/G.2–4, with root progressions by ic6 (major/ minor), ic4 downwards (minor/major: cf. E.7) and ic6 (major/minor once again). Above all this, the rising upper line is diatonically consistent with the E-Dorian mode in which motif e now appears. The harmonic support for this motif may be compared with another characteristic progression from the outer sections of 'From Far, From Eve and Morning' (Example 3.5b) – though in the Fantasia the second chord is heard in first inversion.

From 1919/G.1 (cf. 1910/G.7) to H.10, the music is dominated by the melodic motif first heard as **d**. This is twice interrupted: first by a restatement of motif **a** (at 1919/G.2–3), and then (at H.1–2) by a variant of **a** in which the falling pentatonic line is transferred to the bass whilst the top line presents two versions of motif **e**. The harmonic support for all the statements of **d** comes from Tallis's theme, but at its least characteristic point – namely, the sole appearance of the dominant triad which momentarily introduces two non-modal pcs. Vaughan Williams thus pits what in his own evolutionary terms is the most highly developed fragment of Tallis's theme against material which in the 'evolutionary' opening of the Fantasia was taken to represent primordial folksong. And, just as the variant of **a** combines Tallis's motif **e** and the folksong idea, so are these two principles also conjoined in the manifold repetitions of **d** (see Example 3.6), which expose what Vaughan Williams identifies elsewhere as a 'stock phrase' of folksong (here labelled **d″**) that he once heard emerging from the speaking voice of an excited preacher ('It seemed that I had witnessed the change from speech to song in actual process').[50]

Thus the entire passage, bars 1919/E.1–H.10 (1910/D.7–H.10), does not so much present a counter-evolutionary transition from Tallis's music to English folksong, but rather constructs synthetically a musical bond between them – a relationship which at a broader level Vaughan Williams clearly held to be a matter of historical fact – employing a variety of means to do so. The rudimentary involvement of thematic development in this process, in apparent contrast to Fuller Maitland's views on the requirements of a modern Phantasy, is a reflection of Vaughan Williams's belief that the closeness of the connection lies in the melodic domain, whilst other musical aspects bear most of the responsibility for the distinctions of style and genre involved.

[50] Vaughan Williams, *National Music*, p. 17.

Example 3.6

(a) second orchestra, violin I, bb. H.4–7, showing motif **d″** arising from repetitions of **d**

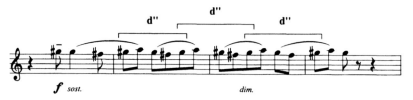

(b) motif **d″** as a 'stock phrase' of folksong (from RVW, *National Music,* p.17)

IV

None the less, the folksong-like viola melody at I.1 ff. represents a significant transformation of genre. The way in which the appearance of motif e near the opening of the melody serves to forge a sense of continuity here may be examined in the light of another remark by Vaughan Williams:

> You will notice that it is in the beginnings and endings of the [folk] tunes that we find most likeness to the church melody. This is just what we should expect. ... If you want to give people something new, start with what they are accustomed to, then having startled them with your new notions let them down gently at the end with the idea that what you have said is not so very new after all.[51]

In line with his view of musical evolution, Vaughan Williams here suggests that ecclesiastical monodies were not merely based on folksong melodies but specifically designed to recall them. But this juncture in the Fantasia would appear to present the opposite phenomenon, if the viola melody is understood to be derived from Tallis's theme. However,

---

[51] *Ibid.*, p. 78.

70

whilst it is undoubtedly possible to find in the viola melody a greater number of motivic links with the Tallis material,[52] only the use of motif e is immediately striking as a cross-reference. In terms of the overall order of events in the Fantasia, this should be taken to refer not to the third phrase of Tallis's theme but to the highly focused initial appearance of e at bars A.3–4, to which the third phrase of the Tallis material also refers back at B.4 and D.1. Analogous links with the earlier part of the Fantasia are made through the folksong 'stock phrase' d″, related to Tallis's motif d, notably in the second orchestra at I.8–9 where it is heard as a direct continuation of d itself. The play of genres continues as the other solo instruments join in what Young calls 'a *fugato* section akin to the string fantasia practice of English composers from Byrd to Purcell'.[53]

From M.1 to the climactic restatement of the viola theme at R.7 comes what Edwin Evans innocently terms the 'development section' of the Fantasia.[54] The layout of this part of the work may be examined in the context of Cobbett/Walker/Fuller Maitland's rather confusing recommendation 'that the development section … be replaced by a movement in slow tempo, which may include also a scherzando'.[55] The sequence of music from M.1 to 1919/O.2 is repeated, with some elisions and transpositional adjustments, from 1919/O.6 to Q.5; and, in so far as this is a development of anything, it is a development of the material which punctuates the folksong-like theme at I.7–J.1. But the tempo is certainly not slower at M.1, and it is far more straightforward to see the entire span from I.1 as a single section whose perceived initial tempo is indeed slower than that of the preceding music despite its being marked *Poco più animato* (originally *Poco animando*). The Fantasia's opening music was at first notated by Vaughan Williams with a time-signature of 8/8 (see Example 3.1) with a quaver pulse of 96 (revised to 112), whereas the viola theme which opens the new section

---

[52] Lionel Pike's thorough analysis of the viola melody ('Tallis – Vaughan Williams – Howells: Reflections on Mode Three', *Tempo*, 148 (1984), pp. 7–8) presents it as 'a tight amalgam of various motifs from Tallis'.

[53] Young, *Vaughan Williams*, p. 47.

[54] Edwin Evans, 'Analysis' [issued with Hawkes Pocket Scores edition of the Fantasia] (London: Boosey & Hawkes, 1943).

[55] See p. 49 above.

at I.1 clearly has a slower crotchet pulse of 63 (revised to 66).[56] The increasing animation from M.1, renewed at 1919/O.6, could even be said to possess something of the quality of a scherzando.

The next point of major textual revision follows a passage which evidently gave Vaughan Williams considerable difficulty in the original composition. At various points in the manuscript one may observe, because they have not been completely erased, Vaughan Williams's outline pencil sketches, which were generally inked in as he made the definitive score. But in a number of places the composer can be seen to have sketched material which was not then confirmed in ink: at bars 8 and A.2 he contemplated an additional iteration of the repeating quaver figures (in the latter case this would have required an extra bar); bar 1910/D.10 was initially sketched differently, as was the continuation after 1910/G.3 (it is interesting that in both these cases the composer's second thoughts were themselves excised from the 1919 version of the score); some melodic details at J.6, J.7, and J.8 were tidied up as he went along; and at M.6 the quavers in the second orchestra viola part were an afterthought. But these minor changes (there may have been others which are now less easily detectable) are as nothing compared with what happens at pp. 23 ff. of the manuscript (i.e. from bar N.4 onwards). On p. 23, which runs from N.4 to N.8, the visible pencil sketches include a great deal which was not confirmed in ink, particularly in bars N.7–8. The sketches on the following page are inconsistent in themselves and bear little or no resemblance to the finished version; indeed, none of them was inked in: the composer simply pasted the final version over the

---

[56] The revised version's faster opening tempo and time-signature (4/4) clearly work against this recognition of a slower tempo in the pastoral section, largely because the new initial tempo ($\downarrow$ = 56) is so much closer to the $\downarrow$ = 66 of I.1. Despite his many markings of $\flat = \flat$ (particularly that at E.5), the composer's rewording of I.1's tempo marking to *Poco più animato* suggests that he expected the music to have already become a little animated in performance by this point, as in fact happens in many of the available recordings. The cumulative result of Vaughan Williams's revisions, and of developments in performance practice, has been to even out the trajectory of the music from its opening to the climax at R.7. In this spirit, the *poco rit.* at 1919/O.5 ought not to be exaggerated; conversely, a performance which attempted to restore some of the original version's formal articulation would broaden significantly at this point (cf. Ex. 3.7), and would maintain a steady tempo in the work's opening section, taking to heart the composer's *Largamente* marking at E.5.

top, having presumably worked out its details elsewhere. But there is a conundrum here, in that the definitive p. 24 contains only four bars (N.9–O.2), even though there is room for five or six and Vaughan Williams habitually did not fail to fill the staves. This would seem to imply that he had already inked-in at least bar 1910/O.3 on p. 25, and thus confirms that the version we have of N.9–O.2 represents the fruit of considerable deliberation. Nor is p. 25 the end of the story, since this page was replaced in its entirety when the score was revised (probably in 1913 rather than 1919). The revision (1919/O.3–5) neatly paraphrases the original 1910/O.3–8 (Example 3.7), enhancing the momentum going into the *Più animato* at 1919/O.6. (In its sequential harmony, which broadly speaking moves downwards in whole-tone steps though with a passing G♭ in the bass, this passage is analogous to the material which introduces the *Più animato* music on its first appearance at M.1.) On p. 26, bars P.4–8 were at first sketched quite differently – essentially ic2 lower – but once this was sorted out the composer's sure-footedness was restored.

What can have caused these difficulties? A closer look at the construction of the music from M.1 to Q.5 reveals it as a mosaic of related fragments, which are joined together to give the impression of continuous thematic development. Phrases of three, three, five, and five bars take the music from M.1 to N.6, building by expansion and variation on the d/d″ phrase previously heard at I.7–9. The modal patterns are familiar from earlier in the work, while the range of harmonies is expanded; from M.4 onwards the succession of underlying diatonic collections follows a consistent progression (one ♭, all ♮, one ♯). The melodic line at bars N.7–9 (where, it will be recalled, Vaughan Williams had considerable difficulty in continuing his sketch) might in the end seem to have been motivically generated from the final part of Tallis's tune (see Example 3.8), but this explanation should be regarded as tenuous in the extreme, even though the *tierce de Picardie* cadence at N.9 is analogous in several details to that which ends Tallis's theme at B.10–C.1. This phrase is varied at N.10–O.2, before a hint of the material which will be used from Q.5 to build the climax, and then the cadential sequence (based on motif d) which the composer chose to condense by paraphrase in the revised score.

In the reprise, from 1919/O.6, there are various inconsistencies in the mosaic-work: the most extraordinary of these comes at P.9 (cf. N.6), where

Example 3.7 bb. 1910/O.3–8

74

Example 3.8
(a) end of Tallis's melody (cf. bb. B.7–C.1, D.4–D.6)
(b) solo violin I, bb. N.7–9

the music takes a harmonic twist which allows the material of N.7–9 to be reprised ic5 lower (P.10–Q.2), only for the next fragment of material (Q.3 ff.) to regain the original pitch level (cf. N.10). Prior to this, the composer's evident indecision about the pitch level of P.4 ff. seems to have been a consequence of having chosen to omit the material of M.7–N.1 altogether in the reprise. Had he eventually revised the score by cutting, say, bars N.10–Q.2, and thus taking the music from M.1 to the climax at R.7 in a single span, his difficulties of construction would have been overcome; yet in the Fantasia's broader context the reprise seems to have the significant function of reuniting the work's antiphonal forces, something which is achieved shortly after P.[57] The resultant formal structure is not characteristic of a 'development section', however, and this may perhaps be taken to confirm that Vaughan Williams purposely avoided writing one, even in the revision.

---

[57] In the 1910 version the two orchestras are in unison at the reprise rather than a few bars later. The 1919 version is misrepresented in the printed score: the manuscript indicates that the second orchestra has joined the tutti by P.2, with some of the individual parts entering during P.1, but the details of this are not shown clearly. Some of the confusion at this point may be put down to the need, in the earlier version, for the players of the second orchestra to remove their mutes, having been marked 'con sord.' at M.3. This matter seems only to have been tidied up at a very late stage

From the *Poco a poco animando* at Q.5, at which point the thematic content has been liquidated, the music proceeds by quasi-sequential harmonic changes, in an implied and unstable 5/4 metre, to the climax at R.7. Here the solo viola melody returns, as Mellers describes it, 'chanted *fortissimo* in a cross between organum and monody'.[58] Mellers is clearly alert to the likelihood of this work resolving the stylistic distance it has opened up between folksong and Tudor music – initially by presenting an 'evolution', later by constructing cross-references – through some kind of synthesis. But this is not the place for it: this *fortissimo* climax is simply the highpoint of the folksong-based section which substitutes for a development. (Even if a 'cross between organum and monody' were imaginable, the somewhat intermediate position of organum along Vaughan Williams's 'evolutionary' line would seem to rule out this genre from any synthesis capable of achieving a large-scale sense of resolution.) Vaughan Williams now uses the full resources of his neo-modal harmony to support the theme, including frequent use of the characteristic falling ic3 progression, which in the revised version of the score is combined, at the *molto allargando* itself, with the Tallis/folksong motif e for the first and only time in the Fantasia. As the music continues beyond this climax the melodic content is liquidated once again: the rhythm dissolves into regular quavers, and the range of articulation is gradually reduced until a simple oscillation is reached at T.1, before at T.5 the music settles, by way of yet another *tierce de Picardie*, on to an E major triad. Vaughan Williams used the ensuing bars again in 1943, to accompany Christian's welcoming acceptance of death in a BBC radio version of *The Pilgrim's Progress*; thus we might take this passage to continue, programmatically, the musical dissolution which precedes it.

V

Vaughan Williams's decision to remove a complete restatement of Tallis's theme from the original version of his score might seem a little over-resolute, and not all commentators have agreed that it effected an overall improvement. As A. E. F. Dickinson puts it, '[the] surviving verse keeps at once a sense of development and recovery, but the proportions of this work,

[58] Mellers, *Vaughan Williams and the Vision of Albion*, p. 56.

with so extended a middle section, remain questionable'.[59] Yet in the context of the dissolution which precedes it, both musical and latterly programmatic, the mundane quality of the original version's first restatement (Example 3.9) seems to be justified only by formal criteria, along the lines of Fuller Maitland's 'A return to the characteristics of the first part of the movement is made'. The definitive version's immediate progress into what Dickinson calls the 'transcendent intimacy' of the music from U.2 onwards[60] – in which the viola obbligato, without directly recalling the folksong-like theme of the Fantasia's middle section, none the less evokes the same musical image by virtue of its sonority, its rhythmic profile, and its largely pentatonic basis – provides the moment of synthesis which Mellers had sought in the earlier, nominally climactic passage.

As suggested above, reading the final part of the work, from T.9 to the end, in terms of Fuller Maitland's complete description ('A return to the characteristics of the first part of the movement is made, but not necessarily a definite repetition; and a developed coda is added as a finale') is comparatively easy in the case of the original version. The varied restatement of Tallis's theme from T.9, and the decorated statement which overlaps it at 1910/V.6, together form 'a return ... but not ... a repetition'; they are concluded at X.4,[61] and at X.5 the 'developed coda' begins. The Fantasia's opening descending pentatonic theme is contrapuntally combined with material based on motifs d and d'', and the final flourish is introduced by a passage Vaughan Williams later excised, which alternates motifs d and e before cadencing with a final use of the falling ic3 progression (Example 3.10). In the revised version, however, the clearly synthetic nature of the music of U.2 ff. gives this passage the immediate aspect of a 'developed coda' – and this leaves only the single statement of motif c at bars T.10–U.1 to stand as a 'return to the characteristics of the first part'.

But, in allowing the work to adhere more closely to the formal niceties of the Phantasy principle, the stanza Vaughan Williams later chose to remove had perhaps violated something far more significant to his

[59] Dickinson, 'The Vaughan Williams Manuscripts', p. 192.
[60] Dickinson, Vaughan Williams, p. 176.
[61] Note that bars W.10 ff. are analogous to E.1 ff., even in the 1910 version of the score. This abbreviated reprise seems to have served as a model for the omission of 1910/D.7–10 in the revised version.

Example 3.9 bb. 1910/U.1–V.9

conception: its responsorial presentation of the first two phrases of Tallis's theme, recalling bars 3–A.3, had retrospectively undermined the 'evolution' so cogently presented at the outset of the Fantasia as the founding premise of its programme. Through the almost unhampered presentation of this in the definitive version of the score, Vaughan Williams, in truly post-modern fashion, now distanced his own style as heard in the work's

Example 3.9 (*cont.*)

middle section from both folksong and Tudor music. This distancing is latent in the earlier version, even rudimentarily in the work's tonal structure – the outer sections being centred broadly on G, the central section on E – but there is a shift in the revision from a somewhat rhetorical presentation of the distinctions among the various styles and style-syntheses involved, which Vaughan Williams achieved more or less in accordance with the tenets of the Phantasy principle, towards a more integrated exposition of such matters in line with his developing personal views on the historical and musical connections between folksong and Tudor church

Example 3.10 bb. 1910/Y.5–8

music. Though the difference is subtle, in revising this, amongst other ground-breaking works, on his return from the Great War, Vaughan Williams contrived by relatively simple means to effect an important shift, developing his Fantasia away from a pre-war dilettante genre into a piece whose measured traversal of a stylistic network opened up a significant part of the space in which he chose to do the remainder of his life's work.

4 Vaughan Williams, Germany, and the German tradition: a view from the letters

HUGH COBBE

Writing from Charterhouse in a letter of October 1889, Vaughan Williams reported to his sister Margaret that his friend, H. V. Hamilton, had been revisiting the school and that they had talked about music until 3:00 am: 'he is going to be a pro. He has been to Bayreuth and is now a Wagnerite. We now have to believe that Mendellsohn[1] is NOT a great composer, that though Beethoven is great he is old fashioned. As to Handel, etc. they are quite out of date.'[2]

This short extract sets out the musical firmament as it appeared to Vaughan Williams and most of his contemporaries at that time. Its central features were German; so the new revelation of Wagner from Germany brought in its train a reassessment of the established German composers who preceded him. The purpose of this essay is to trace, as far as possible in the composer's own words taken from his writings and letters, the development of his view of the German musical tradition (by which I mean the musical tradition emanating from the German-speaking lands of central Europe); a development which took him from accepting this tradition as the mainspring of European music, to regarding it as certainly a vital component but only one amongst several, albeit with a dangerous predominance from which English music needed strong protection. As Vaughan Williams developed his ideas on the need for a truly English national

---

[1] Sic.

[2] Letter printed in U. Vaughan Williams, *R. V. W.*, p. 27. All quotations from published and unpublished letters of Vaughan Williams in this essay are made with the kind permission of Ursula Vaughan Williams. The texts are, unless otherwise stated, taken from originals or photocopies in Mrs Vaughan Williams's possession and have been compiled by the author as part of his project to edit the letters for eventual publication. No attempt has been made to correct grammatical or spelling errors in Vaughan Williams's German or English. All ellipses are editorial.

musical tradition over the early years of the new century, he was as much reacting against the pervasiveness of German models, which had provided the staple fare of music-making and teaching throughout the nineteenth century, as he was creating a good thing in its own right. Thus the views on the German tradition that emerge from his writings, formal and informal, over the years do much to illuminate his conception of the specifically native tradition which he set out to establish.

Vaughan Williams's first mature journey abroad (there had been a childhood holiday in Normandy) was a family excursion in 1890 to Germany, to Oberammergau to see the Passion play and also to Munich, where the composer had his own Wagnerian revelation:

> I went to Munich and heard my first Wagner opera. We found that Die Walküre was down for that evening. ... This was my first introduction to later Wagner, but I experienced no surprise, but rather that strange certainty that I had heard it all before. There was a feeling of recognition as of meeting an old friend which comes to us all in the face of great artistic experiences.[3]

When, in 1890, Vaughan Williams went to the Royal College of Music, where Parry found him musically rather illiterate, his diet naturally continued to be mostly German (though the composer did confess to an overdose of Gounod) and he himself at the time counted Bach, Beethoven, Wagner, and Brahms as the only composers worth considering.[4] Indeed there was nothing unusual about this view of the musical world, and the experience of *Tristan* conducted by Mahler in June 1892 can only have strengthened it. In the same year he went up to Cambridge; there the German tradition retained its position in the forefront of his mind and was further strengthened by the addition of Schubert and Schumann to the pantheon.[5] But during the two further years at the Royal College of Music (1895–7) friendships were formed, above all the fundamental one with Gustav Holst, which started a steady process of detachment.

---

[3] 'A Musical Autobiography', *National Music*, p. 180. The autobiography was published initially in 1950, as part of the first full-length book on the composer, Hubert Foss's *Ralph Vaughan Williams: A Study* (London: Harrap, 1950).

[4] 'A Musical Autobiography', p. 183.

[5] He founded a choral society to perform Schubert masses (U. Vaughan Williams, *R.V.W.*, p. 42).

None the less, by the end of Vaughan Williams's RCM time Wagner still remained in the centre of his thought, as is evident from a letter of October 1897 to his cousin and closest university friend, Ralph ('Randolph') Wedgwood, and from a piece entitled 'The Romantic Movement and its Results', which has only recently come to light.[6] In the letter he replies to Wedgwood, who had asked him what present he would like for his forthcoming marriage to Adeline Fisher:

> I should prize a Wagner full score more than anything, if you really cared to give me one. I should prefer Tristan; if you think that bad for me, then Die Walküre; if that again does not meet your views Siegfried; or if that is too Buoyant, then Meistersinger. I went to make some enquiries and found that they cost from £6 to £8 – that sounds most appalling – but I can only follow your instructions. They cost this if you promise by declaration never to use them for a public performance; if you infringe this they will cost, as the stolid German said 'aabaowt two hundert paownds more'. If you don't want to give me some music I suggest some Meredith ...

In the article, he takes up the controversy between the adherents of Brahms the 'classical' composer, who had died the previous April, and Wagner the 'romantic'. He describes the development of romantic music from Schubert and Weber through Berlioz to Schumann and concludes:

> This is the history of the romantic school – first one art influenced by another; then one art illustrating another, and finally the first glimmerings of a *new art* which combines the dramatic and musical art in one. After Schumann it was for ever impossible to call the new art 'music'; the dramatic element had to be recognized as of equal importance with the musical. To make this new art complete but one step was necessary – to transfer it to its proper home, the theatre – and this was done by Richard Wagner.

Wagner then was the culmination of this historical development, but Brahms was the continuation of the true musical tradition, writing 'pure music from a musical heart'. The future now lay with two separate arts, the 'musical' and the 'musico-dramatic', and the composers who worked in either were in the 'forward movement'; the laggards were those who, without the brains to write either a symphony or an opera, were content to

---

[6] *The Musician*, 1/23 (13 October 1897), pp. 430–1. The paper ran for twenty-eight issues in 1897 before closing.

sit on the fence and to attempt to hide their ignorance both of poetry and music by using such high-sounding titles as 'symphonic poem' and the like (perhaps a dig at Richard Strauss, 'a cook who can serve up mutton with such art that he does not always take the trouble to look for venison'[7]). He concludes: the romantic school 'has lived its life and done its work, and has died an honourable death; to honour it truly is to let it rest in peace'.

This then was his state of mind when, his RCM studies over, he took the opportunity provided by his marriage to Adeline to travel abroad:

> In 1897 I decided to have a few months' study and experience abroad. Stanford wanted me to go to Italy and hear opera at the Scala. He thought I was too Teuton already. He did not want me to take definite lessons with anyone. But I disregarded his advice and went to Berlin. My reason for this choice, I believe, was the extraordinary one that Berlin was the only town at that time where they performed the *Ring* without cuts![8]

Other reasons for his choosing Berlin were a decision to seek the advice of Heinrich von Herzogenberg at the Hochschule für Musik (who suggested, contrary to Stanford's advice, that he study with Max Bruch – whom Vaughan Williams could well have met when Cambridge University awarded him an honorary degree in 1893) and the fact that René Gatty, the brother of his close friends Nicholas and Ivor Gatty, was in Berlin at the time and able to find Adeline and him accommodation.

A vital preparation was of course to acquire a sufficiency of the German language. There seems to be no record that he took lessons, but equally it was impossible to study works of Wagner, for example, or become familiar with the organ music of Bach, without developing at least a nodding acquaintance with the language. The following extract from a letter to his Cambridge friend the philosopher G. E. Moore, written to acknowledge a wedding present, provides some evidence that he had set about preparing himself for his journey:

---

[7] Vaughan Williams makes this remark in his article 'Ein Heldenleben', *The Vocalist*, 1/10 (January 1903), pp. 295–6. Cf. Michael Vaillancourt's discussion of this article and Vaughan Williams's attitude to Strauss in Chapter 2 of the present volume; Vaillancourt's remarks on other aspects of German influence on Vaughan Williams's early works are also germane.

[8] 'A Musical Autobiography', p. 187.

It seems a sort of insult to write and thank you as that is what I am doing to such quantities of *unangenehm* [uncongenial] people (I put that word in to show you that I know some German – I doubt if it does so); but I must try and put on paper how good it is to receive a present like yours in the midst of a wilderness of social duties.[9]

Once settled in Berlin, Vaughan Williams wrote a number of times about his experiences to Wedgwood; three of these letters survive, two written in November 1897 and one in February 1898. They not only provide an account of Vaughan Williams's impressions of Germany but also convey a tone of sardonic amusement which surely reflects the character of Vaughan Williams's circle at Cambridge, linked as it was with the sophisticated Cambridge Conversazione Society, better known as the Apostles.[10]

XI.97
Dear Randolph

Its a long time since I've written to you and so I will tell you a little of what I've been doing – Firstly I am a charter boy that is to say I am a member of the 'Akademie der Künste' for which I paid an entrance fee of 20 marks and then the state pays Max Bruch to give me an hours lesson once a week at his home – so there's an expense the less. We also have German lessons from a tall fat very hearty young man who discourses learnedly on Grimm & Descartes for 1 1/2 hours once a week and makes us read Lessing's 'Nathan der Weise' – very dull. We simply soak in concerts – the best concerts and all the 'Hauptproben' which are just as good take place on Sunday mornings at 12.0 – a most ideal time to listen to music. Also we went to [a] German version of 'Trilby'[11] and to Faust 'Erste Theil'. They are also doing 'Zweiter Theil' but we haven't been to that yet as the concerts take up all the time.

All that has been said against Berlin is absolutely untrue – it's of course not a picturesque place but very bright and cheerful and delightful canals with trees planted all along them. Also here is Potsdam 1/2 hours rail away – with that lovely place Sans Souci the most wonderful artificial garden with its statues and fountains and terraces all on an autumn afternoon with the leaves falling which fitted in beautifully with the general feeling of

---

[9] Letter in the University Library, Cambridge.
[10] Vaughan Williams never belonged to the society, but his close friends George Moore, George Trevelyan, and Ralph Wedgwood were all members. On the society see Paul Levy, *Moore: G. E. Moore and the Cambridge Apostles* (London: George Weidenfeld & Nicholson, 1979).
[11] The novel by George du Maurier, first published in 1894.

sentimental decay. Then across the valley on the other side rise beautiful sham ruins making a classical landscape in the style of Claude. The whole is so beautifully artificial. It was on that journey I helped a policeman to put out a lamp – he was trying to do it with his sword but was not tall enough so I offered to help him whereupon the servant of the Kaiser handed me his sword and I turned it out.

We feed here very nicely – ordinary German Fruhstuck then about 2.0 we go [to] the little restaurant where you get a luncheon of 3 courses and coffee for 1 mark. On opera nights we have buttered eggs, bouillon, rogenbrod,[12] kuchen and tea at home before we go out & tea and kuchen later on when we come in; on other (I was going to say ordinary) days we reverse the process, the buttered eggs & bouillon are self-made.

yrs affec[ntely]

R. Vaughan Williams

The subsequent Berlin letters to Wedgwood retain the same vein of amused detachment combined with an earnest drive to absorb as much of German culture as possible in the time available. Writing later in November he describes seeing the symbolist play *Die versunkene Glocke* by Gerhard Hauptmann[13] and sums up its moral, 'which is that man must always come to grief if he tries to do an "Uebermenschliche Werke" – that is to say he must stop at home with his wife and family and not go off with Rautendelein and build a temple to the sun on the top of a mountain'. Bruch had asked him 'to his at homes "in ze Englisch staile" and said he hoped I should be as successful as I was courageous'. He also sent a 'Letter from Berlin' to *The Musician* devoted mainly to a performance of *The Ring* under Felix Weingartner at the Opera, with Anton van Rooy as Wotan, Ernst Kraus as Siegfried, and Lilli Lehmann as Brünnhilde. We have seen that one object of Vaughan Williams's visit was to hear Wagner without cuts and, accordingly, he devotes a good part of his notice to the benefits of hearing an uncut performance:

> I do not mean to say that Wagner's want of conciseness is not a distinct artistic fault; it is unfortunate that he lacked that faculty of self-criticism which would have led him to revise and compress his work – that would

[12] I.e., Roggenbrot – rye bread.

[13] *Die versunkene Glocke* had first opened on 2 December 1896 in the Deutsches Theater, Berlin.

have been to have repainted the picture – the managers' mutilations are holes cut in the canvas. [14]

However much Vaughan Williams admired Wagner, there are signs here of a reaction setting in, and this began to spread to other German music. By the time of the third surviving letter to Wedgwood, the composer was beginning to articulate his thoughts on how a school of English national music might be developed on the basis of folksong (this some months before the founding of the Folk Song Society and some five years before his own folksong collecting activities began).

Eichhorn Strasse 6.II

[February 1898]   Berlin IV

Dear Randolph

... You will be glad to hear that Max Bruch considers I am a 'guter musiker und ein Talent-voller Componist'[15] and that I have 've-ry o-riginaal ideeas' but my harmonies are 'rather too originell' [;] in fact I meet with much more encouragement – this is of course only for your ears who know that I write things and not for Moore for instance – who would think it ridiculous – You may tell him however that all the living Germans I have heard in Berlin are most feeble folk – it seems to me that the future of music lies between England and Russia but first the Russians must try to give up being original and the English being imitators – I very much believe in the folk tune theory – by which I don't mean that modern composing is done by sandwiching an occasional national tune – not your own invention – between lumps of '2d the pound' stuff – which seems to be Dvorak's latest method. But that to get the spirit of his national tunes into his work must be good for a composer if it comes natural to him, in which case it doesn't matter if what he writes occasionally corresponds with some real 'folk tune' – All this because in the

---

[14] *The Musician*, 1/25 (27 October 1897), p. 464.
[15] The full written reference given by Bruch at the completion of the lessons was as follows:

Herr Ralph Vaughan Williams, der im Winter 1897–98 die unter meiner Leitung stehende Akademische Meisterschule für musikalische Composition besuchte, ist ein sehr guter Musiker und ein talentvoller Componist. Er verdient, allen Musikgesellschaften, Kirchenchören etc. warm empfohlen zu werden. Dr Max Bruch. Mitglied der Königl. Akademie der Künste. Berlin 5. Februar 1898

[Mr Ralph Vaughan Williams, who attended my master-class for musical composition in the winter of 1897–98, is a very good musician and a talented composer. He can be warmly recommended to music societies, church choirs etc. Dr Max Bruch, Member of the Royal Academy of Arts. Berlin 5 February 1898.]

last thing I wrote for Bruch I used a Welsh tune as my 'Haupt Thema' –
unacknowledged of course, – but then 'I made it my own'.

I never answered you about the Wagners. I think in acts is best – but I
would much rather you settled – because I should like the idea that every
detail in it came entirely from you [–] that makes the beauty of a present.[16]

We went to a most wonderful dinner party the other day – all professors
– the two 'hauptsaches' were

(a) The food and drink which kept on going after dinner in this order 9.30 –
11.30:

Cigars, coffee, liqueurs*, belegte brod, caviar, sweets, beer, tea.

(b) The subjects which I discussed with the most brilliant professors of the
Berlin university in this order 9.30 – 11.0:

α. In German: Bach, Wagner, classical, romantic, Shelley, Keats, the Puritans,
the influence of religion on art, Browning, Rossetti, Swinburne, lodgings.

β. In English: The Riviera, Coleridge, Wordsworth, Oxford, Prigs, German
art galleries, Fra Angelico.

Adeline sends you her love,

Yours affec[ntely]

Ralph Vaughan Williams

* Note Have you ever made a practice of liqueurs? If not you have neglected
your opportunities like I have. This must be rectified at our next festlichkeit
together.

Following their stay in Berlin the Vaughan Williamses paid a visit to
Dresden, from where they reported back to René Gatty in Berlin that they
were to hear 'Die Neunte Symphonie' and *Othello*.[17]

It is clear from letters written after their return to England that the
visit to Berlin had made a deep impression on Vaughan Williams musically
and linguistically: while away he had written letters to Gatty entirely in
German and for some time after their return his and Adeline's letters to
their closer friends continued to be spattered with German phrases.
Musically he had found Berlin especially stimulating: writing to Gatty in
about November 1898, he urges him: 'Try and hear some music in Berlin – it
seems so dreadful to be in the very heart of music and not to hear any'.[18]

---

[16] Vaughan Williams is obviously responding to a question from Wedgwood as to
how the Wagner scores, which Wedgwood had given him as a wedding present,
should be bound up.   [17] See U. Vaughan Williams, *R.V.W.*, p. 53.

[18] Birmingham City Archives MS 135.

88

Soon there was another foreign journey, to Haarlem to hear the organ at St Bavo, and later, early in 1899 after leaving his post as organist at St Barnabas, South Lambeth, there was a return to Berlin ('to keep up with the influential people there'[19]) and Dresden. This time they went on to Prague where Vaughan Williams was affected (perhaps reluctantly in view of his earlier strictures on Dvořák's use of national tunes) by the nationalist spirit of Smetana and Dvořák ('I feel awfully national just now – though I have just written an article against "national" music which no magazine has thought fit to accept'). In Prague they saw *The Devil and Kate* and Vaughan Williams wrote to Gatty:

> The Dvorak was very good and characteristic all the time he was with the village scenes, but when he got down to hell he lost himself and became a bad imitation of 'Nibelheim' in the Rheingold. I don't think they are the coming Volk. Smetana and Dvorak were the result of a natural movement but I think they will probably now become cosmopolitan.[20]

There is no record of any further journeys to Germany until his controversial journey to Hamburg in 1938 to receive the Shakespeare Prize, and his view of German music now settled down into a form that seems to have remained with him for the rest of his life. He had established his own personal pantheon of the composers who were especially important to him: Bach – 'one of the three great composers of the world (personally I believe the greatest)'[21] – Beethoven, Brahms, and Wagner. He had also determined that he did not feel sympathetic to the directions in which newer music was going – he hardly ever mentions Mahler for example[22] – nor did he feel that the tradition as a whole was healthy for music in England, though that was not to say that it was not a fully valid national tradition in its own right and on its own territory. It was necessary for the good of his own country's music, in Michael Kennedy's words, 'to achieve...a break with the German or Teutonic late-romantic hegemony that was dominating English music at

---

[19] This and the following quotation are from a letter to Ralph Wedgwood written from Prague in early 1899.

[20] Birmingham City Archives MS 135, printed in U. Vaughan Williams *R.V.W.*, p. 58. Smetana had of course died in 1884.

[21] Vaughan Williams in his 1932 lecture 'Should Music be National?', *National Music*, p. 2.

[22] That is, other than in the 'Musical Autobiography', where Mahler is described as 'a very tolerable imitation of a composer' (p. 187).

the turn of the century'[23] and Vaughan Williams, as is well known, found the key primarily in English folksong. He summed up the matter in his 1932 lectures on 'National Music' at Bryn Mawr:

> ...several of us found here in its simplest form the musical idiom which we unconsciously were cultivating in ourselves ... it freed us from foreign influences which weighed on us, which we could not get rid of, but which we felt were not pointing in the direction in which we really wanted to go.[24]

His preoccupation thus turned deliberately from Germany to folksong, and to other liberating influences and concerns – work on *The English Hymnal*, a growing interest in Tudor music, and, early in 1908, his period of study with Ravel. Kennedy describes the latter stimulus as 'the crux of his development',[25] and thereafter the composer quickly found his own lasting voice in works such as *On Wenlock Edge* and the *Fantasia on a Theme by Thomas Tallis*.

There is little evidence that his mental attitude to Germany and its musical tradition was altered or even intensified by the First World War, despite the losses amongst Vaughan Williams's circle of friends. As became even clearer at the time of the Second World War, Vaughan Williams was too large-minded to allow political and emotional considerations arising from the state of war to sway his view of the music of the enemy country. That stood for good or ill on its own merits. The war was a watershed for the composer in other ways, however. In its aftermath Vaughan Williams found himself transformed all at once from the young rebel to the established senior composer. He received an honorary Doctorate of Music from Oxford and joined the staff of the RCM as a composition professor. He now had the opportunity to develop the views of a new generation of English composers and to help them to find a voice that, like his, was largely independent of Teutonic influences, while at the same time maintaining an awareness of developments abroad. His views on how this should be achieved are well set out in his Bryn Mawr lectures[26] and, in a more private context, in a letter to Edward Dent of 1 July 1928.

---

[23] Introduction to *National Music*, p. vii.
[24] 'The Evolution of the Folk-song', *National Music*, p. 41.
[25] Introduction to *National Music*, p. vii.
[26] See in particular *National Music*, p. 11.

Dear Dent

May I ask you for some advice? A composition pupil of mine at the R.C.M. whom I consider very gifted is anxious to go abroad and study music, especially composition, for 6 months, or possibly longer.

I also think it would be very good for her. Who do you consider the best composition teacher in Europe at present? And which centre do you consider the best for a young student to receive a 'finishing' musical education and generally to improve their musical culture. I expect you will say that the two queries are incompatible, in which case we shall have to make a compromise.

Miss Maconchy[27] is just 19 – plays the piano quite well and has had a thorough grounding at the hands of Kitson and Charles Wood. She has – as I say – in my opinion decided inventive powers but is of course at present like all young people going through a new phase every month. At present she has been badly bitten by Bartok and is of course anxious to study with him, but I rather doubt the wisdom of this. I feel possibly that Respighi or Casella might be good for her – if they ever take pupils. On the other hand neither Rome nor Buda-Pesth would I imagine be good from the point of view of general musical atmosphere and the hearing of plenty of good music etc. Also of course we must consider a place where we could find a nice family for her to live with and so on.

Are Leipzig or Dresden any good nowadays? Prague has been suggested to me – what do you think of that? or I thought of sending her to Ravel but I doubt if he would take any pupils now.

I should be most grateful for your advice. I hope I am not asking too much but I feel I have a certain claim on you in your professorial capacity though I am no longer an undergraduate of your university.

Yrs

R. Vaughan Williams[28]

It is noteworthy that of all the foreign possibilities canvassed by Vaughan Williams, Germany is paid the least attention; and indeed, although his reply does not survive, Dent seems to have supported the idea of Prague, for in the event Maconchy went there to study under the composer and conductor K. B. Jirák, who as an active member of the International Society for

---

[27] Dame Elizabeth Maconchy, 1907–94.

[28] King's College, Cambridge, Dent Archive 1926–27.10, 11. Vaughan Williams had remained on close terms with Dent ever since they had been contemporaries at Cambridge.

Contemporary Music would have been well known to Dent, the Society's President.

Although Vaughan Williams does not seem to have allowed the events of the First World War in themselves to influence his view of German music, the rise of Nazism during the 1930s brought him directly and personally up against international politics. Although he was honoured in 1936 to be offered its first Shakespeare Prize by Hamburg University, the acceptance of the award was not an easy decision. On the one hand his left-leaning political views and even more deeply held beliefs concerning civic freedom meant that he wished to have nothing to do with the increasingly distasteful political regime of the Third Reich; but on the other the award represented in some sense a victory in his long struggle to create a new balance between English and German music. As he wrote in response to the offer:

> I feel that the honour is offered, not so much to me personally, as to the whole of English musical art. Therefore I must put personal questions on one side. Indeed this honour to English music is so unprecedented that I want to make sure that it is made only from a desire to recognise art and learning in this country.
>
> Now, though I wish to avoid the personal side of the question, I feel bound to explain that I am strongly opposed to the present system of government in Germany, especially with regard to its treatment of artists and scholars. I belong to more than one English society whose object is to combat all that the present German *régime* stands for ... I cannot accept this great honour without satisfying my own conscience that I shall not feel in any way hampered in the free expression of my own opinion in accepting it.

On receiving assurances from Hamburg confirming his understanding of the non-political nature of the award, Vaughan Williams felt able to accept and in June 1938 went to Germany to receive the prize. As Ursula Vaughan Williams recounts, during the visit the composer visited Brahms's birthplace and Buxtehude's organ at the Marienkirche in Lübeck, thus reminding himself of the overwhelming contribution to music made by the Teutonic tradition.[29] Indeed, on 10 October 1939, well after war had broken out, he wrote to Elizabeth Trevelyan with reference to whether German music should be broadcast: 'it occurs to me that many musical and sensitive

---

[29] See U. Vaughan Williams, *R.V.W.*, pp. 217 and 221.

people who love German people and German music might for that reason find it an unbearable pain to listen to German music – because it would remind them so forcibly of what Germany had been, what it might have been – & what it still may be – & contrast this with what it is.'

His concern for the increasing number of refugees from the Nazi regime, especially scholars and musicians, and for the consequent state of music in Germany, disturbed him every bit as much as the overweening influence of Germany on British music had in his youth. His contacts with refugees such as the composer Robert Müller-Hartmann, with whom he became close friends,[30] and his membership of the Dorking Committee for Refugees impelled him to write many letters on behalf of those whom he considered to be deserving cases. After the outbreak of war and the internment of German nationals, he was dismayed at seeing friends and musicians such as Müller-Hartmann sent away. In July 1940 the Government published a White Paper setting out arrangements for the release of internees in certain categories.[31] This encouraged him to write to Müller-Hartmann on 6 August:

> I feel sure then, in spite of all, you will still continue to believe in English freedom. The Government were in a terrible emergency and had to adopt, all [of] a sudden whole sale measures which worked unfairly on many perfectly innocent people. May you soon be free to work for the country of your adoption and for the cause we all have at heart.

On 21 August he sent a round-robin letter to senior colleagues urging them to join him in pressing the Home Office to include music in its definition of 'work of national importance',[32] with the result that on 28

---

[30] On Robert Müller-Hartmann, see *Die Musik in Geschichte u. Gegenwart*, vol. IX, cols. 873–4. He had been recommended to Vaughan Williams by Imogen Holst and the two men remained friends until Müller-Hartmann's death in 1950. Vaughan Williams went out of his way to provide Müller-Hartmann with work and to encourage the performance of his music.

[31] *Civilian internees of enemy nationality: categories of persons eligible for release from internment and procedure to be followed in applying for release*, Cmnd 6233, July 1940.

[32] The recipients were Sir Hugh Allen, Sir Granville Bantock, Lord Berners, Sir Adrian Boult, H. C. Colles, Edric Cundell, Sir Walford Davies, Thomas Dunhill, George Dyson, Constant Lambert, Stanley Marchant, Ernest Newman, William Walton, and W. G. Whittaker.

August he was able to report to Sir Granville Bantock, one of those individuals whose support he had canvassed: 'I have had a promise from Sir Cyril Asquith[33] that the case of musicians shall be "sympathetically considered" – So I suggest that we now meet and discuss action & among other things draw up a list of interned musicians'. The result of this initiative was a revision to the White Paper, which now included a category of 'persons of eminent distinction who have made outstanding contributions to Art, Science, learning or Letters', and the appointment of Vaughan Williams himself as chair of an advisory committee charged to recommend which musicians should be released from internment. An early beneficiary of the Committee's work was, of course, Robert Müller-Hartmann.

The release of refugee musicians, however, while certainly a highly desirable end in itself, also awoke Vaughan Williams's old fears about the Teutonic dominance of English music. His dilemma was to reconcile the strong views he held both on artistic freedom and the future political organization of the world with his belief in national cultural independence, which he saw as again coming under threat because of the influx of foreign musicians.

> We all want peace, we all want international friendship, we all want to give
> up the hateful rivalries of nations; we must learn to plan the world
> internationally, we must unite or we shall perish. This is a very different
> thing from that emasculated standardization of life which will add cultural
> to political internationalism...
>   The problem of home-grown music has lately [1942] become acute owing
> to the friendly invasion of these shores by an army of distinguished German
> and Austrian musicians. The Germans and the Austrians have great musical
> traditions behind them. In some ways they are more musically developed
> than we are and therein lies the danger...[34]

---

[33] The chairman of the Home Office Advisory Committee making
recommendations about cases put forward for release.

[34] 'Nationalism and Internationalism', *National Music*, pp. 154 and 156. From
about this time Vaughan Williams was especially enthusiastic about the
movement for Federal Union, which envisaged the post-war political
organization of the world as a system of federated states.

He treated the problem at greater length in a contemporary correspondence with Ferdinand Rauter,[35] who had invited him to be Patron of the newly formed Anglo-Austrian Music Society:

Aug 16[1942]

Dear Dr Rauter

Your letter has opened up a great problem.

I find it difficult to state but I want [to say] as a preface that nothing contained in this letter affects my personal affection for my many Austrian friends; nor my admiration for their art.

The great thing which frightens me in the late peaceful invasion of this country by Austria is that it will entirely devour the tender little flower of our English culture. The Austrians have a great musical tradition, and they are apt to think that it is the only musical tradition and that everything which is different must be wrong or ignorant; they think moreover that they have a mission to impose their culture wherever they go as being the only one worth having.

Now this seems to me to be all wrong.

We cannot swallow the strong meat of your culture (even if we wished to) our stomachs are not strong enough – indigestion & finally artistic putrefaction would result. To try and make England, musically, a dependency of Austria could kill all the musical initiative in this country – destroy all that is vital and substitute a mechanical imitation of your great art – which will have no vitality, no roots in the soil and no power to grow to full stature.

What do I suggest therefore? – We want your art and we want your help – Become Englishmen – try to assimilate our artistic ideals and then strengthen and fertilize them from your own incomparable art – But do not force a 'Little Austria' on England – keeping itself apart from the 'untouchables' and having its own musical life without any reference to the life going on around. This would not only be of no value to our country but would actually be a disservice – because people seeing this little body of musical aristocrats with their art perfected by generations of artistic endeavour would think that was the only art worth having and that they

---

[35] An Austrian musician, 1902–87, who had settled in London in the later 1930s. He published a number of collections of folksongs in cooperation with the Icelandic singer Engel Lund, whom he accompanied, and with Ursula Vaughan Williams. The author is very grateful to Mrs Claire Rauter for making the correspondence between Vaughan Williams and Rauter available to him. Dr Rauter's letter is quoted with her kind permission.

could reap without sowing by a mere mechanical imitation of Austrian music.

As you must already know from your sojourn in England that there is a tendency, clearly, among English people to take it that 'Schmidt' is musical – while Smith is ipso facto unmusical. You must not stand apart and say 'Schmidt is musical – you are not. Your only chance is to become musical Schmidts' – You must help Smith to realise that he is musical, help him to discover where his artistic nature lies hidden and to help it to grow to a full flower.

Yours sincerely
R. Vaughan Williams

This letter is perhaps the clearest exposition we have of Vaughan Williams's attitude towards the German musical tradition, an uneasy mixture of admiration for its contribution to the art as a whole and disquiet lest its influence might, even after forty years, still pose a threat to the English musical tradition he had done much to bring into being.

Rauter's reply was frank and deeply thoughtful:

28, Clarendon Road
26 September 1942 London, W.11
Dear Dr. Vaughan Williams,

I want to thank you very much for your very kind letter. The problem with which you deal in it is very well known to me and I have tried hard to penetrate it and find a solution.

I admit that the Austrians often seemed to have imposed their culture upon other countries. This fact can, however, be understood for two reasons. First of all because the Austrian musician loves and understands his own music as part of his own self. Secondly because he judges foreign from his own tradition, not knowing that other traditions have cultural roots other than his own.

This mistake became obvious when it showed itself in daily life: In discussions between Austrian and British people, of 'facts' which seemed clear and logical to both parties and yet in a quite different way. Many of us came to realize very soon, after arrival in this country, that with the translation of words the translation of real meaning did not follow. No wonder that it took us musicians quite a long time to realize that to an even greater extent the same mistake occurred in the judgement of British music. It is practically impossible to learn a foreign language outside its own country and just as impossible or even more so to understand national

96

music outside its own surroundings. The few musicians in a few Austrian cities who had the rare chance of hearing English musicians or composers could not assess this music or those performers in the right sense and most of it was lost.

The immigration of Austrians to this country has given them the best and only opportunity of re[a]lizing this fact. As far as they were allowed to they tried to root themselves in British soil and be n[o]urished by it. Slowly they began to understand what 'British' means and that the musicality of the British people was existent too, even to an astonishing degree, but different.

Rauter went on to set out what he saw as the aims of the proposed society and to reassure Vaughan Williams that he and his countrymen regarded themselves as deeply in his debt, because of his work for interned musicians:

Now you will understand that we wanted you, the Guardian of British music to protect us and our aims. The formal name of 'Patron' should only be the outer sign of what you have always been: our helper and our friend.
Very sincerely yours
F. Rauter.

The response from Rauter is particularly interesting, in that it makes clear that, for their part, Germans and Austrians had difficulty in understanding English music. His eloquent plea for the threatened musical culture in which he had grown up in effect turned Vaughan Williams's own arguments on behalf of English music back on him. Certainly now he accepted the honour, remarking 'I need hardly say that if there is any danger of the tradition which produced Haydn, Mozart & Schubert disappearing we must make every effort to preserve it'.

This exchange of letters forms an appropriate conclusion to this essay, summing up a coherent development through the composer's career on the question of German music: an initial assumption that the German tradition lay at the heart of all that is serious in music followed by a growing determination that, though he did not belittle Germany's contribution to music (his lifelong music-making with the Leith Hill Musical Festival at Dorking centred around the performance of choral music by Bach), he did not believe that it provided a springboard for the development of English music. He was in fact probably right to fear the new influx of refugee musicians, many of whom became influential writers, critics, and teachers in their adopted country. It could be argued that, since they could not, for reasons which Rauter sets out, feel at ease with his English idiom, they inevitably lent some impetus to that swing of the critical pendulum away from Vaughan Williams's music which took place towards the end of his life and in the years following his death. It is perhaps only now, after nearly a century, that the critical equilibrium has been achieved for which Vaughan Williams strove.[36]

---

[36] The author would like to thank Paul Banks, Howard Ferguson, Michael Kennedy, Oliver Neighbour, Michael Oliver, Claire Rauter, and especially Ursula Vaughan Williams for information and advice during the preparation of this essay.

5 Scripture, Church, and culture: biblical texts in the works of Ralph Vaughan Williams

BYRON ADAMS

For William Austin

Shortly after the première of his operatic Morality *The Pilgrim's Progress*, given at Covent Garden on 26 April 1951, Ralph Vaughan Williams received a 'long and interesting' letter from Rutland Boughton, composer of the once popular opera, *The Immortal Hour*, founder of the Glastonbury Festival, and sometime apologist for the Communist Party.[1] Dated 12 May and written in response to a radio broadcast of *The Pilgrim's Progress*, the letter contains one particularly provocative sentence. After railing at David Willcocks and Sir Steuart Wilson (then Organist of Worcester Cathedral and Deputy General Administrator of the Royal Opera House respectively) for rejecting his suggestion that the work be mounted in a cathedral at the next Three Choirs Festival, Boughton writes: 'The anti-Christians have got such a hold on our life that they are afraid of Christian vitality in Christian buildings (and by the way your Pilgrim seems to be afraid of his Christian name) – still more of admitting Christian thought into our theatres'. His insightful aside concerning Vaughan Williams's change of the protagonist's name from Bunyan's 'Christian' to 'Pilgrim' elicited a highly revealing reply: 'I on purpose did not call the Pilgrim "Christian" because I want the idea to be universal and apply to anybody who aims at the spiritual life whether he is Xtian, Jew, Buddhist, Shintoist or 5th Day Adventist'.

This declaration testifies both to Vaughan Williams's democratic belief in the validity of all religious traditions and to his desire to address spiritual concerns through his music. But it also offers a rare glimpse into the complex and sometimes contradictory relationship that existed between the composer's spiritual life, the evolution of his artistic aims, and

[1] The correspondence between Boughton and Vaughan Williams appears in Kennedy, *Works*, p. 313.

99

the many religious texts which he chose to set. In this regard, Vaughan Williams's use of biblical texts is of particular interest, illuminating the development of his personal beliefs and his desire to create an aesthetic that would embrace his visionary impulses, as well as casting new light on the cultural nationalism which led him to honour the liturgy and musical traditions of that unique institution, the Church of England. Furthermore, Vaughan Williams's explanation to Boughton reveals how willing he was to alter basic aspects of a text in order to suit his own purposes, an attitude that was to prove crucial in the composer's dealings with scripture.

Vaughan Williams was uncompromising concerning the composer's prerogative in setting a text. A. E. Housman's publisher informed Vaughan Williams that a biographer wished to publish letters the poet had written that bitterly castigated the composer for omitting an entire stanza from 'Is my team ploughing?' (*On Wenlock Edge*). Vaughan Williams replied:

> You may print anything you like. If the biographer consents, I think I ought to be allowed my say, which is that the composer has a perfect right artistically to set any portion of a poem he chooses provided he does not actually alter the sense: that makers of anthologies, headed by the late Poet Laureate have done the same thing – I also feel that a poet should be grateful to anyone who fails to perpetuate such lines as:
>
> The goal stands up, the keeper
> Stands up to keep the goal.[2]

Vaughan Williams may have had some flickering scruples about modifying the meaning of one of Housman's lyrics – and by excising those transparently phallic lines from 'Is my team ploughing?' he has indeed significantly altered the sense of the poem – but he goes even further when setting religious texts. Vaughan Williams does not scruple in stripping a biblical passage of its context and modifying its meaning by juxtaposition with other texts, sometimes biblical, but often taken from sources quite foreign to the Bible, such as Thomas Hardy or Walt Whitman. (In contrast, Vaughan Williams is scrupulously careful when setting poetry to reflect its prosody in his music.)

This manipulation of fragments provides insight into the development of Vaughan Williams's inimitable and complex personal system of

[2] Kennedy, *Catalogue*, p. 48.

100

belief and epitomizes his response as an artist to the cultural assumptions of his time. The intellectual and spiritual tension created in Victorian England by the rival claims of the old religion and the new rationalism was woven into the very fabric of the composer's family. His father, who died when Vaughan Williams was two years old, was an Anglican clergyman. His mother, a descendant of Josiah Wedgwood, was a strict Christian with Evangelical leanings; at the same time she was a niece of Charles Darwin. Echoes of the controversy created by the publication in 1859 of the first edition of *The Origin of Species* continued to resonate in both family and country well past the composer's birth thirteen years later. Faint murmurs of the raging debate over his august relative's theories penetrated even into Vaughan Williams's nursery. When he enquired of his mother what the book was about she gave the following quaint, if sensible, reply: 'The Bible says that God made the world in six days, Great Uncle Charles thinks it took longer: but we need not worry about it, for it is equally wonderful either way'.[3]

There is no conclusive evidence to suggest that Vaughan Williams ever read his Great Uncle Charles's controversial book. His evolutionary view of music history, a thread running throughout the Mary Flexner Lectures he delivered at Bryn Mawr in 1932 and published two years later under the title *National Music*, was for the most part derivative, filtered through the writings of Hubert Parry, his revered teacher at the Royal College of Music. Vaughan Williams acknowledged Parry's influence upon his own thought in the first chapter of *National Music*: 'Hubert Parry, in his book, *The Evolution of the Art of Music*, has shown how music like everything else in the world is subject to the laws of evolution, that there is no difference in kind but only in degree between Beethoven and the humblest singer of a folksong'.[4] (One notes in passing the suggestive title of Parry's book, as well as his admiration for the ideas of Herbert Spencer.[5]) Like Parry, Vaughan Williams simply appropriates the outlines of evolutionary theory for his own historical purpose. In the fourth and fifth chapters of *National Music*, loosely organized under the title 'The Evolution of the Folk-song', general principles of evolutionary theory are applied to social

---

[3] U. Vaughan Williams, *R.V.W.*, p. 13.   [4] *National Music*, p. 6.
[5] R. Vaughan Williams and G. Holst, *Heirs*, p. 96.

and cultural phenomena as Vaughan Williams describes in an unsystematic and democratic fashion the gradual communal creation of folk music. Elsewhere in *National Music* this adaptation of Darwinian hypotheses is somewhat uncomfortably allied with a Hegelian view of the historical development of music, a 'development' conceived very much in the tradition of Herder's *Entwicklung*. Vaughan Williams studied history at Cambridge in the early 1890s and it seems highly unlikely that he could have remained unacquainted with the work of Hegel (we know that the composer's friend G. E. Moore attended the philosopher John McTaggert's famous Cambridge lectures on Hegel in 1894).[6] Nevertheless, Vaughan Williams's occasional attempts to apply Hegelian philosophy to music may derive from Parry once again, whose writings are profoundly teutonophile in many aspects of their intellectual ancestry.

However and whenever he may have sampled the fruit of the tree of knowledge regarding the theory of evolution or the philosophy of Hegel, Vaughan Williams was aware as a schoolboy of the conflict between rationalism and religion. As his intellectual independence increased, so did his scepticism of the religious beliefs held by his parents. As Ursula Vaughan Williams writes in her biography of her husband, 'He was an atheist during his later years at Charterhouse and at Cambridge, though he later drifted into a cheerful agnosticism: he was never a professing Christian'.[7] His impulse towards atheism was further encouraged at Cambridge, where he was an undergraduate from 1892 to 1895. Through his cousin Ralph (Randolph) Wedgwood, Vaughan Williams entered a circle that, as noted above, included G. E. Moore, as well as G. M. Trevelyan and Bertrand Russell. All of these relations, friends, and acquaintances were members of the notorious semi-covert intellectual society known as the Apostles. Nine of the twelve undergraduates who founded the society in 1820 took holy orders, but seventy years later the Apostles were anti-clerical and emphatically non-Christian.[8] Vaughan Williams was close enough to this circle to be considered as an 'embryo', or prospective member, of the Apostles during his first year at Cambridge, but his candidacy never progressed beyond the

---

[6] Paul Levy, *Moore: G. E. Moore and the Cambridge Apostles* (London: George Weidenfeld & Nicolson, 1979), p. 125. [7] *R.V.W.*, p. 29.

[8] Levy, *Moore*, p. 67.

initial stage.[9] Perhaps the extensive musical activities which consumed most of his time militated against his election to the society. (This was probably for the best, for one cannot imagine the sensitive, romantic, and emphatically heterosexual young composer feeling at ease among the frank sexual discussions and revelations – by tradition couched exclusively in terms redolent of schoolboy homo-eroticism, even when the experiences under discussion were of a heterosexual nature – that frequently coloured meetings of the Apostles.[10]) Yet Vaughan Williams's atheism doubtless hardened in this radical milieu. In a letter to Michael Kennedy, Bertrand Russell recalled that Vaughan Williams had the reputation at Cambridge of being a 'most confirmed atheist' who once walked into Hall at Trinity College and exclaimed, 'Who believes in God nowadays, I should like to know?'.[11]

In light of this rhetorical question, it is not surprising that during his early creative period Vaughan Williams completely avoided using biblical texts. Apart from some juvenilia and student exercises, he did not set a verse from the Bible until 1913, by which time he was over forty years old and an established composer. With the minor exceptions of a few hymns and some modest incidental music written for a dramatization of Bunyan's *The Pilgrim's Progress* given at Reigate Priory in 1906, he avoided Christian poetry as well. Indeed, Vaughan Williams did not use texts even remotely associated with the Judeo-Christian tradition in a major work until 1911, when he set poems by George Herbert in the *Five Mystical Songs* for baritone, chorus, and orchestra.

Vaughan Williams instead attempted to express his visionary impulse during this period by selecting the verse of such contemporary poets as Dante Gabriel Rossetti, Robert Louis Stevenson and, later and more successfully, Walt Whitman. Bertrand Russell introduced Vaughan Williams to Whitman's poetry in 1892,[12] and the impact of the American poet on the composer was immediate, profound, and lasting. Vaughan Williams chose passages from *Leaves of Grass* for two major choral works, both presented at the Leeds Festival: *Toward the Unknown Region* in 1907, and the massive *A Sea Symphony*, first sketched in 1903 and given its première seven years later

---

[9] *Ibid.*, p. 53.   [10] *Ibid.*, p. 140.   [11] Kennedy, *Works*, p. 42.
[12] *Ibid.*, p. 82n.

in 1910. Whitman's language echoes that of the psalms, employing long lines and parallelism to evoke a sense of spiritual exaltation and express universal truths. These epic verses served Vaughan Williams and other English composers of the time, such as Stanford and Holst, as an attractive alternative to the Bible.

Whitman, though, was not merely a substitute for the Bible. It is difficult to imagine exactly how liberating his poetry must have been for those English readers who discovered him during the latter part of the nineteenth century. Whitman repeatedly insisted on the equality and intrinsic dignity of all peoples; he criticized the constricted social and sexual mores of the period; and he clearly preferred to be outdoors communing with nature than in polite urban company. This contrasted bracingly with the parlour-bound stuffiness of most late Victorian verse, and his hearty pantheism and utopian fervour offered a welcome antidote to the fustiness of Victorian Christianity. Whitman's work thus received a warm welcome from such radicals as Russell, and, because of its frank homo-eroticism, Edward Carpenter and John Addington Symonds. Vaughan Williams, himself a convinced if undogmatic radical on political and social issues, was profoundly affected by Whitman's poetry: he carried a pocket volume of *Leaves of Grass* throughout the First World War,[13] and, in the final month of his life, confessed to Michael Kennedy his continuing enthusiasm for Whitman's poetry.[14]

The visionary strain which Whitman shared with the New England Transcendentalists was combined with an obsessive celebration of the real, earthy life around him. Whitman's ability to maintain a balance (however precarious) between the transcendent and the commonplace, and his insistence on the honest expression of vast, oceanic emotions, must have seemed particularly attractive to a young composer in 1892, especially one just beginning a long struggle to reconcile style and authenticity in his own music. By drawing texts from Whitman for his first important large-scale choral works, Vaughan Williams was able to express a yearning for transcendence unmarked by conventional religious associations, and he could articulate as well the fiercely democratic convictions that he and the poet held in common. (He does not let the American off lightly, however, for despite his manifest love for Whitman's poetry, Vaughan Williams manipu-

---

[13] U. Vaughan Williams, *R. V. W.*, p. 129.   [14] Kennedy, *Works*, p. 100.

lated texts from *Leaves of Grass* for *A Sea Symphony* with the same ruthlessness that he demonstrated later with verses drawn from the Bible or the choleric Housman's truncated poem.) Reading Whitman may also have helped Vaughan Williams conceptualize the particular kind of cultural nationalism that he fervently promoted in his own career. Whitman, like Vaughan Williams, frequently moves in a rhetorical space which is poised between the national and the universal. Although intensely American – for only Matthew Arnold has crammed into his poetry as many place-names of his native land – Whitman always used the national as a means to reach the universal, even as he aspired towards the spiritual beyond by fully and alertly observing the streets of his native Manhattan. In like manner, Vaughan Williams's sense of national identity was never confining or parochial.

By the time he set the overtly Christian verse of George Herbert in 1911, Vaughan Williams had developed into a passionate cultural nationalist. He began collecting English folksongs in 1903, and subsequently wrote a series of essays proposing folksong as a crucial element in the creation of a new, uniquely English, musical syntax. The most controversial of these early articles, 'Who Wants the English Composer?', was written in 1912 and is headed by eight lines of Whitman's *Song of the Exposition*; this cogent and polemical essay defined Vaughan Williams's nationalist aims in terms both blunt and sincere:

> Art, like charity, should begin at home. If it is to be of any value it must grow out of the very life of himself [the artist], the community in which he lives, the nation to which he belongs. ... Have we not all about us forms of musical expression which we can purify and raise to the level of great art? ... The composer must not shut himself up and think about great art, he must live with his fellows and make his art an expression of the whole life of the community.[15]

In a later essay published in 1942 under the title 'Nationalism and Internationalism', he wrote, 'I believe that the love of one's country, one's language, one's customs, one's religion, are essential to our spiritual health'.[16] It was this almost mystical belief in the importance of identifying

---

[15] 'Who Wants the English Composer?' *The R.C.M. Magazine*, 9/1 (Christmas Term 1912), pp. 11–14. [16] *National Music*, p. 154.

with the community around one that enabled Vaughan Williams, despite his early rejection of organized religion, to come to value the Church of England as not merely an institution of the English State, but an integral part of the 'whole life' of his national community.

Vaughan Williams's involvement with the musical tradition of the Anglican church had begun in earnest with his discovery of the great service music from the Tudor period, edited during the first thirty years of the twentieth century by E. H. Fellowes, Sylvia Townsend Warner, and others. Tudor church music, and especially the verse anthems of Byrd and Gibbons, had as great an influence as folksong on the development of Vaughan Williams's style. Furthermore, between 1904 and 1906 he devoted the bulk of his time to compiling and editing the *English Hymnal*. Through his work on this revolutionary hymnal, Vaughan Williams significantly raised the standards of English hymnody, enriching and rejuvenating an important national musical tradition. The tunes which he composed especially for the hymnal, such as 'Down Ampney' ('Come Down, O Love Divine', no. 152) and 'Sine Nomine' ('For All The Saints', no. 641), as well as the folksongs he arranged as hymns, such as his beloved 'Dives and Lazarus' ('Kingsfold', no. 574), entered into the musical life of a vast community of English-speaking congregations, which treasures them to this day. One notes with interest that his first mature setting of a biblical text followed by only one year the publication of 'Who Wants the English Composer?', and that it was intended for the national church. In 1913 he set the Prayer Book version of Psalm 148 as an Anglican anthem for mixed a cappella choir, entitled 'O Praise the Lord of Heaven'. The composer continued to adorn the Anglican musical tradition throughout his career, producing three anthems, four canticles, nine motets, an Evening Service, an entire set of Services, several examples of Anglican chant, and twenty hymn-tunes.

Vaughan Williams's music for the Anglican church expressed his appreciation of the church's role as a reliquary of English cultural traditions. He would have agreed with Matthew Arnold that, 'Man worships best, therefore, with the community; he philosophizes best alone'.[17] Like

[17] Matthew Arnold, *Collected Prose Works*, ed. R. H. Super, 11 vols. (Ann Arbor: University of Michigan Press, 1960–77), vol. V, p. 197. For a discussion of Vaughan Williams's early settings of Arnold's poetry see Oliver Neighbour's chapter in the present volume.

Arnold, Vaughan Williams rejected theological dogma, valuing Christianity instead for its ethical code and social utility. Just as Arnold's rational critique of religion, with its dismissal of traditional metaphysics and emphasis on verification, led directly to the positivist philosophy of G. E. Moore,[18] so Vaughan Williams's early scepticism of received religious faith, although less systematically developed than Arnold's, led him to an atheism reinforced by the influence of Moore and his circle at Cambridge.

The trends which influenced Arnold and his contemporaries, and which would later have a role in moulding Vaughan Williams's intellectual attitudes, had their basis in the German tradition of textual criticism that arose in the late eighteenth century. Applying such tools as philology and the Higher Criticism, German scholars precipitated a profound cultural crisis when they ascribed a communal inspiration to such texts as the *Iliad* and the Bible, effectively refuting the theory of a single author for the former, and casting grave doubt on the historical accuracy and divine authority of the latter. The impact of these ideas was keenly felt throughout the Victorian intelligentsia.[19] Whether or not Vaughan Williams was directly exposed to the contentious debates engendered by them, this strain of textual scholarship certainly influenced his personal beliefs, as is clear from *National Music*. As he documents the communal development of folksong in the fourth chapter of *National Music*, he adduces the work of the distinguished classicist Gilbert Murray in support of his theories.[20] In one of the passages Vaughan Williams quotes, Murray echoes the central thesis of an early exemplar of close textual criticism, Friedrich August Wolf's 1795 *Prolegomena to Homer*: 'The Iliad and the Odyssey represent not the independent invention of one man, but the ever-moving tradition of many gen-

---

18 See Ruth apRoberts, *Arnold and God* (Berkeley and Los Angeles: University of California Press, 1983), p. 229; also Levy, *Moore*, pp. 217–18.

19 I am indebted to the second chapter, 'The Fathers of Higher Criticism', of apRoberts, *Arnold and God*, for most of the historical information contained in this paragraph.

20 Gilbert Murray (1866–1957), Regius Professor of Greek, Christ Church, Oxford. In addition to his influential books, such as *The Rise of the Greek Epic* (1907), Murray was well known as a translator of classical drama. He was an acquaintance of Vaughan Williams, who set sections of Murray's translation of *The Bacchae* of Euripides for an ill-fated choral ballet which was to have been danced by Isadora Duncan (see U. Vaughan Williams, *R.V.W.*, p. 94).

erations of men'.[21] Not only does Vaughan Williams cite Murray's description of the process of communal creation, he also notes that Murray places the Bible in the same class as the *Iliad*: 'Can we not truly say of these [folksongs] as Gilbert Murray says of that great national literature of the Bible and Homer, "They have behind them not the imagination of one great poet, but the accumulated emotion, one may almost say, of the many successive generations who have read and learned and themselves afresh re-created the old majesty and loveliness. ... There is in them, as it were, the spiritual life-blood of a people."'[22]

By considering the Bible a series of folk texts created over generations in the same manner as one of his beloved folksongs, Vaughan Williams gave himself permission to jettison the aversion to Christian dogma that had kept him, a card-carrying atheist throughout his early career, from using biblical texts without discomfort. He deeply loved the Authorized Version of the Bible and he recognized its central position in the development of English language, culture, and society, expropriating like most other English artists an anthology of Middle Eastern historical and poetic texts, considering their translations as uniquely English as 'Bushes and Briars'. Given his freedom from religious belief or vision of a conventional or institutional kind, and his commitment to the notion of art as social expression, he felt no constraints in selecting and adapting these texts for his own devices, just as he freely selected, arranged, and developed folksongs throughout his career, transforming them in the process and making them utterly his own.

In view of the complex interweaving of these variegated strands of personal development and cultural influence, it is not surprising that a certain confusion has developed among commentators on the role of religion in the life and work of Vaughan Williams. His declarations of rational humanism and atheism appear to be at odds with the visionary fervour of many of his major works. After 1920 this apparent dichotomy between words and works became more pronounced, as Vaughan Williams composed in rapid succession a series of scores based on biblical, liturgical, or otherwise overtly Christian texts: the two large motets 'O Clap Your Hands', a setting of Psalm 47 published in 1920, and 'Lord Thou Hast Been Our

---

[21] R. Vaughan Williams, *National Music*, p. 29.   [22] *National Music*, p. 23.

Refuge', whose text is taken from Psalm 90, and which appeared the following year; the darkly beautiful motet 'O vos omnes', written in 1922 for Terry and the choir of Westminster Cathedral; the Mass in G minor, composed 1920–21 for Holst and his Whitsuntide Singers; and the pastoral episode in one act after Bunyan, *The Shepherds of the Delectable Mountains*, which was premièred at the Royal College of Music in 1922. As late as 1922, he dealt with this apparent contradiction summarily by declaring of the liturgical Mass in G minor, 'There is no reason why an atheist could not write a good Mass'.[23] Behind blunt statements of this sort, so characteristic of the man, there lie fascinating layers of ambiguity and conflict. Ursula Vaughan Williams touches upon this conflict without attempting to explain or reconcile it: 'Although a declared agnostic, he was able, all through his life, to set to music words in the accepted terms of Christian revelation as if they meant to him what they must have meant to George Herbert or to Bunyan'.[24]

The tendentious and often-heard argument that Vaughan Williams was some sort of *chrétien malgré lui* can be quickly dismissed as wishful thinking on the part of confused admirers and commentators. His religious dilemma was that of a person innately and deeply spiritual, yet far too intelligent to accept unquestioningly the historical reality of the Christian myth. As a child of his time, and as a member of the Darwin family, Vaughan Williams had to grapple with and resolve as best he could the competing claims of rationalism and faith. Unlike his Darwin relatives or his Cambridge friends, however, Vaughan Williams was an instinctive and essentially empirical artist faced with the complicated task of evolving an aesthetic position within which he could work securely.

While the rational critiques of Arnold, and the philosophical systems of Moore and Russell, challenged his intellect and influenced his rejection of Christianity, they offered little help in his search for a viable aesthetic position. A visionary artist simply cannot develop an aesthetic theory based solely on rationalistic or positivistic elements that banish anything remotely resembling traditional metaphysics. For Vaughan Williams, art,

---

[23] U. Vaughan Williams, *R. V. W.*, p. 138.
[24] *Ibid.*, p. 138.

especially music, was the medium through which both creator and participant could experience what lies beyond the boundaries of sensory experience. He restated this point again and again in his writings, as in his brief 'musical autobiography': 'The object of art is to stretch out to the ultimate realities through the medium of beauty'.[25] With a remarkable and wholly characteristic generosity, he consistently declined to impose upon others an exclusive interpretation of the meaning of his music, respecting listeners by allowing them to approach his work by their own individual paths: 'A work of art is like a theophany which takes different forms to different beholders'.[26]

Furthermore, a visionary artist who was committed to the European tradition of national culture could not have done without the metaphoric vocabulary and metaphysical concepts, mostly derived from the Bible, that provide the foundation upon which the very concept of 'nation' uneasily rests. Expressed in large part through a love of the Anglican musical tradition, and of the language of the Book of Common Prayer and the Authorized Version, Vaughan Williams's cultural nationalism led him to select texts whose metaphors spoke directly to the English community through a common religious heritage. The composer 'drifted into a cheerful agnosticism' around the early 1920s, developing a private system of belief that rejected Christianity's claims to a unique validity among other religious traditions while preserving the power of its myth and metaphor through his music. By removing biblical passages from their original surroundings and juxtaposing them with other texts, he manipulated their context and subtly modified their import – powerful metaphors are thus used to generate new meanings.

In many of his major works that draw text or subject matter from the Bible, Vaughan Williams found a way of qualifying the literal meaning through the introduction, in one way or another, of secular elements. Even in his oratorio *Sancta Civitas*, where the source is exclusively biblical (the Book of Revelation), he attached a disclaimer in the form of an epigraph. The score is prefaced by a quotation in Greek from the *Phaedo* of Plato, a translation of which reads:

---

[25] 'A Musical Autobiography', *National Music*, p. 189.
[26] *National Music*, p. 3.

Now to assert these things are exactly as I have described would not be reasonable. But that these things, or something like them, are true concerning the souls of men and their habitations after death, especially since the soul is shown to be immortal, this seems to me fitting and worth risking to believe. For the risk is honourable, and a man should sing such things in the manner of an incantation to himself.[27]

By employing this excerpt the composer clearly sets aside a Christian interpretation of the biblical text that follows, while pointing towards a reason for its selection. While the inscription from Plato is meant to distance the composer from the literal meaning of the biblical passages he has chosen, it also serves to guide performers and listeners of *Sancta Civitas* towards his symbolic intent. Part of the beauty of a living symbol is its inexhaustible potential for interpretation on multiple levels of meaning. By combining textual and musical symbolism, the composer gave his listeners the freedom to find their own meaning for both words and music.

Vaughan Williams always sought to reach the authentic through the symbolic. In a revealing sentence from his luminous essay 'The Letter and the Spirit', Vaughan Williams is quite explicit about the value he places on the power of the symbolic in art: 'The human, visible, audible and intelligible media which artists (of all kinds) use, are symbols not of other visible and audible things but of what lies beyond sense and knowledge'. In the next paragraph he asserts that, 'the symbols of the musical composer are those of the ear – musical sounds in their various combinations'.[28] Such views about symbolism in art are utterly consonant with Vaughan Williams's predilection for authors whose work is pervaded by symbols – Whitman, Bunyan, Blake, and Herbert, as well as minor symbolists such as Seamus O'Sullivan and Fredegond Shove. Ursula Vaughan Williams is a poet whose use of symbolism is both pervasive and highly sophisticated. Given these predilections, it is likely that Vaughan Williams considered the Bible to be a trove of symbolic texts, rather than the truth sent from above.

Furthermore, the quotation from the *Phaedo* is a reaffirmation of the composer's essentially Platonic aesthetic, and an implicit repudiation of the positivism espoused by his erstwhile associates at Cambridge. In the few

---

[27] Kennedy, *Works*, p. 194.   [28] *National Music*, p. 122.

years between the composition of the Mass in G Minor in 1921, when he asserted that 'There is no reason why an atheist could not write a good Mass', and the completion of *Sancta Civitas* in 1925, when he affixed the quotation from the *Phaedo*, the icy hardness of Vaughan Williams's doctrinaire atheism may have begun to thaw into agnosticism. In particular, as both the text of *Sancta Civitas* and the Greek epigraph suggest, he seems to have begun cautiously and intermittently to entertain the possibility of some form of life after death. Viewed in light of its epigraph, the text of *Sancta Civitas* is meant on at least one level as a symbolic statement concerning the survival of the soul after death. At the conclusion of the work, after a stirring depiction of the war between the kings of the earth and the forces of heaven, and a sensuous and highly dissonant lament over the destruction of the alluring secular city of Babylon, the New Jerusalem descends from heaven adorned in radiant music, perpetually celebrating within its environs the mystical marriage of the Bridegroom and the Bride. Vaughan Williams would again invoke this powerful symbol of a Holy City where all conflict is reconciled to great effect at the end of *The Pilgrim's Progress*.

The reasons for Vaughan Williams's fitful and protracted progress from a Cambridge atheist to a symbolical agnostic are difficult to determine with any certainty, given the ambivalence that lies at the very heart of his personality, not to mention the care with which he guarded his inner privacy. It is certainly true that the transcendent strain permeates a great deal of his work, from *Toward the Unknown Region*, written near the beginning of his career, to the Ninth Symphony, completed in the last year of his life. It is equally undeniable that the pieces composed in the years immediately after the First World War reflect a marked intensification of the mystical and symbolic elements of his work. Scores written immediately after the composer's demobilization from active service in 1919 include *A Pastoral Symphony*, completed in 1921; the Mass in G Minor; *The Shepherds of the Delectable Mountains*; and, as the culmination of this strain in his work, *Sancta Civitas*. In 1938, exasperated by fatuous remarks concerning *A Pastoral Symphony* by Constant Lambert and others, Vaughan Williams disclosed that the symphony was explicitly associated with his time as a private in the Royal Army Medical Corps, stationed at the front in France:

> It's really war-time music – a great deal of it incubated when I used to go up
> at night with the ambulance waggon at Ecoives and we went up a steep hill
> and there was a wonderful Corot-like landscape in the sunset – it's not really
> lambkins frisking at all as most people take for granted.[29]

Although certain commentators have attempted to shrug off the impor-
tance of Vaughan Williams's wartime experiences,[30] it was in fact a harrow-
ing ordeal for the sensitive composer, aptly characterized by Ursula
Vaughan Williams's stark comment that 'Working in the ambulance gave
Ralph vivid awareness of how men died'.[31] In that very ambulance at
Ecoives, filled with the wounded, the dying, and the dead, Vaughan
Williams first conceived the radiant anguish of *A Pastoral Symphony*. He
may well have planned other works at that time, such as the *Shepherds of the
Delectable Mountains*, which, after all, takes as its subject the passage of its
protagonist through the River of Death into the Celestial City.

Surrounded by death, then, he may have found respite in the vision of
a serene existence beyond earthly cares, disappointments, and losses. To
articulate this ambivalent longing, Vaughan Williams employed the symbolism offered by Christian eschatology, drawing texts from the Bible for
Sancta Civitas and other scores; but it never was an expression of faith in a
particular creed. Later, when his dear friend and colleague Gustav Holst
died in 1934, he wrote:

> Some years ago I had the privilege of writing about Gustav Holst. I
> remember saying then that 'perhaps he will lead us into regions where it will
> be difficult to follow.' He may have now found in new regions that which his
> music ever seemed to be seeking. . . . All art is the imperfect human half-
> realization of that which is spiritually perfect. Holst's music seems especially
> to be a quest after that which in early life we can only partially fulfill.[32]

Two weeks before his own death, when asked by Sylvia Townsend Warner
how he would choose to be reincarnated in the next life, he responded seriously: 'Music, he said, music. But in the next world, I shan't be doing music,
with all the striving and disappointments. I shall be being it.'[33]

---

[29] Letter of 4 October 1938, quoted in U. Vaughan Williams, *R.V.W.*, p. 121.
[30] See, for example, Andrew Porter, 'The Open Road', *The New Yorker*, 66/17
(28 May 1990), p. 96.   [31] *R.V.W.*, p. 122.   [32] *National Music*, p. 151.
[33] Sylvia Townsend Warner, *Letters of Sylvia Townsend Warner*, ed. William
Maxwell (London: Chatto & Windus, 1982), p. 168.

Vaughan Williams not only arranged biblical passages in order that the symbolism of the text coincided with the symbolic import of his aesthetic purpose, he also on occasion employed the expressive qualities of his music in order to construe the words in a manner quite contrary to their orthodox interpretation. By careful choice of musical idiom he deconstructs the text, shattering its original import to bits in order to rebuild it closer to his heart's desire; in other words, in such works it is the music itself, rather than textual manipulation, which is used to place both composer and listener at a remove from the literal meaning of a biblical text.

The most radical example of this procedure is found in the *Magnificat* for contralto, solo flute, and orchestra, written for Astra Desmond and premièred at the Three Choirs Festival in 1932. In a letter to Holst, Vaughan Williams wrote that he hoped 'to lift the words out of the smug atmosphere which had settled down on [the *Magnificat*] from being sung at evening service for so long (I've tried to get the smugness out; I don't know if I have succeeded – I find it awfully hard to eradicate it)'.[34] He need not have worried, for not only did he eradicate any lingering whiff of stale ecclesiastical incense, he reinterpreted the text in a manner utterly at variance with its context in the Gospel according to Luke. The composer clothes the pristine narrative of the Annunciation with richly textured music of unabashed sensuality, as overtly and unashamedly erotic as his earlier *Flos Campi* (for viola solo, small wordless chorus, and chamber orchestra), premièred in 1925, which drew its inspiration, as well as the Latin quotations placed above each movement, from the *Song of Songs*. While the hypnotic, oscillating chords which open the *Magnificat* have often justly been compared to Holst's music, surely they are equally reminiscent, in their oriental voluptuousness, of the incantatory swaying harmonies that pervade 'L'Indifférent', the last movement of Ravel's *Shéhérazade* of 1903. Vaughan Williams's use of the solo flute is close in spirit to Ravel's 'La flûte enchantée', the second movement of that gorgeous song-cycle, and also recalls, again incongruously, another milestone of musical erotica, Debussy's *Prélude à l'aprés-midi d'un faune*. Furthermore, the mood, sonority, and certain of the melodic contours of the *Magnificat* anticipate in an uncanny fashion

---

[34] R. Vaughan Williams and G. Holst, *Heirs*, p. 79.

sections of a work premièred thirteen years later, Messiaen's *Trois petites liturgies de la Présence Divine*, which features prominently a women's chorus and revels in a potent and eerie admixture of sensuality and religiosity. Indeed, both the sound and spirit of Vaughan Williams's lapidary score is far from any hint of association with either the traditional view of the Annunciation story or the Anglican liturgy. Ursula Vaughan Williams quotes her husband as saying that, 'he thought of the flute as the disembodied, visiting spirit and the alto solo as the voice of the girl yielding to her lover for the first time'.[35]

In addition to the various methods of treating a biblical text outlined above, Vaughan Williams freely combined verses from the Bible with other texts in order to articulate a social or political message. For his anti-war cantata *Dona Nobis Pacem*, premièred in 1936, the composer compiled a text drawn from the Roman liturgy, Whitman's *Drum Taps*, and a famous speech delivered by John Bright to the House of Commons in February 1855 at the height of the Crimean War, along with nine passages from the Old and New Testaments. Here the Bible is used for a quite different purpose than in *Sancta Civitas*. Forming the conclusion to the work, but placed immediately after Bright's speech, the biblical passages are used to express Vaughan Williams's hope for a purely terrestrial peace on earth, rather than as a symbolic evocation of 'that which lies beyond sense and knowledge'. The section of Bright's speech used in *Dona Nobis Pacem* itself contains a biblical allusion, to the Passover story found in Exodus (12:21–3): 'The Angel of Death has been abroad in the land; you may almost hear the beating of his wings. There is no one as of old ... to sprinkle with blood the lintel and the two side-posts of our doors, that he may spare and pass on.'

Vaughan Williams's placement of this speech gives the biblical selections that follow a distinctly modern and secular implication. Set to joyous, extroverted music, the biblical fragments are manipulated so as to call for a political peace on earth, a call which is intensified by its proximity to Bright's sombre reminder of the human cost of war in an age without miracles. This interpretation is at variance with the Bible verses in their original context, either the covenant promises which God made to the Israelites in

---

[35] *R.V.W.*, pp. 121–2.

the selections from the Old Testament (such as Micah 4:3) or the spiritual peace promised by the birth of Christ in the single verse chosen from the New Testament (Luke 2:14). Vaughan Williams ends his cantata on a note of quiet urgency, as the soprano sings, alone and unaccompanied, the words 'Dona nobis pacem'; perhaps the composer's active participation in the Federal Union, an organization that worked towards the creation of a united Europe, had given him an idea of how difficult it was (and is) to achieve even the most precarious 'peace on earth'.

A particularly moving and telling example of textual juxtaposition is found in a late work, the large-scale Christmas cantata for three soloists, chorus, and orchestra entitled *Hodie*, which was given its first performance during the 1954 Three Choirs Festival. Compiled from the Gospels of Luke, Matthew, and John, as well as the poetry of Milton, Herbert, Drummond, Ursula Vaughan Williams, and anonymous medieval sources, the text of this work tells, with one exception, the familiar Christian story in conventional, if fresh and elegant, terms. The exception is a muted, deeply felt setting for baritone soloist and orchestra of Thomas Hardy's 'The Oxen', which casts its gently sceptical and rueful shadow upon the surrounding texts:

> So fair a fancy few would weave
> In these years! yet, I feel
> If someone said on Christmas Eve,
> 'Come; see the oxen kneel,
> In the lonely barton by yonder coomb
> Our Childhood used to know,'
> I should go with him in the gloom,
> Hoping it might be so.

Here, in the midst of the joyous celebration of Christmas, is a cry for the innocent faith of childhood from a speaker who has lost it, and experienced all the attendant pain and uncertainty that comes in the wake of that loss. By choosing this poem, Vaughan Williams clearly allies himself with Hardy, whose lost childhood faith was not replaced by adult belief. One can imagine that in setting this haunting lyric, the elderly composer addresses the listener directly, stepping, as it were, from behind his curtain of aesthetic distance to sing of his nostalgia for a kind of faith irrevocably lost long ago.

Although he closely followed the philosophical developments of his time, Vaughan Williams never attempted to explain his views in consistent, logical terms. He loved the language and symbolic potential of the Bible, yet he approached it neither in the spirit of unquestioning acceptance nor of deliberate critique. He sought instead to fix a constantly evolving inner vision using the symbols at his disposal, in the union of words and music. Moreover, he offered his vision to his nation and, by interpreting the traditions of that nation, to the world in a way he hoped would move others as deeply as he himself was moved. Throughout his own long pilgrimage, Vaughan Williams never doubted for a moment that the language of music fully expressed the thoughts, hopes, doubts, and convictions, at once mutable and deeply held, that made up his spiritual life.

6 Vaughan Williams's folksong transcriptions: a case of idealization?

JULIAN ONDERDONK

Anyone who would today seek to assess Vaughan Williams's activities as a folksong collector cannot ignore the changes that have occurred in British folksong studies over the past thirty years. Modern scholarship has come to see folksong less as a collection of individual songs and repertories than as one part of a fluid social and cultural process, in which the meaning of a song is defined by the circumstances of performance and audience reception. Developing alongside these notions have been equally specific ideas about what constitutes reliable collecting work. In the words of the folklorist A. E. Green, an accurate collector not only takes note of the performance context, but sees to it that 'air and text be from the same informant; that the air be transcribed as far as possible as sung; that the text be complete in so far as the informant knows it, no less and no more, and failing this, if collation has been undertaken, that the nature and extent of the collation be made clear'.[1]

As the basis on which all present-day collecting work is to be undertaken, these criteria have also become the standard against which past collecting work is judged. In recent decades an historical branch of folksong scholarship has emerged that seeks to evaluate the work of the pioneer collectors of the 'First' Folk Revival, Cecil Sharp, Frank Kidson, Lucy Broadwood, and Ralph Vaughan Williams among them.[2] Observing that

---

[1] 'Foreword' in Frank Kidson, *Traditional Tunes: A Collection Of Ballads And Airs* [1891], facsimile edition (Wakefield, 1970), p. vii. For a survey of the new emphasis in folksong research see Michael Pickering, 'Recent Folk Music Scholarship in England: A Critique', *Folk Music Journal*, 6 (1990), pp. 37-64.

[2] For an overview and references to sources see Richard Sykes, 'The Evolution of Englishness in the English Folksong Revival, 1890-1914', *Folk Music Journal*, 6 (1993), pp. 450-60.

the methods of these collectors fell far short of the standards defined above, modern folklorists claim that their predecessors signally failed to record folksong as it was truly sung in the early years of this century. The charge has caused a stir in the folk-music community since it directly challenges the early collectors' well-publicized belief in their notational accuracy and 'scientific' methods of collection. But it is the conclusions that the folklorists draw from their observations that have proven most controversial. They suggest that, far from viewing folksong with 'scientific objectivity', Sharp and his contemporaries in fact idealized the music they were collecting. Influenced by an emerging ruralist nationalism that sought reassurance and inspiration in England's pre-industrial past, collectors imbued folksong with almost mythical powers of social and cultural renewal. They hailed it as the 'voice of the people', a cultural artifact uniquely expressive of the feelings of the nation, and promoted it as a means to reform popular musical taste. But since the realities of traditional music-making were much more complex and disorderly than this idealized image would admit, turn-of-the-century collectors necessarily (though on the whole unconsciously) simplified and distorted what they found. The evidence, folklorists assert, is in their biased collecting methods and flawed editorial practices. Collectors sought folksong only in isolated rural areas, rejected those songs not meeting preconceived criteria, and reduced the variational complexity of traditional singing to a minimum.

While it cannot be said that the individual folklorists pursuing this critique concur in all particulars, their general thrust is nevertheless one of a cultural materialism or sub-Marxism grounded in the discipline of social history. All have centred their analysis on the social and cultural separation of middle-class collector and working-class singer and have related their findings to historical contexts. They also agree that the collectors' idealization, or mediation, of traditional song was, like the emerging nationalism it reflected, part of a potent cultural politics whose effect was to reinforce the existing power-structure at a time of national uncertainty. In these terms, folklorists assert that the collectors' promotion of folksong constitutes what historians have called an 'invented tradition' – a bid to invest authenticity and authority in revived or newly minted cultural forms by means of dubious appeals to antiquity, as a means of confronting perceived problems in the social order.[3] Such promotion also conforms to the Gramscian model of hegemonic renewal, in which ruling groups acquire political legitimacy through the assimilation of selected aspects of lower-class culture.[4] Hence the current insistence on judging the early collectors by the standards of modern scholarship: this, it is argued, provides the acid test that demonstrates the strength of their class-orientation and prejudice. For in proving that collectors failed to record folksong precisely 'as sung', it shows that they were interested only in the *idea*, their own idea, of folksong. Instead of viewing it as the cultural process it authentically was, collectors saw folksong only as a sort of collectible item, a simplified and abstracted – indeed purged – version of the real thing. Far from documenting the reality of traditional song and its singers (as they claimed to do), collectors were in fact indifferent to that reality, unknowing victims of their own cultural needs and ideological priorities.

In testing the validity of this argument as it pertains to Vaughan Williams, we must concede from the beginning that his methods of collecting do often fall short of those of modern scholarship – and often on the very issues outlined above. Maintaining the erroneous and sentimental belief that the intrusion of printed ballad sheets had 'corrupted' a purely oral process of text transmission, he disregarded the words of half of his collected songs. Exaggerating the musical and cultural backwardness of the 'typical' folk-singer, he pursued the great majority of his collecting in isolated rural areas and rejected songs betraying the influence of urban popular music. He also failed to record personal facts concerning many of his singers, their names and places of residence, their occupations and backgrounds, where and how they learned their songs, etc. But if these failings seem only to confirm that he idealized and seriously misrepresented folksong, we must realize that they are frequently offset by attitudes and practices that suggest the very opposite – that do demonstrate an interest in the singer's social reality and that do faithfully record the facts of traditional music-making. For example, if he disregarded the words of many collected songs, he did so because he was on the lookout for texts which in his opinion most

---

[3] See Eric Hobsbawm and Terence Ranger, eds., *The Invention of Tradition* (Cambridge: Cambridge University Press, 1983). For a broader discussion of Vaughan Williams and the ruralist movement see Alain Frogley's chapter in the present volume.

[4] See T. Jackson Lears, 'The Concept of Cultural Hegemony', *American Historical Review*, 90 (1985), pp. 567–93.

bore the impress of the singer's own personality, and therefore gave little attention to those that were clearly stock-in-trade. If he theorized folksong as narrowly rural and unlettered, he nevertheless did not ignore singers who were both literate and town-dwelling when he encountered them; indeed, evidence suggests that he actually favoured these singers' songs in the course of publication. If he neglected to record personal information concerning many of his singers, he was none the less careful to note down the places where and dates on which they sang to him. Even if he failed to record all he could about his singers, examination of his activities within the Folk Song Society shows that he was instrumental in urging fellow collectors to obtain such information in their own work.[5]

The truth of the matter, quite simply, is that Vaughan Williams's collecting work was inconsistent, and his views on folksong often contradictory. On the one hand, he romanticized and idealized folksong and distorted its musical and cultural realities. On the other, he neither sentimentalized his singers nor falsified their repertories and, most importantly, he faithfully recorded the facts of folksong performance. The significant point, however, is that the contradiction exists at all. It is one that, to date, the folklorists in their account of Vaughan Williams have consistently overlooked. Observing that he was one of the leading figures of the Folk Revival, they have simply taken for granted that his methods were fundamentally deficient and have given little thought to the possibility of alternative judgements. The real problem undoubtedly lies in the fact that no single study devoted exclusively to Vaughan Williams's collecting work has yet appeared from within the folklorists' critique;[6] as a

[5] This summarizes some of the main points discussed in my forthcoming New York University Ph.D. dissertation, 'Vaughan Williams and Folksong: English Nationalism and the Sensibility of Pastoral'.

[6] When his work has been discussed at all, it has generally been only in the context of other collectors. See Vic Gammon, 'Folk Song Collecting in Sussex and Surrey, 1843–1914', *History Workshop Journal*, 10 (1980), pp. 61–89; Dave Harker, *Fakesong: The Manufacture of British 'Folksong' 1700 to the Present Day* (Milton Keynes: Open University Press, 1985), Chap. 9; and Georgina Boyes, *The Imagined Village: Culture, Ideology and the English Folk Revival* (Manchester: Manchester University Press, 1993), Chap. 3. Appearing outside the orbit of the folklorists' critique is Roy Palmer, ed., *Folk Songs Collected By Ralph Vaughan Williams* (London: J. M. Dent and Sons, 1983), which reproduces and traces the history of 121 songs from the manuscript collection. An introduction and extensive notes contain valuable information about Vaughan Williams's collecting methods and procedures.

consequence, their opinions have rested on an insufficiently detailed knowledge of his folksong work as a whole. In particular, relying exclusively on his essays and contributions to the *Journal of the Folk Song Society* (henceforth *JFSS*), the literary organ of the Revival, they have largely ignored the single most important source pertaining to the topic, his manuscript folksong collection.[7] While the material contained therein – written annotations, field drafts and sketches, pasted-in and written-out verbal texts – often confirms the folklorists' suspicions, it no less frequently refutes them as well. Certainly, it demonstrates that any monolithic conception of Vaughan Williams's motivations and practices, conscious or unconscious, must inevitably constitute a serious oversimplification.

It is with the intention of correcting the folklorists' distorted perspective, therefore, that I undertake this examination of Vaughan Williams's collecting work – using the standards of modern scholarship, of course. Space does not permit, however, the consideration of his record in all the areas of collecting activity emphasized by those standards (I have in the brief overview above attempted to give an idea of his success or failure with

---

[7] Compiled principally between December 1903 and September 1913 and consisting of 829 items (tunes both with and without text, as well as texts without music), the manuscript folksong collection effectively exists in two stages, a preliminary 'field' stage and a final 'official' stage. The former consists of the pencil drafts he noted 'in the field', directly from the mouths of the singers themselves; the latter, generally written in ink, of the fair copies made from the field notes. It is the second stage that alone constitutes the 'official' collection and unless otherwise stated it is from this that all subsequent manuscript examples and illustrations in this chapter are drawn. The British Library has grouped the collection into Additional MSS 54187–91; the members of this series will here be indicated by the five-digit shelfmark alone (e.g. '54187'). (The pencil field drafts are found in Add. MSS 50361, 57294, and 59535–6, as well as scattered throughout 54187–91.) For general descriptions and inventories of the official collection, see Kennedy, *Catalogue*, pp. 261–95; Palmer, *Folk Songs*, pp. viii–xxii; and the handwritten inventory by Rosamund Strode, 'R.V.W. Folksong Manuscript Collection: General Descriptions And Check Lists' [31 pp., 1967], photostat and accompanying materials held in the Vaughan Williams Memorial Library (henceforth VWML), English Folk Dance and Song Society, London. My thanks to Rosamund Strode for much help and advice, and for the herculean labours involved in compiling her invaluable catalogue; and to Ursula Vaughan Williams for permission to quote both music and text from the folksong manuscripts.

respect to some of them). I propose pursuing instead a detailed examination of his collecting achievement in just one of these areas: that is, his attention in transcription to the melody of folksong as sung by his singers. There is a singular appropriateness in this, not merely because Vaughan Williams was (by his own admission) most interested in folksong tunes, or because it is his treatment of the music of folksong that will naturally most interest the readers of this volume. More to the point, the question of transcription lies at the very heart of the folklorists' attack and offers the best possible introduction to the debate. Indeed, in their view, evidence that the early collectors misrepresented folksong as sung offers conclusive proof that they unconsciously idealized folksong. After all, it was to their notation of tunes, not to their collection of texts or their attention to singers' personal histories, that the collectors' claims to 'scientific accuracy' principally referred.

This was clearly the case with Vaughan Williams, who stressed the accuracy of his (and others') melodic transcriptions.[8] It cannot be denied that evidence of melodic misrepresentation and distortion is to be found in his treatment of tunes. But juxtaposed to and sharing space with such misrepresentation is evidence of a genuine interest in and careful focus on the facts of folksong performance. The situation, in short, is precisely that occurring in other areas of his collecting work – a simultaneous idealization of and close attention to the social and musical reality of folksong. Again, it is in the inconsistency that the interest lies, and the opportunity for critical revision resides. Indeed, as I hope to suggest in this essay, a thorough understanding of Vaughan Williams's achievement even in one aspect of his collecting work may be grounds to revise the folklorists' reading of the historical significance of the Folk Revival as a whole and its role in the emerging ruralist nationalism of the time.

*

---

[8] Cf. Vaughan Williams's statement: 'But nowadays a new spirit animates the collector: he wishes to preserve and put before the public exactly what he has heard – neither more nor less – and we can be sure that whatever we find in the collections of modern investigators is an accurate transcript of the songs of the traditional singers' (R. Vaughan Williams, *English Folksongs*, pamphlet published by the English Folk Dance Society, n.d. [1912], p. 4).

Perhaps the best place to begin is with the tunes that Vaughan Williams did manifestly alter in the course of transcription. To understand how he could do this while also believing that he was maintaining notational accuracy, it is useful to recall his description of folksong as 'a series of individual variations on a common theme'.[9] He meant two things by this: that folksong had been evolved over generations of singers, of course, but also that each folksong embodied the singer's personal response to a common repertory of songs. It was in this spirit that he spoke of the 'normal version' or the 'norm of the tune'[10] – the single-stanza melody which it was believed the singer had in mind and which formed a sort of exemplar or point of departure for variation and embellishment. And it is this attempt to recapture the melodic 'original', the tune behind the performance, that often explains the alterations and changes he made when publishing the tunes.

Compare, for instance, the manuscript and published versions of 'The Basket of Eggs' (see Example 6.1).[11] What Vaughan Williams has created here, in effect, is an 'ideal' version of the tune, a sort of abstracted account of the melody as it may have existed prior to performance. In all cases, the changes tighten the melodic structure, uncovering parallels that Vaughan Williams believed had been obscured by the particular rendition at which he had been present. Hence the removal of the crotchet rest in

---

[9] Vaughan Williams, *English Folksongs*, p. 11.
[10] *JFSS* no. 14 (1910), p. 20.
[11] In this and all subsequent examples taken from manuscript, I have provided quasi-diplomatic transcriptions which attempt to reproduce all musical notation just as it appears in the original, but which also introduce slight changes for purposes of reading ease. For example, since it is the function of these transcriptions to facilitate melodic analysis, I have removed all underlaid verbal text (omissions are acknowledged in all cases individually). This in turn has made it possible to beam certain quaver and semiquaver notes which (because of the presence of text) had appeared unbeamed in manuscript. Since space is limited, my transcriptions also disregard manuscript staff changes whenever possible, though numbers in square brackets above individual bars indicate the original location of shifts from one staff to another. All other additions are also bracketed. Transcriptions of songs taken from the *JFSS* follow similar procedures: underlaid text has been removed and some beaming has been introduced, especially where this facilitates comparison with the manuscript version of the tune. My thanks to the English Folk Dance and Song Society for permission to print musical examples from the *JFSS*, and to Malcolm Taylor, VWML librarian, for unstinting hospitality and encouragement.

Example 6.1 'The Basket of Eggs'

(a) MS, 54191, f. 80ᵛ

(b) *JFSS* no. 7, p. 103

[Transposed from key of D]

bar 2, the attendant pushing forward by a beat of the remainder of the phrase, and the excision of the upper variant in bar 4. These alterations not only regularize the melody – the retained (lower) variant in bar 4 now avoids an awkward shift into 4/4, for example – they clarify the rhythmic and melodic coherence of the tune as a whole: with the alteration in bar 2 and the removal of the upper variant, the first and second halves of the melody are now shown to be perfectly symmetrical. This holds good even down to the two phrases making up each half, as well as to the presence before each of them of framing anacruses (upbeats to bars 1 and 5). The alterations also clarify the melody's antecedent – consequent (and domi-nant – tonic) construction.

Nor is it only through the modification of specific passages or the selection of variants that Vaughan Williams seeks to establish this 'normal version'. Sometimes the reconstruction is effected through the switching or privileging of sung variants, as in 'The Sheffield Apprentice' (see Example 6.2). Here, Vaughan Williams does not actively change what was sung but instead *rearranges* it to create the best possible version. Variants which in manuscript had appeared subordinate and secondary are, generally speak-ing, elevated to primary status in the *JFSS* version, while those that had been primary in manuscript take their place below (note the word 'better' and

Example 6.2 'The Sheffield Apprentice'

(a) MS, 54191, f. 111ᵛ

(b) *JFSS* no. 8, p. 169

the written instructions to the copyist above the second, 'variant' staff in the manuscript version). The reason for the switch is obvious: it creates an 'ideal version' that displays the tune's melodic coherence to maximum effect. The 'new' bars 1–2 parallel the 'original' bars 13–14, and in like manner bar 9 now echoes bar 5. But note how while taking these 'better' variants, he fails to show similar favour to the variants in bars 11 and 15. The choice apparently owes in the first case to the fact that the 'original' layer of bar 11 offers more contrasting melodic interest than the variant (entered in

126

smaller notes) – at a point (end of third phrase) when such contrast is desirable – and in the second to the fact that the 'original' bar 15 exactly parallels the cadence of the first phrase. The tune is thus given a stronger sense of closure and coherence than would have been the case had all the subordinate variants been used; coherence, moreover, that is not cloyingly repetitious.

Further examples might be shown,[12] but they would only confirm what is already clear: that the primary attraction of folksong for Vaughan Williams was the musical coherence and structural tautness that he perceived within it. It is no coincidence that his essays on folksong often stress such tautness and present melodic analyses by way of illustration.[13] The point, however, is that in endeavouring to bring out these structural features he has actively manipulated, to the point of alteration and omission, what was sung to him. In so doing, he breaks the cardinal rule of modern collecting and automatically subjects himself to the worst of the folklorists' charges. At fault, clearly, is his dedication to a concept – the 'normal version' – whose emphasis on an essentially unchanging single-stanza 'original' could not help but result in the suppression (or at least down-playing) of the strophic variations which the singer naturally introduced in performance. Such a dedication suggests that he was not above seeing (and treating) folksong as a set of collectible objects. Attempting to record not so much the singer's personal response to a common repertory of songs as that repertory itself, these transcriptions document Vaughan Williams's willingness to sacrifice the individual to a concept of community, the reality of folksong to an idea of it.

Needless to say, folklorists rely heavily on these arguments in making their case against the revivalists. As they see it, any collector failing to notate and preserve each and every stanza of a singer's performance runs the risk

[12] For example, in publishing four closely related versions of 'Maria Martin' together in *JFSS* no. 7 (1905), pp. 118–19, Vaughan Williams alters a crucial note in the third phrase of the fourth version in order to bring it into line with the first three versions (manuscript transcription in 54191, f. 40ᵛ). In publishing 'The Ploughboy's Dream', he omits an irregular 2/4 variant from an otherwise regular 4/4 tune (compare 54188, f. 15ᵛ and *JFSS* no. 8 (1906), p. 203).

[13] See Vaughan Williams's analysis of 'Searching for Lambs' in *National Music*, pp. 19–20; also the various melodic analyses in his 'Dance Tunes', *The Music Student*, 11/12 (August 1919), pp. 453–7.

of misrepresentation. In practice, this has meant that only those collectors who advocated the use of the phonograph for song collection – Percy Grainger, principally – have escaped censure. Predictably, Vaughan Williams's indifference and even aversion to the phonograph have been held against him. Nor on one level is such criticism unjust or unfounded. He reportedly described Grainger's verse-by-verse transcriptions as 'mad'; observing that the singer would inevitably introduce alterations with every performance, he believed making a detailed transcription of a single performance to be 'a waste of time'.[14]

Such dismissiveness is clearly in evidence in his treatment of one of the few phonograph recordings he did make, that of Mrs Verrall's rendition of 'Covent Garden'.[15] The transcription is unique because it exists in manuscript in two forms. First is the transcription made directly from the phonograph recording and consisting of all five verses as sung by Mrs Verrall (see Example 6.3; ditto signs indicate the melodic repetition of the corresponding bar from the first verse).[16] The other version, itself a transcription of the first, appears elsewhere in the same manuscript and telescopes these five verses into a single-strophe 'normal version' (see Example 6.4).[17] The violence done to the melody as sung is self-evident. In a way now familiar to us, the editorial decision to omit sung variants – notably bars 1–2 of verse 4 and the dotted rhythms in the last phrase of verse 3 – serves to tighten the tune melodically and rhythmically. Especially noteworthy here is the addition of a quaver beat to bars 2, 6, and

---

[14] Michael Yates, 'Percy Grainger and the Impact of the Phonograph', *Folk Music Journal*, 4/3 (1982), pp. 265–75; see in particular p. 267, n. 9. For a critical view of the early collectors' attachment to the 'normal version' and their dislike of the phonograph see Harker, *Fakesong*, pp. 160–5 and pp. 206–9.

[15] Whatever his attitude concerning the phonograph, Vaughan Williams did use it to transcribe thirty-one of the tunes in his collection. Twenty-three of these – though not 'Covent Garden' – were transcribed in the company or at the request of fellow collectors G. B. Gardiner and Mrs E. M. Leather, who sometimes sent him recordings via the post. Seven of his recordings have been preserved and copied on to tape at the VWML. (See Yates, 'Percy Grainger', pp. 273–4.)

[16] Note that Vaughan Williams writes the third verse out of order, below the others. Certain rhythmic differences – the repeated D's in bar 10 of verse 2, the occasional repeated semiquavers in verse 4 – are the product of textual articulation and are not 'variants' *per se*.

[17] This second version also appears, just as in the manuscript, in *JFSS* no. 8, p. 195.

Example 6.3 'Covent Garden', first manuscript version, 54189, ff. 211ᵛ–212ʳ

14, a procedure that brings what had been irregular 3/8 bars into conformity with the 2/4 norm.[18]

Strong as this evidence may be, however, it fails to tell the whole story. Vaughan Williams may have simplified and distorted folksong as sung, but

---

[18] Doubtless, Vaughan Williams viewed these 3/8 bars as singer 'errors' (see below), especially since the singer performed two of them – verse 5, bar 6 and verse 3, bar 14 – in a clear 2/4. Note also Vaughan Williams's omission of the repeat of the second half of the tune, which was clearly indicated in the first manuscript version.

129

Example 6.4 'Covent Garden', second manuscript version, 54190, f. 98ᵛ

Example 6.5 'The Cruel Father and the Affectionate Lover', manuscript version, 54188, f. 8ʳ (text omitted)

Note * He sang F decidedly

examination of manuscript and printed sources shows that this was by no means always the case. Indeed, far from always ignoring the singer's individual melodic contribution, evidence suggests that he was often quite prepared to *emphasize* it – even when to do so obscured melodic coherence and regularity. The treatment accorded 'The Cruel Father' (see Example 6.5) offers an excellent example, for it illustrates not only Vaughan Williams's habit of thinking in terms of a 'normal version' of a tune, but also his ability to overcome that habit. As the quaver C's in parentheses in bar 4 indicate, a reconstructed 'normal version' was clearly on Vaughan Williams's mind as he wrote out this fair copy (the reiterated C's at this juncture would make the first and third phrases exactly parallel, thereby tightening the structure of the tune as a whole). But see the asterisk occurring there and the inscription that appears below, 'He sang F decidedly'. It is these quaver F's, not the C's, which appear in the *JFSS* version (not shown). Here, at least, reality triumphs over idea.

It does so even more dramatically in the case of 'Fare Thee Well', the manuscript transcription of which appears in Example 6.6 (the original page of manuscript is reproduced in Plate 6.1).[19] The considerably worked-

---

[19] Original staff changes are retained in this transcription (cf. Plate 6.1).

Example 6.6 'Fare Thee Well', manuscript version, 54190, f. 199ᵛ (text omitted)

over quality of this draft shows it to have been a sort of battleground for the competing claims of 'sung' and 'reconstructed' folksong. Vaughan Williams was evidently puzzled by the metre of this tune as performed by the singer, since he initially entered it (staves 1 and 2) without bar-lines. Only later did he try to organize the rhythm, first by numbering beats and adding sporadic bar-lines to staves 1–2, and then by writing out a new version on staves 4 and 5. This later draft is of the 'normal version' variety: an attempt at 'regularizing' the melody into a constant 6/4, it results in the introduction of arbitrary pauses (bar 3), distortions of rhythm (bar 8), even alteration of the melodic line (bars 6–7). (The numbers above staves 1–2 clearly predate staves 4–5, and both are written in the same dark ink, which contrasts with the lighter hue of the original layer of staves 1–2; staff 6, meanwhile, carries an alternative 6/4 attempt at bars 3–5 of staff 4.) The remarkable thing, however, is that in publishing this tune in the *JFSS* Vaughan Williams abandons this attempt at normal-version 'reconstruction', and opts instead for a reading that comes close to the shifting, irregular phrasing (staves 1–2) actually sung by the singer (see Example 6.7).

131

Plate 6.1 Vaughan Williams's transcription of 'Fare Thee Well', British Library Add. MS 54190, f. 199ᵛ

Example 6.7 'Fare Thee Well', published version, *JFSS* no. 8, p. 201 (text omitted)

While these examples show that Vaughan Williams was indeed capable of forfeiting the pursuit of a putative melodic original in deference to the facts of performance, certain other transcriptions reveal something more significant still: they suggest that he was in fact attracted to precisely those tunes that bore most vividly the imprint of the singer's own personality. The manuscript version of 'Henry Martin', for example, consists of two very different complete verses, one quite regular and concise, the other irregular and much extended. In the *JFSS*, however, only the irregular verse appears.[20] While it is justifiable to censure Vaughan Williams for failing to

[20] Compare 54190, f. 160ᵛ and *JFSS* no. 17 (1913), p. 302.

Plate 6.2 Vaughan Williams's transcription of 'The Captain's Apprentice', British Library Add. MS 54191, f. 74ᵛ

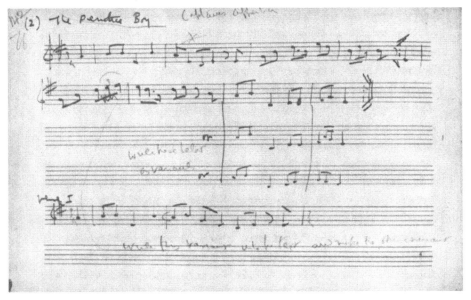

publish all the variants he had collected, his choice is none the less revealing. No less striking, especially in view of our observations on 'The Sheffield Apprentice' above, is the switch of variants he proposes when preparing the famous 'Captain's Apprentice' for publication (see Plate 6.2). As is indicated by the written comment to the copyist in staff 6 – 'write this variant into the text and make the other a variant' – he wished to switch what had been the 'primary' bar 2 with the variant below. The result, duly reproduced in the *JFSS* (not shown), is yet another irregular melody, with a 4/4 bar now appearing within a 3/4 tune.[21] That this alteration stemmed simply from personal preference seems likely when we consider that Vaughan Williams quoted only this form of the tune in his orchestral work *Norfolk Rhapsody No. 1* (composed 1905–6, revised 1914). Certainly, the irregularity lent emphasis to his reference in the *JFSS* commentary to 'the wild character of this remarkable tune'.

Many similar examples could be cited, but the message seems clear enough: that Vaughan Williams transcribed folksongs in two ways. In

[21] *JFSS* no. 8, p. 161.

certain circumstances, he seeks the original behind the performance; in others, only the performance itself. But why should this be? How are we to explain why Vaughan Williams in certain instances reconstructs the 'norm of the tune' but in others carefully attends to the singer's peculiarities – even, in the case of 'The Captain's Apprentice', apparently seeking to 'enhance' them? The answer is a complex one and, on one level at least, demands an appreciation of the difficulties facing the collector. After all, singers were often of advanced age, and uncertain in both memory and voice, facts which (in Vaughan Williams's opinion) rendered some of them incapable of executing the song they had in mind. Admissible or not, this belief probably lies behind a number of the alterations he chooses to make, as when he introduces a blank bar into one tune with the comment 'bar missing?' or when, in the course of publishing another, he rewrites a bar as he feels it should have been sung.[22] Lest this make Vaughan Williams appear too ready to correct 'errors', however, there are instances in his manuscript collection where he leaves untouched even those passages about which he is sceptical. Below one tune laden with accidentals, for example, he writes: 'Doubtful – but he sang it like this'. Under an irregular two-bar repetition in a different song, he comments: 'I think he must have forgotten here but he sang it the same each verse'.[23] As much as these statements betray a lingering watchfulness for a garbled 'normal version', they demonstrate with equal force his interest in preserving anything characteristic or intentional.

For this is just the point. In deciding whether to reconstruct the melodic original or to leave a tune as sung, Vaughan Williams was motivated by an interest in recording anything characteristic. This goes far beyond any concern to correct 'errors' – clearly, anticipation of vocal or memory failure cannot explain all the alterations he makes – and instead highlights his genuine interest in singers' individual melodic contributions. But not just any contribution: rather, only those that are in his view

---

[22] The rewritten bar appears in his transcription of 'Just as the Tide was Flowing' (compare 54191, f. 102ᵛ, and *JFSS* No. 8, p. 173); 'bar missing?' in his transcription of 'Banks of the Shannon' (54187, f. 24ʳ).

[23] 'Doubtful' appears in his transcription of 'The Robin's Petition' (54191, f. 97ᵛ); 'I think he must have forgotten' in his transcription of 'Young Jimmy' (54187, f. 19ʳ).

Example 6.8 'New Garden Fields', manuscript version, 54189, f. 40ᵛ

unique or exceptional – in a word, 'artistic'. Nothing illustrates this better than a comparison of his treatment of Mrs Verrall's 'Covent Garden' (Examples 6.3 and 6.4 above) with that accorded another song recorded on phonograph, Mr Locke's 'New Garden Fields' (see Example 6.8). As with 'Covent Garden', Vaughan Williams here writes the recorded verses one below the other, with ditto signs to mark melodic repetitions of the first verse. In this case, however, there is no later manuscript version that serves to reduce and simplify the melodic variants of the original transcription. Indeed, the tune appears in the *JFSS* (not shown) just as in the manuscript, with all three verses intact.[24] The explanation for the difference of treat-

---

[24] *JFSS* no. 17, p. 334. The published version occasionally differs slightly from the manuscript version in rhythmic and melodic detail. The discrepancy is explained by the fact that Vaughan Williams collected this song jointly with George Butterworth and adopted many of his notational suggestions in preparing it for publication. See Butterworth Folk Music Manuscripts (Vol. 7b), VWML.

ment is obvious. Mr Locke's singing of 'New Garden Fields' is far more varied and richly ornamented than is Mrs Verrall's in 'Covent Garden'. Whereas in the latter there are only two or three places where variation or embellishment appear, in the former there are at least ten (and this despite the fact that it is a whole two verses shorter). With one exception, no two phrases are similar, and the final cadence is interpreted in three different ways.

Thus it would seem that the decision either to record the tune as sung or to 'reconstruct' a normal version ultimately depended on Vaughan Williams's interest in separating the 'exceptional' performance from the 'unexceptional'. Here again we see the outlines of the belief that every collected tune embodies the singer's response to a pre-existing repertory of songs. Judging each performance against a presumed 'original', Vaughan Williams determines which renditions display the most, and which the least, individual characteristics, and treats each accordingly. The practice at once supports and qualifies the folklorists' critique. For if it is true that so selective a method is grossly unscientific, the motivation behind it is nevertheless one which the folklorists cannot wholly criticize: an interest in preserving precisely those performances that bear most clearly the traces of a singer's own personality. Vaughan Williams may not have brought a modern consistency and uniformity to his transcriptional methods – for one thing, such selectivity begs the issue of what was and was not 'exceptional' – but it is that very inconsistency, ironically, that demonstrates his interest in and respect for the singers' individual contributions. Certainly, it belies the claim that he was wholly indifferent to the reality of traditional culture or to the individuals comprising it.

*

It might be tempting to ascribe Vaughan Williams's two distinct transcriptional methods to two different motivations – one ideological, the other purely musical. In this scenario, his violation of folksong as sung would be attributed to his idealization of the communal idea, his faithfulness to the 'exceptional' performance to his compositional interests. While there is undoubtedly some merit to this notion – Vaughan Williams was evidently drawn to the more irregular, open-ended tunes in his melodic borrowings from folksong[25] – it is on the whole misleading. It would mean, in effect, that both transcriptional methods were ideologically motivated since, in the case of the 'exceptional' tunes, notational precision was prompted only by a larger musical ambition, namely the establishment of a national school of composition. This would in turn remove the possibility that Vaughan Williams was motivated by a genuine interest in the singers themselves and the culture they embodied. In view of what we have seen above, however, this assertion cannot be sustained. How otherwise are we to explain Vaughan Williams's treatment of 'The Cruel Father' (Example 6.5 above), where he notes the details of so regular, even impersonal a performance (a candidate, if ever there was one, for 'normal version' treatment)? Or his approach to 'The Robin's Petition' and 'Young Jimmy' (see n. 23), where despite doubts about vocal and memory failure he records exactly what he hears? The conflict encoded in Vaughan Williams's transcriptional inconsistency is one not between the communal ideal and a larger musical agenda, but rather one between the communal ideal and the individual reality.

It is a conflict, finally, that lies at the very heart of the Folk Revival and of the emerging ruralist nationalism of which it was emphatically a part. More than the merely escapist fantasy or proactive strategy of a self-serving middle- and upper-class elite (the folklorists' interpretation of the movement), that nationalism was also the means by which this elite addressed itself to questions of positive social reform. Arising in a period of transition from an outmoded Victorian Liberalism to new forms of political and economic centralization, it was part of a cultural initiative designed to protect the national interest by encouraging social cohesion and inter-class cooperation. As such, it was an ambiguous and deeply contradictory force – on the one hand concentrating cultural authority in the hands of the few, but on the other inspiring a genuine belief in the need for a better, more egalitarian society.[26] It is this ambiguity that the folklorists, in their

---

[25] Elsie Payne, 'Vaughan Williams and Folksong: The Relation Between Folksong and Other Elements in his Comprehensive Style', *The Music Review*, 15 (May 1954), pp. 103–26.

[26] For a discussion of the radical origins of the period's ruralist nationalism, see Peter C. Gould, *Early Green Politics: Back To Nature, Back To The Land, And Socialism In Britain 1880–1900* (Brighton: Harvester Press, 1988).

one-dimensional reading of the ruralist impulse, fail to grasp. Vaughan Williams and others could both falsify and faithfully attend to the realities of folksong precisely because the question of 'rural England' was itself the flashpoint of the era's social and cultural uncertainty. Separated by reason of class and education from their object of study, they could not help but idealize (and ultimately misrepresent) folksong. But imbedded in that idealization was a very real interest in and respect for working-class life, one born of an unyielding faith in a firmly democratic future.

Vaughan Williams never rid himself of certain romanticized notions about traditional music. Embracing the evolutionary theory of cultural 'survivals', he emphasized the 'spontaneous' and 'unselfconscious' nature of folksong, and contrasted it with the more fully 'conscious' approach of the art-music composer. The singing of folksongs, he believed, was 'only a half-conscious act', the product of the singer's 'unrecognized artistic instinct'.[27] And yet, in the course of his own collecting work, he found reason to qualify these assertions. He discovered evidence of musical literacy among his singers and, on at least two occasions, admitted the possibility that singers consciously invented tunes themselves. But as he wrote in 1912, just as the great bulk of his collecting work was nearing completion:

> Then the scoffer comes along, and he says: 'I expect the [singer] was having you on; I believe he made [the song] up himself.' To which I answer that it is quite possible that to a large extent he did, and that for that reason it is all the more valuable to me. ...The more I see of folksong the more important I believe the impress of the individual to be.[28]

[27] Vaughan Williams, *English Folksongs*, pp. 10, 12.   [28] *Ibid.*, pp. 12–13.

7   Vaughan Williams and British wartime cinema

JEFFREY RICHARDS

In his 1912 article entitled 'Who Wants the English Composer?', Vaughan
Williams set out his understanding of the role of the composer in society.
The composer 'must live with his fellows and make his art the expression of
the whole life of the community', cultivating 'a sense of musical citizenship';
he should as a servant of the state 'build national monuments'; and he could
'take and purify and raise to the level of great art' the popular forms of
musical expression.[1] These remained central strands of his philosophy, and
in the supreme national crisis of wartime he put his beliefs into practice by
entering the sphere of film music, which had hitherto gone largely ignored
by critics, but was an integral part of people's lives and entertainment, and
was precisely one of those forms of national expression to be taken and
purified and raised to the level of great art.

Just as British films attained a 'golden age' in the 1940s, so too did
British film music. As John Huntley noted in his classic study *British Film
Music* (1947), 'Almost every modern [British] contemporary composer has
nowadays made some contribution to the film'.[2] It was the war that made
the difference. Personal commitments to the struggle against Fascism led
artists and intellectuals in unprecedented numbers to put their talents to
the service of the national effort, to celebrate the united struggle of a free

---

[1] Hubert Foss, *Ralph Vaughan Williams: A Study* (London: Harrap, 1950), pp.
    200–1. The article originally appeared in *The R.C.M. Magazine*, 11/1 (Christmas
    Term 1912), pp. 12–15. The author would like to acknowledge with gratitude
    the advice and assistance of the following in the preparation of this paper: Dr
    Alain Frogley, Dr Anthony Aldgate, Dr David Kershaw, Mr John Clegg, Mr
    James Chapman, the staff of the British Film Institute Information Library,
    and the National Film Archive Viewings Service.
[2] John Huntley, *British Film Music* (1947; reprint edn., New York: Arno Press,
    1972), p. 11.

people against a monstrous tyranny. The composers who did so included Sir Arnold Bax, Constant Lambert, Lord Berners, Lennox Berkeley, Noel Mewton Wood, and William Walton. Many of their scores were arranged as concert suites and performed both in live concerts and on BBC radio, which regularly featured film music throughout the war; some were also issued on gramophone records.

Vaughan Williams and film music

It is not surprising that Vaughan Williams, generally acknowledged as the doyen of Britain's composers of serious music, should have thrown himself enthusiastically into the wartime film effort. In a 1940 broadcast talk on the role of the composer in wartime, he called for the composer to 'serve the community directly through his craft if not through his art'.[3] But he added: 'Art is a compromise between what we want to achieve and what circumstances allow us to achieve. It is out of these very compromises that the supreme art often springs: the highest comes when you least expect it.' The same rationale could be applied to Vaughan Williams's entry into film music. His introduction came through Muir Mathieson, long established as the leading musical director in films. During the war he was Director of Music for the Ministry of Information and responsible for commissioning the scores for their film productions. Mathieson had clear views about the role of music in the documentary. He saw it compensating in part for the absence of the star names, Technicolor, and large-scale publicity campaigns from which feature films benefited: 'Music plays a doubly important part, providing, as it must, a larger than usual share of the entertainment. Music can help to humanize the subject and widen its appeal. Music can make a film less intellectual and more emotional. It can influence the reaction of the audience to any given sequence'.[4]

His first wartime encounter with Vaughan Williams, however, was in connection with the MoI's only major feature film production, *49th Parallel*. Mathieson recalled visiting Vaughan Williams at his Dorking home to ask whether he might consider composing the score for the film.

---

[3] R. Vaughan Williams and G. Holst, *Heirs*, pp. 90–3.

[4] Muir Mathieson, 'Music for Crown', *Hollywood Quarterly*, 3 (1948), p. 323.

> When I went to see Vaughan Williams at his country home in the spring of
> 1940, I found him strangely depressed at his inability to play a fuller part in
> the war. He felt that the musicians had done little to express the spirit and
> resolve of the British people. At this time he was 'doing his bit' by driving a
> cart round the village and countryside, collecting scrap metal and salvage. ...
> I told him the story of *49th Parallel* and tried to show how the cinema could
> help to achieve those very objects for which he was striving. ...He set to work
> right away – and remember this was the first time he had ever consented to
> write for the screen.[5]

Vaughan Williams set down his ideas about composing for films in an essay
he contributed to the *R.C.M. Magazine* in 1945.[6] 'Film composing is a
splendid discipline, and I recommend a course of it to all composition
teachers whose pupils are apt to be dawdling in their ideas, or whose every
bar is sacred and must not be cut or altered'. He believed that 'film music is
capable of becoming, and to a certain extent already is, a fine art but it is
applied art and a specialized art at that', and that 'the film contains the
potentialities for the combination of all the arts such as Wagner never
dreamt of'. Ideally all the arts involved should come together at the beginning, but standard practice was unfortunately such that the constituent elements were instead 'segregated and only reassembled at the last moment',
preventing film from realizing its true potential.

There were two ways of writing film music, 'one [is that] in which
every action, word, gesture or incident is punctuated by sound'. That
approach he felt was too scrappy. He preferred 'to ignore the details and
intensify the spirit of the whole situation by a continuous stream of music',
which could be modified where appropriate 'by points of colour superim-
posed on the flow'.

Vaughan Williams's method of work was different from that of the
Hollywood film composers. In Hollywood the composer would normally
run the rough-cut of the picture first in its entirety, then reel by reel, and in
consultation with the director, producer, film editor, and music editor,

---

[5] Huntley, *British Film Music,* pp. 56–7.
[6] 'Film Music', *The R. C. M. Magazine,* 40/1 (February 1944), pp. 5–9. It was
subsequently republished in Huntley, *British Film Music,* pp. 177–82 and in R.
Vaughan Williams, *National Music,* pp. 160–5, where it appears as 'Composing
for the Films'.

would agree a set of cues and a set of timings; the composer would then rapidly write the music required. Owing to the speed demanded of the composer, his music would often be orchestrated by someone else, as he continued the task of preparing the main themes. The score would then be recorded with the film running on a screen behind the orchestra; timings were made, and the recorded music was finally dubbed on to the soundtrack and mixed with the dialogue and sound effects.[7]

Vaughan Williams worked in a much more detached manner. He would receive a script and a set of cues, and often composed his score before the film was even finished. He then left it to the musical director to fit it to the finished film, remaining ever-ready to make whatever adjustments and alterations the director required. This procedure enabled him to pursue his philosophy of providing a score consisting of a continuous stream of music paralleling the action rather than, as in Hollywood, underlining the action and often the dialogue. The scores of *The Loves of Joanna Godden, Scott of the Antarctic,* and *Coastal Command* were all delivered in this way. His method of writing had a beneficial by-product. Because he was writing continuous passages of music, coherent and self-contained in their own right, it was easier to arrange the film scores into concert suites, something which he did on a number of occasions.

He was very fortunate in the musical directors he worked with, who held his music in the highest regard. Muir Mathieson was musical director on *49th Parallel* (1941), *Coastal Command* (1942), *The Flemish Farm* (1943), *The People's Land* (1943), and *Stricken Peninsula* (1945). *Coastal Command* was Vaughan Williams's first pure documentary assignment and his music fulfilled exactly the role that Mathieson envisaged for documentary scores. Mathieson recalled that for *Coastal Command*, Vaughan Williams 'composed a delightful score which met with the unqualified approval of everyone both inside and outside the unit'.[8] The respect with which the music was treated was recalled by sound recordist Ken Cameron:

> When we heard the music, we knew that here was something great, something indeed finer and more alive than any music we had ever had

---

[7] Tony Thomas, *Music for the Movies* (South Brunswick, New York and London: A. S. Barnes & Co., 1973), pp. 26–30.

[8] Muir Mathieson, 'Music for Crown', p. 324.

before. Nor did we waste. On the rare occasions when the music was slightly too long or too short to match the existing picture, then it was the visual material which suffered the mutilation. The music for *Coastal Command* is as V.W. composed it. It is, in fact, the picture.[9]

Mathieson subsequently created a concert suite from the *Coastal Command* score, as he did later from the music for *England of Elizabeth*. Vaughan Williams's other musical director was Ernest Irving, of Ealing Studios, who commissioned, conducted, and supervised the scoring of *The Loves of Joanna Godden* (1946), *Scott of the Antarctic* (1948), and *Bitter Springs* (1950). Like Mathieson, Irving believed in recruiting the best of contemporary composers to write for Ealing's films, and during the war he drew on the services of William Walton, Lord Berners, John Ireland, Alan Rawsthorne, Gordon Jacob, and Frederic Austin. He wrote in 1943: 'There is no reason why a master should write more effective film music than a hack, for artistic merit and authenticity of style have no "film value" per se, but it is pleasing to record that in point of fact they do'.[10] Irving's mediation was crucial in ensuring that the music of *Scott of the Antarctic* emerged to the composer's satisfaction, a debt in recognition of which Vaughan Williams dedicated to Irving the *Sinfonia Antartica*.

There are several ways of looking at Vaughan Williams's film music, all of which overlap and interpenetrate. The primary focus of this essay will be on the propaganda role of the wartime film scores. But this cannot easily be separated from the composer's construction of Englishness, a central theme of his work both during and after the war, and we need briefly to consider this broader issue as a backdrop to the more specific concerns of propaganda. Vaughan Williams was profoundly convinced that music must be national in its origin, endorsing Hubert Parry's view that 'style is ultimately national', and rejecting the idea that the 'artist invents for himself alone'. Anyone who set out to be cosmopolitan, he thought, must fail. 'The greatest monuments of music...have worldwide appeal, but first they must appeal to the people and in the circumstances where they were created. ...Every composer may reasonably expect to have a special message for his own people. ...Many young composers make the mistake of imagining they can be

---

[9] Huntley, *British Film Music*, p. 111.
[10] Ernest Irving, 'Music in Films', *Music and Letters*, 24 (1943), pp. 223–35.

universal without at first having been local. What a composer has to do is to find out the real message he has to convey to the community and say it directly and without equivocation ... if the roots of your art are firmly planted in your soil, and that soil has anything individual to give you, you may still gain the whole world and not lose your soul.'[11]

Such views accorded well not only with the imperatives of wartime, but also with broader trends in British film-making during the 1940s and 1950s. Vaughan Williams's view of nationalism in art parallels almost word for word that of Sir Michael Balcon, the head of Ealing Studios. His studio was committed to making films projecting Britain and the British character. He wrote in his autobiography: 'My ruling passion has always been the building up of a native [film] industry with its roots firmly planted in the soil of this country'. He rejected in retrospect the 1930s policy of importing American stars and trying to make cosmopolitan films, testifying to his 'growing conviction that a film, to be international, must be thoroughly national in the first instance, and that there is nothing wrong with a degree of cultural chauvinism'.[12] In 1945 Balcon outlined a programmatic schedule for post-war film-making that demonstrated a high level of civic responsibility and patriotic pride: 'The world must be presented with a complete picture of Britain. ...Britain as a leader in Social Reform, in the defeat of social injustice and a champion of civil liberties; Britain as a patron and parent of great writing, painting and music; Britain as a questing explorer, adventurer and trader; Britain as the home of great industry and craftsmanship; Britain as a mighty military power standing alone and undaunted against terrifying aggression'.[13]

It is no coincidence that Vaughan Williams worked for Ealing on three films (*The Loves of Joanna Godden, Scott of the Antarctic, Bitter Springs*) or that his film oeuvre embraced many of the same themes: the resistance to tyranny and the championship of civil liberties figured strongly in *49th Parallel, Stricken Peninsula*, and *The Flemish Farm*; exploring and adventuring in *Scott of the Antarctic* and *Bitter Springs*; industry and craftsman-

---

[11] R. Vaughan Williams, *National Music*, pp. 3, 9, 11.

[12] Michael Balcon, *Michael Balcon Presents: A Lifetime of Films* (London: Hutchinson & Co., 1969), pp. 48, 61.

[13] Jeffrey Richards and Anthony Aldgate, *Best of British: Cinema and Society 1930–70* (Oxford: Blackwell, 1983), pp. 99–100.

ship in *Dim Little Island*; and virtually all the themes were recapitulated in *The England of Elizabeth*.

Yet Vaughan Williams's principal definition of Englishness in his films, as elsewhere in his work, lay deeper still, in the pastoral and in the visionary. His great achievement was to unite the two. The rural myth, pumped out in poems, novels, paintings, and music since the 1880s, had a direct effect on evocations of the national character. The Englishman was said to be at heart a countryman and his character – thanks to his rural roots – to be based upon the principles of balance, peacefulness, traditionalism, and spirituality.[14] In wartime the countryside was a peculiarly potent image. For while cities could be blitzed and bombed, the countryside remained – eternal, timeless, self-renewing, and indestructible, a fitting symbol for Britain at bay. The musical symbol of all this was folksong. Vaughan Williams believed that song was the basis of all music and that purely instrumental music was a later development. Folksong was 'the spiritual lifeblood of the people' – intuitive, oral, applied, purely melodic, an art which grows straight out of the needs of a people'. Church music derived from folk music and Vaughan Williams saw in church music a continuous tradition of organized response to the need for spiritual expression. By applying folk-tunes to the words of well-loved hymns in *The English Hymnal* he effectively fused the two great expressions of the people's music, implementing his own stated belief: 'The composer must love the tunes of his own country and they must become an integral part of himself'.[15] The pastoral image and the centrality of folksong received full expression in *The People's Land* (1943), *Dim Little Island* (1949), *The Loves of Joanna Godden* (1946), and *The England of Elizabeth* (1957), while the visionary aspects of Englishness were expressed in *Scott of the Antarctic* (1948) and *The Vision of William Blake* (1958).

But how did Vaughan Williams reconcile his intense English nationalism with his socialism? Easily – as he outlined in 1942: 'We all want peace, we all want international friendship, we all want to give up hateful rivalries of nations; we must learn to plan the world internationally, we must unite

[14] On this phenomenon, see Martin J. Wiener, *English Culture and the Decline of the Industrial Spirit, 1850–1980* (Cambridge: Cambridge University Press, 1981).

[15] R. Vaughan Williams, *National Music*, p. 23.

or we shall perish. This is a very different thing from that emasculated standardization of life, which will add cultural to political internationalism.' Vaughan Williams believed that political internationalism could coexist perfectly comfortably with cultural nationalism. 'I believe that love of one's country, one's language, one's religion, are essential to our spiritual health...that all that is of value in our spiritual and cultural life springs from our own soil; but this life cannot develop and fructify except in the atmosphere of friendship and sympathy with other nations'.[16] It is not therefore surprising to find this 'quintessential English composer' providing the music for films about other countries, both in Europe (Belgium for *The Flemish Farm*, Italy for *Stricken Peninsula*) and in the Commonwealth (Canada for *49th Parallel* and Australia for *Bitter Springs*).

In addition to questions of propaganda and of Englishness, there is one other aspect of Vaughan Williams's film music that should not be forgotten, namely its relationship to the rest of his work. His film music cannot be isolated from his other music: it is all part of an organic whole in which there is both continuity and development. Although Vaughan Williams's film scores certainly use gestures familiar from his music in other genres, they also inspired and generated new work, most notably, of course, *Sinfonia Antartica* developing out of the score for *Scott of the Antarctic*. Vaughan Williams very much enjoyed writing film music, as both Ursula Vaughan Williams and Michael Kennedy testify.[17] He relished the challenges it threw up, for instance to provide music to illustrate an outbreak of foot-and-mouth disease in *Joanna Godden* or penguins on the ice in *Scott*, subjects that would have been unlikely to come his way in the normal run of things. But the experience of writing for films also enriched his musical language as a whole, his flexibility, his use of orchestral colour, and his freedom in writing.[18] Since film music is the ultimate in programme music, a close examination of the films Vaughan Williams chose to score and how he went about it may tell us more about the meaning of his 'serious music', for which he was notoriously reluctant to accept the programmatic interpretations offered by critics.

---

[16] *Ibid.*, pp. 154–9.
[17] U. Vaughan Williams, *R.V.W.*, p. 239, and Kennedy, *Works*, p. 259.
[18] Hugh Ottaway, 'Scott and After: The Final Phase', *The Musical Times*, 113 (1972), pp. 959–62.

Wartime propaganda

At the centre of Britain's propaganda effort in World War Two was the Ministry of Information (MoI), its task to 'present the national case to the public at home and abroad'. To this end, it was responsible for the preparation and issue of national propaganda, the control of news, and the maintenance of morale. Lord MacMillan, the first Minister of Information, laid down the principal themes for propaganda in a memorandum to the War Cabinet. They were: what Britain was fighting for, how Britain fights, and the need for sacrifice if the war is to be won. There was to be a particular emphasis on British life and character, showing 'our independence, toughness of fibre, sympathy with the underdog, etc.'.[19]

49th Parallel was the only full-length feature film to be financed by the MoI. Afterwards, the Ministry concentrated on financing a programme of short documentary films, leaving the commercial industry to provide the features, although the MoI retained control of the allocation of film stock, suggested themes and subjects through its ideas committee, and provided technical assistance instead of finance. But it invested heavily in *49th Parallel*, which emerged as one of the great films of the war and one of the best works of Britain's premier film-making team, Michael Powell and Emeric Pressburger. On *49th Parallel* Powell directed, while Pressburger provided the original story and co-wrote the script with Rodney Ackland. According to Powell, the aim of the film, which was shot partly on location in Canada, was 'to scare the pants off the Americans, and bring them into the war sooner'.[20] It sought to pay tribute to Canada, to stress Canadian – American friendship, and to outline programmatically the evils of Nazism. Powell and Pressburger lined up a distinguished roster of stars (Leslie Howard, Eric Portman, Laurence Olivier, Raymond Massey, Anton Walbrook) to play the leads.

The film told the gripping story of a stranded crew of Nazi submariners making their way across Canada towards the neutral United

---

[19] On the Ministry of Information and wartime British cinema see Anthony Aldgate and Jeffrey Richards, *Britain Can Take It*, rev. edn. (Edinburgh: Edinburgh University Press, 1994).

[20] Michael Powell, *A Life in the Movies* (London: William Heinemann Ltd., 1986), p. 347.

States and encountering *en route* various representatives of democracy. An uncommitted French-Canadian trapper (Laurence Olivier) turns against the Nazis when they maltreat the 'racially inferior' Eskimos. An immigrant community of German Hutterites, led by Anton Walbrook, demonstrates the workability of a system of democratic equality, cooperation, and Christian love. A donnish aesthete Leslie Howard, who is writing a book on Red Indian customs and culture, beats one of the Nazis to a pulp when the Nazi burns his 'decadent' books and pictures. Finally, an ordinary Canadian soldier (Raymond Massey), the grumbling, individualistic, democratic 'Everyman', takes on and defeats the ruthless Nazi superman commanding the fugitives (Eric Portman). The Nazis are thus effectively depicted as standing for cruelty, tyranny, racism, arrogance, and philistinism. The action of the film encompasses the whole of Canada from the icy wastes of Hudson Bay to the grain-filled prairies, from the deep dark forests and lonely limpid lakes to the frontier where at one end the mighty crashing Niagara Falls marks the undefended boundary with the United States.[21]

Vaughan Williams's score was clearly regarded as a major prestige coup and he was billed as one of the stars of the film, the credits reading: 'Leslie Howard, Laurence Olivier, Raymond Massey, Anton Walbrook, Eric Portman, and the music of Ralph Vaughan Williams in *49th Parallel*'. Given Vaughan Williams's preferred method of work, his score inevitably functions very much more as a series of musical interludes than as the sort of cohesive and integrated musical texture, intimately tied to the action on screen, that Erich Korngold and Max Steiner achieved in Hollywood films.

The prelude is a broad, stately theme which musically encapsulates the breadth and majesty of Canada. It is followed by a visual evocation of contrasting Canadian landscapes, of mountains, wheatfields, rivers, and

---

[21] For an account of the making of the film and an analysis of it see Aldgate and Richards, *Britain Can Take It*, pp. 21–43; Powell, *A Life in the Movies*, pp. 346–84; and Kevin MacDonald, *Emeric Pressburger* (London: Faber and Faber, 1994), pp. 159–82. Given that most of the films discussed here are not in general circulation, and that their scores are for the most part neither published nor recorded, it has been necessary to include here a good deal of basic description of both visuals and music. In the area of CD recordings, it is pleasing to be able to report that Naxos has recently announced a series of releases of Vaughan Williams film scores. The first of these (Marco Polo 8.223665) has appeared; it contains the Prelude to *49th Parallel*, the suites from *Coastal Command* and *Flemish Farm*, and *Three Portraits from the England of Elizabeth*.

cities, accompanied by a sweeping passage of music featuring 'O Canada', the Canadian national anthem. As the scene changes to the Gulf of St Lawrence, a submarine rises, to a dark-toned version of *Ein' Feste Burg*, the Lutheran hymn, which develops into sinister variations; an ironic comment, surely, on the perversion of German faith by the Nazis. This theme recurs in the urgent pursuit music that accompanies the submarine's escape northwards to elude pursuing Canadian planes. As the submarine passes icebergs, we hear eerie, sombre music which contains the first seeds of the *Scott of the Antarctic* score. Then a menacing falling staccato figure punctuates the texture, a phrase that recurs throughout the Nazis' flight across Canada. At Hudson's Bay trading post, cheerful flowing music accompanies scenes of Eskimos in their kayaks and at the first appearance of the French-Canadian trapper (Laurence Olivier), we hear a jaunty version of 'Alouette'. A folksong figures too in the encounter with the Hutterite girl (Glynis Johns), who is first discovered singing a German song, 'Lasst uns das Kindlein Wiegen'; it seems to be English folk music, however, with vigorous dance patterns, that accompanies the Hutterite harvest. The Nazis walk across Canada to music with an appropriately regular tread. From Banff on Indian Day, evoked by a snatch of heavily rhythmic material, the Nazis flee to agitated music echoing the pursuit, with the atmosphere intensified by a recall of the menacing phrase earlier associated with the submarine. When the Nazis encounter Leslie Howard at the lake, their conversation takes place against a piece of piano music, impressionistic, light, and delicate. The film ends with a reprise of the prelude as the beaten Nazi is shunted back across the border from the United States to Canada. Throughout, the music is either functional or atmospheric, heightening emotion or scene setting. It is mostly competent rather than outstanding.

But Vaughan Williams was well aware of what elements within the score could be retrieved. A suite was prepared which featured in a festival of British film music in Prague in 1946, but this was subsequently suppressed by the composer.[22] It consisted of the most substantial passages from the film. They are listed by Michael Kennedy as: (i) Prelude; (ii) Warning in a

---

[22] Huntley, *British Film Music*, p. 57; Frank Howes, *The Music of Ralph Vaughan Williams* (London: Oxford University Press, 1954), p. 362.

dance hall; (iii) Hudson's Bay; (iv) Nazis on the prowl; (v) Hutterite settlement; (vi) Indian festival; (vii) The lake in the mountains; (viii) Nazis on the run; (ix) Epilogue.[23] All but the second of these items appears in the film. There is no warning in a dance hall, which must represent an episode cut from the film before release. The prelude survived, however, to be recorded by Bernard Herrmann for an LP of British film music in 1976.[24] It was also arranged for organ by Christopher Morris in 1960, and was set to words as an anthem, *The New Commonwealth*, by Harold Child, librettist of *Hugh the Drover*, for unison voices with piano or orchestral accompaniment. Its optimistic and uplifting sentiments stress international brotherhood and emphasize the tune's hymn-like properties. *The Lake in the Mountains* appeared as a solo piano piece under that title and dedicated to Phyllis Sellick in 1947. The music had largely been lost in the film, heavily damped down under dialogue between Leslie Howard and Eric Portman. It emerged as a tranquil, impressionistic piece, opening with an English pastoral melody, sounding like gentle running water, overshadowed by a sudden threatening shift from B♭ to F♯ minor. After the pastoral melody is elaborated, it returns to F♯ minor, developing the air of menace and ending with a bleak D minor. There is no musical reason for the shift but in the context of the film it signals the arrival of the Nazis in the hitherto peaceful location.

The Nazi theme recurred in the scherzo of the Second String Quartet, composed in 1943–4. The Sixth Symphony has often been seen as Vaughan Williams's response to the war. Sir Malcolm Sargent for instance called it, 'A frightening symphony. ... Here we have a complete testament of a man who, in his seventies, looks back on the human sufferings of his time. I never conduct the Sixth without feeling that I am walking across bomb sites. ...Chaos, despair, desolation and the peace that flows from desolation.'[25] Vaughan Williams always denied the validity of such interpretations. But his film music gives us an important interpretative clue to the inspiration for such works. The Second String Quartet is a product of the same period of musical development as the Sixth Symphony and can be seen to share the same mood. The first three movements are bleak, anguished, and jagged,

---

[23] Kennedy, *Works*, p. 179.   [24] Decca PFS 4363.
[25] Charles Reid, *Malcolm Sargent* (London: Hamish Hamilton, 1968), p. 357.

and the scherzo repeats over and over again the stabbing motif that accompanied the Nazis in *49th Parallel*, the title of which Vaughan Williams marked in his score against this movement.[26] The finale is also a product of his involvement in the cinema. The movement is marked 'Greetings from Joan to Jean'. The Jean is Jean Stewart, violinist of the Menges Quartet and the dedicatee of the piece. The Joan is St Joan, and the main theme of the movement comes from the composer's sketches for a score to a film about St Joan that never materialized.[27]

Although details about the film are lacking, it can only be the long-mooted film version of Bernard Shaw's play. In 1943 film tycoon J. Arthur Rank formed a partnership with Hungarian producer Gabriel Pascal to make three Shaw films. Pascal had already produced film versions of *Pygmalion* (1938) and *Major Barbara* (1940). Shaw had entrusted him with exclusive rights for filming his plays, and films of *St Joan*, *Caesar and Cleopatra*, and *The Doctor's Dilemma* were planned. Shaw was working on the scenario and given Pascal and Shaw's commitment to employing leading composers (Arthur Honegger scored *Pygmalion* and William Walton *Major Barbara*), it seems highly likely that Vaughan Williams was approached to do the music; and that, given his usual working methods, he had started sketching the score before filming was completed. Shaw had originally intended that the score for any film version of *St Joan* would be written by John Foulds, who had composed the highly praised score for the stage play in 1924. But Foulds had died of cholera in India in 1939.[28] What Foulds and Vaughan Williams shared was a deep sense of spirituality in their music, which was what was required for this subject.

But the project was abandoned. This was due in part to the difficulty in finding a suitable actress to play Joan – Greta Garbo, Katharine Hepburn, Wendy Hiller, Deborah Kerr, and Ingrid Bergman were all considered at various times and rejected for various reasons. But more seriously, the MoI, who had the final say on film projects, objected that 'it would be the most injudicious time to make a film about St Joan and remind [our] French allies of England's little mistake in burning their saint'.[29] Shaw and Pascal switched their attention to *Caesar and Cleopatra*, which became notorious

---

[26] See Kennedy, *Catalogue*, p. 186. [27] *Ibid.*
[28] Malcolm MacDonald, *John Foulds* (Rickmansworth: Triad Press, 1975), pp. 47–8.
[29] Valerie Pascal, *The Devil and His Disciple* (London, 1971), p. 103.

as one of the most expensive films in British history. The film movement of the Second String Quartet preserves what would have been Joan's theme, a serene and spiritual melody which concludes the turbulence and agony of the first three movements on a note of uplift. Is there not a key here to Vaughan Williams's thinking? The bleakness and cruelty of war (embodied in the Nazi theme from *49th Parallel*) is transcended ultimately by the faith and spirituality of St Joan, who died in the service of her country against cruel invaders. 'Nowhere', writes Hubert Foss of this movement, 'has Vaughan Williams written music so philosophical, so resigned, so restful in simplicity'.[30]

If *49th Parallel* was Vaughan Williams's contribution to 'why we fight', his next film, *Coastal Command*, showed 'how we fight'. Produced by the Crown Film Unit and directed by J. B. Holmes, this film – like other notable wartime documentaries such as *Target for Tonight, Fires Were Started, Merchant Seamen,* and *Western Approaches* – utilized men and women of the armed forces playing themselves. This seventy-one-minute film, tightly constructed and impressively shot, does for Coastal Command what the more celebrated *Target for Tonight* did for Bomber Command. A narrator introduces the film, explaining that behind the drama of attacks lies the 'ceaseless, patient, humdrum vigil of patrol', and the film takes us to Portferry Bay in Scotland from where Sunderland flying boat *T for Tommy* is sent to protect a convoy. Their patrol is uneventful but they sight and report a German sub, which is sunk by their relief, a Catalina flying boat. The German raider *Düsseldorf* is reported to be leaving Norway. *T for Tommy* is sent to shadow it. Hudson bombers and Beaufighters take off from Iceland to sink the ship. She is duly crippled. The Sunderland is sent in to report on the damage, gets information back but is hit by flak and loses its port engine. Attacked by a Junkers 88, the Sunderland is rescued by an Australian-crewed flying boat and limps back to Portferry. As the skipper, Lt Campbell, visits his injured men, he tells them that they are to be transferred to West Africa. The film is a highly effective dramatized re-creation of the work of Coastal Command. Like so many wartime films, it is a study in British character. Both on the flying boat *T for Tommy* and back in the control room, the prevailing mood is one of quiet dedication, unselfcon-

---

[30] Foss, *Ralph Vaughan Williams*, p. 172.

scious professionalism, self-deprecating good humour. It fulfils the MoI criteria of showing how we fight, the nature of the British character, and the need for sacrifice (crew members are wounded during the aerial battles).

Vaughan Williams's score for *Coastal Command* is consciously heroic, celebrating the deeds of the RAF but also seeking to evoke the national character. It opens with a vigorous prelude which encapsulates the main musical themes of the score, including a folksong-like theme that recurs throughout. A piece of mood music evokes Portferry in the Hebrides and *T for Tommy* floating at anchor – a delicate, wistful evocation of sea, wind, and mystery, which again looks forward to Scott. The attack on the U-boat is urgent and arresting with a hint of Satan's dance from *Job*, a sea-shanty rhythm but orchestral and agitated. Three percussive chords signal the crash of the bombs on the U-boat. But Ken Cameron's observation that the music took precedence over the visuals is borne out by the fact that the three chords occur in the music after the bombs have fallen and the submarine has been sunk.

An expansive and majestic theme, recalling the end of the Fifth Symphony, covers the return of the Sunderland, a more solemn tune its subsequent departure to shadow the *Düsseldorf*. As the Hudsons take off in Iceland, the main theme of the score is reworked. The music revs up along with the planes and then soars gracefully into the sky with the strings, across the rugged landscape of Iceland and into the clouds, tailing off gently with a clarinet recapitulation of the main theme. As the Sunderland searches, strings are plucked to indicate the ticking of a clock; the tempo increases as the search goes on, with the basic motif repeated with variations. Then as the Beauforts attack the broad heroic theme becomes aggressive. As the Sunderland goes in close, there comes the passage marked by Vaughan Williams 'quiet determination', the musical encapsulation of 'how we fight', depicted by the heroic theme taken up on clarinet and oboe. The tone gradually darkens as the plane emerges from the clouds and then full-blooded brass chords signal the flak hitting home. The attack music is repeated, as Beaufighters come to the rescue, and after a final triumphant surge of the heroic theme, there is the serene landing music, followed by an expansive, optimistic ending as the team takes off for West Africa.

In 1942 Muir Mathieson constructed a seven-movement suite from the music for *Coastal Command*, which he dedicated to the RAF. It included: (i) title music; (ii) the island station in the Hebrides; (iii) taking off at night; (iv) Hudsons taking off from Iceland; (v) the Battle of the Beauforts; (vi) the Sunderland goes in close 'quiet determination'; (vii) the JU88 attack and finale.[31] In 1992 Christopher Palmer added the U-boat attack to Mathieson's original selection. Both suites reverse the order of the Beaufort attack and the 'quiet determination' movements from that in the actual film. The CD recording of *Coastal Command*[32] reveals it to be a richly textured, deeply felt score well worth retrieving and a marked advance on the music for *49th Parallel*.

The Flemish Farm (1943) was made with the cooperation of the Belgian government in exile and the Air Ministry, and was based on a true story. Directed by Jeffrey Dell and written by Dell and his then wife, Jill Craigie, the film opens in 1940 with the last five planes of the Belgian Air Force fighter squadrons stationed on a Flemish farm near the coast. When news of the Belgian surrender comes through, the commandant, Major Lessart (Clive Brook), orders the regimental standard to be destroyed to prevent it falling into enemy hands. It is formally buried at sea. When the Germans bomb the farm, the surviving planes take off, with two friends, Matagne (Philip Friend) and Duclos (Clifford Evans), sharing the cockpit of one aircraft. A year later in Britain, where both are now serving with the RAF, Matagne reveals to Duclos that he had secretly buried the real flag on the farm, at Lessart's orders, and the sea burial had been staged to fool the Germans. Also he reveals he had secretly married the farmer's daughter, Tresha (Jane Baxter), and she had helped him bury it. He plans to return and retrieve the flag. But Matagne is killed in the Battle of Britain and Duclos gets permission to go instead. Parachuting into Belgium, Duclos makes contact with Lessart, now leading the local resistance, reaches the farm, and with Tresha's help retrieves the flag. The remainder of the film concerns his adventures as he escapes across Belgium and France to safety. Before he leaves Belgium, however, he learns that Lessart has given himself up to the Germans, who have taken hostages for the murder of one of their agents. Lessart confesses to the murder and is shot but the hostages are released. Duclos, however, succeeds in getting the flag back to Britain where it is presented to the Belgian squadron of the RAF.

---

[31] See Kennedy, *Catalogue*, p. 181.   [32] See n. 21.

The film fulfils completely the MoI's stress on the need for sacrifice if the war is to be won. The film is constructed as a series of heroic sacrifices. The lovers Tresha and Matagne sacrifice their happiness together so that he can serve in the Air Force in England; Matagne sacrifices his life in the Battle of Britain; Lessart sacrifices his life to save the hostages. But all this is worthwhile because the struggle against tyranny and Fascism will go on. The Air Force standard becomes a holy relic, a symbol of resistance, faith, and struggle, the guarantee that Belgium will continue to fight, whatever the cost, until the war is won and freedom restored. Several characters in the film comment on the symbolism of the flag, and the Germans' desperation to lay hands on it shows that they appreciate this equally.

The film is richly scored, illustrating a variety of moods and episodes, with the emphasis on heroism, sacrifice, and spiritual uplift. The title music, full of fanfares, contains what sounds like a Flemish hymn or folksong, which recurs throughout the film, as when the flag is located on the farm. The music heard during the burial of the flag is noble and elegiac, with a stirring fanfare to indicate continuing defiance. By contrast, there is a wistful, lyrical love theme surging up as the lovers kiss in the barn at dawn before parting forever (though most of the music is lost beneath the dialogue); a jaunty little tune, likened not inaptly by A. E. F. Dickinson to a calypso,[33] as Duclos walks through the town and meets Lessart at a café; and menacing music to accompany the Germans' search of the cart conveying Duclos and the flag from the farm. A slow, sombre passage building up with a crescendo dramatizes Lessart's last walk towards German headquarters. Then there is quite a lengthy passage of escape music, similar to the exciting and agitated passages accompanying such episodes in previous films, but also including a heroic march theme that is repeated and reworked. There is a final recapitulation of the main theme as the flag is re-presented to the squadron.

Vaughan Williams thought well enough of this music to retrieve much of it for a twenty-six-minute concert suite, *The Story of a Flemish Farm*. It consisted of seven movements: (i) the flag flutters in the wind; (ii) night by the sea, farewell to the flag; (iii) dawn in the barn, the parting of the lovers; (iv) in the Belgian café; (v) the Major goes to meet his fate; (vi) the

[33] A. E. F. Dickinson, *Vaughan Williams* (London: Faber and Faber, 1963), p. 443.

dead man's kit; (vii) the wanderings of the flag.[34] This enabled the music to assume a more permanent form and to get a proper hearing. In the film itself, for instance, the music accompanying Duclos' examination of the dead Matagne's kit is the merest snatch, and the lovers' music was considerably banked down behind the dialogue. The suite was premièred at the Proms on 31 July 1945 with Vaughan Williams conducting the London Symphony Orchestra at the Royal Albert Hall. *The Musical Times* considered it the best of that season's novelties. Their review confirms the coherence and musicality of Vaughan Williams's film scores:

> One feared that film music separated from the action it is meant to describe and emphasize might lose some of its vividness, or perhaps that the duties imposed by the brisk doings on the screen had robbed the composer of the liberty of developing his ideas freely. The event proved such fears to be completely unfounded. Not only has each period full development, but each episode contrasts with the rest as effectively as the main sections in any well-built symphony. Between the war-like tunes that rightly begin and close the suite Vaughan Williams has provided chapters cast in very different moods. One describes the parting of two lovers with extraordinary tenderness; the other is concerned with the search amongst the effects of the dead airman who has given his life to save his comrades. This is an eerie affair with perfectly simple but most striking orchestral effects. This suite has come to stay, and is sure of being as popular with the sophisticated as with the unsophisticated.[35]

Regrettably the suite has rarely been heard in concert since, but the newly issued CD recording provides an excellent opportunity to reappraise this fine score. Apart from the suite itself, Vaughan Williams recalled that two of the themes written for the film, but not included in the final score, were the germs of the opening themes of the second and fourth movements of the Sixth Symphony.[36] Given the subject, mood, and context of the film, this further suggests that we should see Vaughan Williams's Sixth Symphony as his war symphony.

In 1943 Vaughan Williams provided the score for a ten-minute Technicolor documentary, *The People's Land*, produced for the National

---

[34] See Kennedy, *Catalogue*, p. 185.
[35] *The Musical Times*, 86 (1945), p. 285. The review is signed F.B.
[36] Dickinson, *Vaughan Williams*, p. 444.

Trust by Strand Films. It was clearly conceived in the spirit of 'The People's War' propaganda thrust endorsed by the MoI. The only overt mention of the war comes at the end when narrator Freddie Grisewood declares that the land had been defended against every foe by the hearts and hands of many generations and the people were now the guardians of this trust. But the emphasis on the people runs through the film. We are told it was the people and not the state who set up the National Trust in 1895 and it is the people who have the responsibility of protecting the more than 1000 properties and sites, and over 150,000 acres held in public trust in perpetuity. The properties are also used by the people, as city-dwellers go to the country to refresh themselves by communing with nature.

The visual images of the film strongly encapsulate the rural myth, as the commentary declares that England has 'some of the loveliest country, the prettiest villages, and the largest, ugliest, and most vigorous cities in the world', the implication being that while the cities are necessary and unavoidable, human kind is most at peace and most truly itself if it can escape to the country. Then intertwined are the threads of tradition, continuity, and heritage, on the one hand, and popular use, on the other. Both are themes valuable to wartime projections of Britain and British heritage.

Not surprisingly Vaughan Williams turns to folksongs and on occasion to popular tunes to create a continuous sound picture, the People's Music, underscoring the beauty and variety of 'The People's Land'. The film opens with the White Cliffs of Dover, the front line against invasion, and then the camera sweeps across the Sussex downs. Vaughan Williams begins with the strains of 'As I walked out one May morning' and this is developed into a sweeping pastoral statement, which modulates into a succession of tunes accompanying visual sequences that stress continuity and tradition. Strong chords and solemn ritual music underpin images of the Castlerigg stone circles at Helvellyn in the Lake District; medieval pageant music accompanies shots of the stronghold Bodiam castle, built by a follower of the Black Prince; Tudor-sounding 'Love will find out the way' accompanies Little Moreton Hall in Cheshire, 'still lived in by the family who built it in the days of Queen Elizabeth', sturdy pastoral strains a Westmorland farm, and the jaunty, folksy 'Chairs to mend' the village of West Wycombe – a cross-section of the varied roster of National Trust properties. The film then gives examples of popular use of the properties. Cyclists scud along country roads to variations on 'Pop goes the weasel', boy scouts hike into the hills to 'John Barleycorn' in march-time, children toboggan down a hillside to 'Boys and girls come out to play', an angler catches fish to a lilting snatch of 'Rakish Highland man' and entomologists pursue butterflies in the fens to the wistful, plaintive strains of 'The springtime of the year'.

Finally, the Lake District and mention of the Lake poets leads on to visionary pastoral music, and as mountaineers ascend the Lake District hills, repeated rising phrases finally culminate in surging notes of triumph when the summit is reached. The film ends as it began, with the White Cliffs of Dover; a round tour of the beauties of Britain in just ten minutes, and an entrancing, lively, and inventive miniature tone-poem which cleverly reinforces the messages of the film, messages close to Vaughan Williams's own heart, projecting an England of rural beauty, spiritual peace, open access, continuity, tradition, and folksong.

Vaughan Williams's last propaganda assignment was the fifteen-minute documentary film, *Stricken Peninsula* (1945), directed for the Army Film Unit by Paul Fletcher and released by the MoI. It deals with the Allied reconstruction programme for newly liberated southern Italy, undertaken at a time when the liberation of the north was still not completed.

The film opens with a shot of the ruins of Pompeii and dissolves to the ruins of present-day war-damaged Naples. The narrator outlines the problems faced by the Allies in this area, where because there was no organized resistance to the Fascists (as there was in the north), there has been a complete collapse of moral and political structures. Each of the facets of the reconstruction work is explained over shots which show it being undertaken.

Reconstruction begins with the clearing of rubble and the digging of graves. In the countryside, farmers recover hidden seed corn, salvage farm machinery, and begin to plough and plant even before minefields have been cleared. In the cities, there is no power, light, fuel, transport, or food distribution, and the black market flourishes. So the Allies organize soup kitchens and food distribution, relief for the unemployed and a campaign of inoculation against typhus which checks the growing epidemic. Hospital equipment is brought out of hiding and new hospital wards established. Bridges and railways are repaired. But this is all threatened by lack of power. The Nazis dynamited the main city generator. An old discarded generator is brought out, refurbished and put into operation, and trolley buses and street cars begin to run again. Fresh fruit and vegetables are brought in from the countryside and sold. A free press is restored, so that people can read and write whatever they like. The political process resumes, with free political meetings, trade unions (banned under the Fascists) restored, and the workers organizing to rebuild the factories. Education is being reintroduced purged of Fascist textbooks and indoctrination, so that the new generation can be instructed in the meaning of liberty. The process of reconstruction is slow and painful and there is an enormous amount to do, but the forces to tackle the job are mobilizing.

The *Documentary News Letter*, keeper of the conscience of the British Documentary movement and scourge of the inauthentic, reviewed the film, and called it

> one of the more remarkable films to result from Service shooting. Paul Fletcher has examined his subject from a traditional documentary standpoint. Here is no newsreel coverage but an attempt to select and analyse episodes in the story of liberation, and to assemble them into a picture which will give not only the material facts but also the mood and feeling of Italians suddenly fallen between the two stools of Nazism and liberation...the film leaves us feeling that here is a vast national problem with the full solution still to be found.

Its propaganda value, DNL thought, 'salutary and excellent. The realities of war's aftermath presented with considerable artistry.' But the music was another matter: '*Stricken Peninsula* is severely handicapped by what in the reviewer's opinion is an execrable musical score by Dr Vaughan Williams. Whatever musical qualities are present achieve no marriage with visual or commentary. One is conscious only of obtrusive and disagreeable noise intruding between the audience and a moving story.'[37]

This is both unfair and inaccurate. As in *The People's Land*, Vaughan Williams provides what is in effect a miniature tone-poem, this time on the theme of reconstruction. A noble theme behind the credits introduces the idea of aspiration; then, over the ruins, bleak, austere music, akin to the second movement of the Sixth Symphony, sketches the desolation and dislocation left by the war. This modulates into a lively, optimistic march as the

---

[37] *Documentary News Letter*, 5 (1945), p. 77.

reconstruction begins, and this reconstruction theme returns with variations over each initiative: the repair of the transport infrastructure, the
trolley buses running again, the schools reopening. The bleakness returns
over scenes of urban desolation, but develops over scenes of well-run hospital wards into music of spiritual uplift, akin to the final movement of *Job*.
Slow, heavy, threatening chords accompany news of the dynamiting of the
power generator, but the music then directly echoes the slow and repeated
cranking up of the machinery and finally the triumphantly whirring and
spinning pistons: a sound picture of a generator being refurbished and
brought on stream that recalls the planes revving up in the score of *Coastal
Command*. As political meetings revive, preceded by a procession of bands-
men, an orchestrated version of a cheerful Italian folksong is heard. Finally,
after a last light reworking for strings of the reconstruction march over
shots of children at play, the score surges back into the spiritual theme from
the hospital scenes, as the narrator concludes that the forces are mobilizing
and the work is underway. The score could, like so much of Vaughan
Williams's film music, stand on its own, as an atmospheric and economical,
but musically sophisticated and multi-layered evocation of the various
facets of post-war reconstruction.

Winning the peace

Stricken Peninsula was Vaughan Williams's last wartime film project. His
post-war film scores, dominated by the Ealing productions, merit a detailed
study in their own right. [38] But one of them deserves inclusion in the present
discussion, offering as it does a particularly succinct expression of several of
the themes of the war films, and also a belated collaboration between
Vaughan Williams and a closely kindred spirit who was one of the most
famous British film-makers of the war years. Humphrey Jennings was the
great poet of the World War Two documentary, his lyrical, richly textured
films capturing something of the soul of the nation at war. In his films the
propaganda objectives of 'why we fight' and 'how we fight' often impercep-

---

[38] Vaughan Williams's post-war film scores and their relation to Englishness will
be examined in detail in my forthcoming book, *Films and British National
Identity* (Manchester: Manchester University Press, 1996).

tibly merged. Jennings saw England as a family, believed that life had a pattern and a purpose, and in his Festival of Britain film, *Family Portrait*, celebrated the British as a people who loved public pomp (pageantry and tradition) and private domesticity (the fireside, the garden). Jennings's love of England centred on three basic principles: his admiration of the common people, his instinctive belief in individualism but always within community, and his love of culture. Gerald Noxon says of Jennings that he had been influenced in his formative years by Shakespeare and Marlowe, Milton and Bunyan, Constable and Blake: 'The works of these men remained in Humphrey's background as a permanent frame of reference. Their kind of Englishness was Humphrey's kind of Englishness.'[39] English music was integral to his films: Handel, Elgar, Purcell, Vaughan Williams; popular songs; folksongs; hymns; dance-band music. He planned a documentary on the London Symphony Orchestra which was unfortunately never made.

In all this Jennings can be seen as a soul-mate of Vaughan Williams, who was widely seen to be, in the words of his longtime friend and Oxford University Press editor Hubert Foss, 'a great Englishman', essentially English to be ranked alongside Milton, Shakespeare, William Blake, and Thomas Hardy.[40] Foss's book on Vaughan Williams, published in 1950, is valuable as an indication of the terms in which the composer was perceived in the 1940s and 1950s. Specifically Foss sees Vaughan Williams as sharing Milton's 'strong feeling for the English language', 'the remote mysticism' and wide imagination of Blake, the 'humanity...understanding...and kindly but incisive humour' of Shakespeare, the attention to human detail and broad philosophical truth of Hardy.[41] Jennings admired Vaughan Williams enormously, writing of his respect for the composer's 'absolute humility, humanity – following his own sure company with bravura' and again of 'his creative fire and with it his tenacity and above all his humility'.[42] Vaughan Williams was therefore an obvious collaborator and although they did not work together during the war they came together for

---

[39] Aldgate and Richards, *Britain Can Take It*, pp. 228–9.
[40] Foss, *Ralph Vaughan Williams*, p. 11.   [41] *Ibid.*, pp. 10–11.
[42] Kevin Jackson, ed., *The Humphrey Jennings Film Reader* (Manchester: Carcanet, 1993), pp. 146–8.

161

Dim Little Island, produced in 1949 by Wessex Films for the Central Office of Information, successor of the MoI.

The ten-minute film was in essence a peacetime propaganda film, designed to tackle 'post-war blues', the idea that the country, bankrupt, rationed, and depressed after the long cold winter of 1947, was going to the dogs. The film was constructed as a meditation on the past, present, and future, by four men: the cartoonist Osbert Lancaster, the industrialist John Ormston, the naturalist James Fisher, and the composer Ralph Vaughan Williams.[43]

Lancaster begins by setting out the current view that Great Britain is 'rather a dim little island', 'hopelessly unmusical' and 'now as always going to the dogs'. He examines the painting 'The Last of England' (1852) to demonstrate that in 1852 people felt the same, whereas looking back we see it as a time of optimism and expansion. Ormston points out that for nearly a century British shipyards built ships better and cheaper and quicker than elsewhere but the industry was run down before the war reactivated it. James Fisher celebrates the value of wild nature ('It's interesting. We learn from it. It's beautiful, and we refresh ourselves with it. It's fun – we take pleasure in it'). Shots of smoking chimneys and cobbled streets are contrasted with the free expanses of the open countryside. Over scenes of the Pennine Hills, an unaccompanied male voice sings the folksong 'Dives and Lazarus' and Vaughan Williams speaks:

> Listen to that tune – it's one of our English folk-tunes. I knew it first when I was quite a small boy, but I realized even then that there was something not only very beautiful, but which had a special appeal to me as an Englishman. It dates from a time when people, of necessity, made their own music, and when as has been well said – they made what they liked, and liked what they made. I like to think of our musical life as a great pyramid, at the apex of which are our great virtuosi and composers of international renown. Then immediately below this come those devoted musical practitioners, true artists who by precept and example are spreading the knowledge and love of music in our schools, our choral societies, our music festivals. Then comes

43 Vaughan Williams later denied all knowledge of the film. Michael Kennedy, *Works*, p. 200, suggested that he may have worked on the film under another title. This suggestion is confirmed by *The Humphrey Jennings Film Reader* which indicates that the working title for the film was 'Awful Old England'.

the next layer of our musical structure, that great mass of musical amateurs who make music for the love of it, and play and sing for their own spiritual recreation in their own houses. And then behind that again we have our great tunes which like our language, our customs, our laws are the groundwork upon which everything must stand. So perhaps we are not too unmusical after all. Nevertheless, our music has lain dormant. Occasionally indeed a candle would shine like a good deed in a naughty world. Byrd, Purcell, or Arne. And lately the candles have become more numerous [the title pages of scores by Elgar, *Enigma Variations*, Vaughan Williams, *A London Symphony*, Bax, *Tintagel*, and Britten, *Peter Grimes*, are seen]. For people have come to find a special message in our music which that of other nations, however skilled and imaginative, cannot give them.

Fisher argues that we must protect our national landscape and resources. Ormston says we can still build ships as well as anyone, 'if we can get supplies and we don't take things too easily'. Lancaster says: 'Doubtless were we a rational race, the spectacle of our present position would overwhelm us. But then we have always been, thank heaven, deaf to appeals to reason', and he cites Dunkirk as an example of a successful act defying rational argument. Vaughan Williams ends his contribution:

> So – the fire is ready. It only requires a match to relight it, to set the whole ablaze. Some great upheaval of national consciousness and emotion. The Elizabethans experienced this and as a result, they produced poetry and music that has never been surpassed. Have we not also experienced lately such a national upheaval? And is this not the reason why, during the late war, those who had never taken music seriously before began to crowd our concert halls from Kensington to Harringay to hear symphony concerts? Today our music which for so long had seemed without life is being born again.

The last words of the film are: 'Who can talk of an end when we are scarcely at the beginning?'.

Vaughan Williams's contribution is a succinct statement of the views he had been advancing for many years. Jennings's vision meshes directly with his. The little film is constructed as a celluloid symphony in four movements with themes that intermesh: (i) the idea that the country is going to the dogs as an illusion; (ii) the strength and viability of Britain's ship-building trade and her role as an island race; (iii) the beauty and value of nature;

(iv) the strength and importance of our musical life as representing the soul of the nation. Jennings discovered a ship called *British Genius* of which he gives us a triumphant close-up shot, and the film's images tell us that the *British Genius* consists in the facts that we are good sailors, proud crafts-men, love nature, and make our own music – all ideas to which Vaughan Williams could easily and readily respond. The war is seen as a catalyst to promote the national parks, ship-building, and the revival of musical life, and these ideas intertwine just as the shot of the ship's girders on Tyneside dissolves into the waving reeds of the Mindsmere marshes.

Vaughan Williams's score – a short prelude and occasional musical interludes – consists of orchestrated versions of folk tunes: 'Pretty Betsy', 'The Pride of Kildare', and, notably, 'Dives and Lazarus'. The latter is first heard sung by an unaccompanied folk singer, who is then joined by the orchestra; at Vaughan Williams's mention of great tunes the music swells into a solemn and majestic version of the folksong, resembling but not exactly matching any of the *Five Variants of Dives and Lazarus* brought together by Vaughan Williams in his orchestral work of that name, written some ten years earlier.

Conclusion

What then can Vaughan Williams's involvement in wartime cinema tell us about him? Above all, it shows that he fulfilled absolutely his own oft-stated definition of the composer as a citizen, contributing to the life of the nation. He committed his skills and artistry to the struggle against Fascism in the most popular way possible, by scoring propaganda films. His basic tech-niques – use of recurring themes, incorporation of folk and popular mate-rials, sharp contrasts of mood – were not in themselves original; but the quality of musical materials, and the subtlety and skill used in their deploy-ment, gives a new depth and emotional coherence to the images that they accompany, and in a way that perfectly matches the best intentions of the film-makers. And he fulfilled exactly the criteria laid down by the Ministry of Information for films about 'why we fight' (*49th Parallel*), 'how we fight' (*Coastal Command*), and 'the need for sacrifice if the war is to be won' (*The Flemish Farm*). His musical projection of the war effort centres squarely on the concept of 'The People's War', the dominant idea of Britain's wartime propaganda policy. In none of the films he scored is there a single individual hero. Throughout, it is the people who are collectively the hero. They are contributing as citizens to the defence of democracy (*49th Parallel, Coastal Command, The Flemish Farm*), in the interests of a shared heritage (*The People's Land, Dim Little Island*), or the restoration of civilized values (*The Stricken Peninsula*). They do so to the accompaniment of 'the People's Music', as Vaughan Williams draws freely and joyously on hymns, folk-songs, marches, and dances to celebrate their efforts. After the war he used films to express his personal vision of the nation in a way which would uplift and inspire in the post-war situation, and would underline his interpretation of Englishness as both visionary and pastoral.

In terms of Vaughan Williams's general musical development, this study has offered further evidence for the close musical and philosophical interweaving of the film music with the rest of the composer's output. But it is not simply a case of 'more of the same'; the film music can be seen as distinctively complementary as well as consanguine. Thus the profound and aching pessimism of the Sixth Symphony, which the film evidence gives us further encouragement to view as Vaughan Williams's war symphony, must be set against the positive recognition of heroism, sacrifice, and struggle in his film output (*The Flemish Farm, Coastal Command, 49th Parallel*). It was through another film project, *Scott of the Antarctic* (1948), that Vaughan Williams was to find a balance between these two strands of his music of the 1940s, a balance that was to influence all his subsequent work: as Hugh Ottaway has suggested, *Scott* achieved a synthesis that enabled Vaughan Williams to move from the acute pessimism of the Sixth Symphony to a final phase of 'tragic but resilient humanism'.[44] But that is another story.

[44] Ottaway, 'Scott and After', p. 961.

165

8   Rhythm in the symphonies: a preliminary investigation

LIONEL PIKE

Rhythm has been unjustly neglected in studies of Vaughan Williams's music. In this respect he has been overshadowed by such composers as Stravinsky, Bartók, and Walton;[1] Vaughan Williams seems to have been regarded by many as a kind of wandering rustic who fantasized endlessly in a pastoral rubato, and as a result the rhythmic subtleties of his music have still not been appreciated or properly investigated. In fact, the composer developed across the course of his career a supple and complex approach to rhythmic control. Most impressive of all is his handling of large-scale processes, and the following discussion takes examples from three of the symphonies in order to show how vital is the role played by rhythm in Vaughan Williams's symphonic logic.

A number of features central to the discussion that follows – overlapping or elided phrases, unexpected phrase extensions, interpolated elements, diminutions effected by repeating or imitating a single bar – have clear classical precedents. This should come as no surprise: as part of his compositional apprenticeship Vaughan Williams often used classical movements as detailed structural blueprints for his own work, and in later life he recommended such modelling to his pupils.[2] Yet Vaughan Williams's

---

[1] Frederick Rimmer, in 'Sequence and Symmetry in Twentieth-Century Melody' (*The Music Review*, 26 (1965), pp. 35–40), compares Vaughan Williams's use of rhythm unfavourably with that of some other major twentieth-century composers. Rimmer's case is seriously weakened, however, by his failure to observe the working of rhythm in the symphonies as whole entities (or, for that matter, in complete individual movements). By isolating melodies which are, in many cases, purposely constructed so as to make a particular rhythmic point in the larger context in which they appear, he shows that he has not understood Vaughan Williams's techniques at all.

[2] See Vaughan Williams, 'A Musical Autobiography', in *National Music*, pp. 192–3.

use of such procedures is rarely classical in effect; what is striking is his ability to adapt them to new contexts and to absorb them fully into his own highly distinctive musical language. In like manner, his lifelong interest in the interplay of duplet and triplet rhythms may well have originated in the music of Brahms, but it became an integral part of his own stylistic fingerprint.[3]

[3] As is customary, I assume in the following discussion that 4/4 is simply a multiple of a duple metre, and describe all such multiples as duple. Elsewhere I reduce the mathematics to the prime numbers two and three wherever possible.
  The manner in which Vaughan Williams's approach to rhythm built on classical precedents, and developed from the relatively simple to the highly complex across his career, is beyond the scope of the present investigation and merits a separate study in its own right. The composer's pre-1914 music offers particularly fertile ground. There are, for instance, detailed parallels to be drawn between the march-like slow movement of Beethoven's Piano Sonata Op. 2 No. 2 and the march sections of the finale of A London Symphony, which was first performed in 1914. In the passage cited in n. 2 from his 'Musical Autobiography', Vaughan Williams identifies the Beethoven movement as a structural model that he had found particularly helpful during his early years. The main rhythmic lessons appear to have been gained from observing how Beethoven set up a steady, four-square phrase structure and then subtly disrupted this at strategic moments, by phrase overlaps, and by augmentation and diminution of phrase units. Like Beethoven, Vaughan Williams sets up a regular tread at the start, but later counters this by introducing phrases of a single bar, by expanding the basic two-bar segment (there is a three-bar pattern in bars 42–4, for instance), and by changing the overall length of the main theme. But Vaughan Williams does not model his music slavishly on Beethoven. For example, between bars 24 and 52 he experiments with various methods of disrupting the established phrase structure, none of which owes anything to Beethoven. Most notable, perhaps, is the countersubject of bars 24 ff., which is worthy of Elgar (Vaughan Williams spent some time in his youth studying Elgar's scores: see Vaughan Williams, 'A Musical Autobiography', p. 148); but it is probably his own originality that suggests the addition of a two-bar phrase at bars 47–8 and the minim triplet at bar 52. All these elements help to break up the regularity of the march pattern, and they point towards the approaches that Vaughan Williams would take in his later music. Denigrators of 'English Pastoral' composers have often labelled the triplet as a facile device that evokes all too readily an earthy, folksy, country feeling; that may be true for some composers, but it can be demonstrated that in Vaughan Williams triplets and elements of conflict between duple and triple often form a powerful part of the musical argument.

Symphony No. 5: Scherzo

Vaughan Williams began work on the Fifth Symphony in 1938, and it was first performed in 1943. Without the experience gained in his earlier works Vaughan Williams could not have written this scherzo, though it is difficult to point to specific influences that may have acted upon the piece. The movement has a complex rhythmic structure; indeed, at times it seems more like a counterpoint of rhythms than of pitches. The result, both here and in the Sixth Symphony, owes much to Vaughan Williams's love of Tudor polyphony, in which independent contrapuntal lines proceed with only scant regard to the regularly recurring pulse. The scherzo starts with a written-out *accelerando*, the quick 3/4 organized first as three bars of dotted minims, then four bars of minims in a hemiola pattern, then as crotchets (see Example 8.1). As a result, the macrorhythm[4] of the opening does not settle: it consists of units of three, four, five, four, and three bars respectively, leading to a series of imitative entries based on the opening, the parts entering at the distance of a single bar (such close imitations are particularly apt to disguise any macrorhythm). The melodic line at Figure 1 falls into five-bar phrases (subdivided into 2 + 3), an effect that is almost immediately thrown into relief when the theme is repeated at bar 1.3, this time with a regular grouping of 2 + 2 in the double-bass and the viola. The rhythm is further complicated by the first violin which does not conform to either the 2 + 3 or 2 + 2 pattern (see Example 8.2). The Dorian line of the first violin is thus distinguished from the Aeolian tune of the flute, piccolo, and clarinet by rhythmical as well as tonal means. The complications are halted at Figure 2 by homorhythmic downward sweeps; wind and strings alternate antiphonally, first bar by bar and then in hemiola rhythm.[5] The 1+1 antiphonal exchanges and the hemiola represent a clear attempt to impose a regular two-bar macrorhythm on the music. At bar 2.6 the stretto imitation of the opening material, with entries one bar apart, does nothing to suggest that either a five-bar or a two-bar macrorhythm is predominant; nevertheless, a five-bar pattern is traceable because significant features

---

[4] I shall refer to rhythmical groupings encompassing more than just a few notes – usually rhythms spread over more than a single bar – as belonging to 'macrorhythm'.

[5] This device is an expansion of a process introduced in the preceding few bars.

Example 8.1 Symphony No. 5, II, Scherzo, bb. 1–24

tend to be spaced in multiples of five bars. At Figure 3 the 2 + 3 tune of bar 1.1 is combined with the 2 + 2 bass, only to be interrupted by the antiphonal downward sweeps of Figure 2, in their hemiola form. It is an alternation that neatly prepares the rhythmic structure of the second subject.

The second subject (bar 3.18) contrasts dotted minims with an accompaniment in 'stamping-dance' style: from time to time this accompaniment uses hemiola patterns, derived from bars 4–7 and foreshadowed more closely in bars 2.5–6 and 3.5–6. The melodic line also contrasts dotted minims with groups of six quavers: the outline of these runs implies subdivision into two groups of three (see Example 8.3). The implied background duplet grouping (♩. ♩.), which cuts across the intermittent pairs of undotted crotchets in the lower parts, prepares one of the features of the central trio. The three levels of macrorhythm evident in bars 1.13 ff. are from time to

Example 8.2 Symphony No. 5, II, Scherzo, bb. 1.13–23

time matched by a threefold variety of accentuation of a single two-bar segment: from bars 4.6–8, for example, the rhythm falls into ♩. ♩. ♩. ♩. (violins), ♩. ♩. (oboe and horns), and ♩ ♩ ♩ (implied by the bass). Such complications are not evident in every bar of the second subject, although other rhythmic devices abound. The oboe tune beginning at bar 4.5 exhibits a 4 + 3 + 4 + 2 + 3 structure, the three-bar and two-bar phrases creating an effect of stretto within the tune itself. This is heard, however, against a string (and, later, a bass) background in regular two-bar phrases (some enlivened by hemiolas) that start a bar later than the oboe tune, and are thus for a time out of phase with it. The first three-bar phrase of the oboe tune, of course, changes the relationship of the tune to the bass pattern.

The trio section, which begins at Figure 8, starts by recapitulating the material of the movement's opening; this is counterpointed against the

Example 8.3 Symphony No. 5, II, Scherzo, bb. 3.18–21

antiphonal downward sweeps, now scored for strings alone. The new element that causes the listener to regard this passage as a trio is played by the horns and lower woodwind. It is a chorale-like tune[6] featuring duplets but cast overall in regular three-bar phrases – indeed, the trio contrasts with the scherzo precisely because it is in a settled macrorhythm throughout (even if the downward sweeps at the opening evoke the two-bar groupings used for that idea earlier). Though the sense of relaxation felt by the listener is partially induced by the strong melodic definition of the central material, it is equally the result of the rhythmic resolution at this point in the music (see Example 8.4). The release of tension in the trio does not involve the removal of all contrasting elements: the lines of its main tune are interspersed, for example, with features derived from the frame that surrounds this central section. The result feels something like a chorale-prelude. At Figure 12, for example, two lines of the 'chorale' are punctuated with a stamping rhythm that includes a hemiola and downward sweeps in quavers whose melodic line creates groups of three (see Example 8.5). The return of the scherzo section (beginning at bar 14.11) has a different feel from its first appearance. It begins staccato and contains more counterpoint than formerly; but the biggest divergence begins at bar 17.3. At this point the second subject gets no further than its first two dotted minims before duplets break in upon it. The duple effect created by the quavers of bar 3.21 (organized into two three-note groups by their melodic shape) is thus writ large. The change to 2/4, with the minim equal to the dotted minim of the preceding passage, propels this development of the duplet rhythm, though the

---

[6] The tune had been foreshadowed in bars 5.10–13.

Example 8.4 Symphony No. 5, II, Scherzo, bb. 9.16–10.1

opening chords of the second subject still interrupt from time to time, and 3/4 sometimes returns in counterpoint with 2/4. The 2/4 bars are at first in 2 + 2 groupings, with occasional three-bar phrases interpolated.

The steady three-bar macrorhythm of the trio acts on the music at Figure 21 by reorganizing the 2/4 motion of the preceding passage into bars of 3/2, so that the duplet quavers are rearranged into a larger three-beat macrorhythm. In bar 21.2 the note-values of the bass part return to the durations heard at the start of the movement: Vaughan Williams makes these minims permeate the texture, thus creating a written-out *rallentando* to balance the written-out *accelerando* of the opening. 3/4 returns briefly for the wispy ending to the movement.

The combination of duple and triple rhythms is developed in the Passacaglia that forms the symphony's finale, where there is an uneasy relationship between the basic triple time and the tendency of the first of the two main Passacaglia themes to fall into duple segments. Vaughan Williams ends the Passacaglia by transforming the material into 4/4. This idea of a conflict between duple and triple rhythms had been foreshadowed in the finale of *A London Symphony* (where the two are in combination more than in conflict), but in the Fifth Symphony the rhythmic devices play a much larger part in the argument. Furthermore, whereas influences from a number of other composers are traceable in *A London Symphony*, in the Fifth the ideas are more characteristically Vaughan Williams's own.

Symphony No. 6

Vaughan Williams uses the idea of a conflict between duple and triple elements as the whole basis of his rhythmic argument in the Sixth Symphony

Example 8.5 Symphony No. 5, II, Scherzo, bb. 11.16–12.4

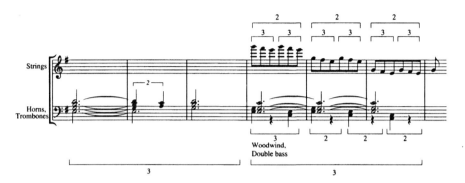

(1944–7). It is easy to equate triple time with dance, with vitality, and thus with the 'life' of a passage; duple rhythms have much more solidity, and can more easily seem heavy-footed: as Hans Keller has remarked, 'other things being equal, an undistinguished idea in triple time will sound better defined, more "individual", more rhythmic in fact, than one in duple or common time, which forms a more neutral background'.[7] Vaughan Williams juxtaposes these two basic kinds of rhythm in the Sixth Symphony – a fact that has scarcely been noticed by commentators. It is true that there is a tonal argument underpinning the work; but there is equally an underlying rhythmic struggle. The idea had already been foreshadowed in the Fifth Symphony, and it may have been suggested by J. S. Bach's fugue in D minor from Book II of the '48' – a fugue in which the subject and countersubject are carefully delineated and distinguished from each other by rhythmic means. Bach's subject uses triplets while his countersubject uses duplets: whenever in the fugue one hears triplets one knows that Bach is dealing with subject material; by contrast, whenever he uses duplets one knows he is using countersubject material.

Vaughan Williams makes the juxtaposition of two and three very clear in the first two bars of his Sixth Symphony, where the opening three-note phrase (A♭–G–E initially) is presented first in triplets, and then shifts immediately to duplets. Yet the duplet semiquavers have to be phrased in groups of three so as to maintain the three-note shape (see Example 8.6).

---

[7] 'Wolfgang Amadeus Mozart (1756–1791)', in *The Symphony*, ed. Robert Simpson, 2 vols. (Harmondsworth: Penguin Books, 1966), vol. I, p. 57.

Example 8.6 Symphony No. 6, I, bb. 1–2

Example 8.7 Symphony No. 6, I, bb. 4.5–6

Such combinations and conflicts of duple and triple elements permeate the work. Although the time signature is 4/4, runs of semiquavers grouped into threes are prominent during the first movement; the resulting syncopation is very clear when both semiquavers and quavers are simultaneously grouped into threes, as in bars 1.7 and 1.8, and 1.10 ff. The outcome of these syncopations is a second subject in G minor that adopts a 'light-music' style, superimposing 4/4 and 12/8, and organizing the duplets of the 4/4 tune into jazzy groups of three (see Example 8.7).

At this point in the work the influence of triple grouping is very strong, having virtually overtaken the duple elements. The 'light music' theme, of which much is made in the exposition, never returns, though Vaughan Williams later uses it as the accompaniment to a new B minor theme which supplants it as the second subject proper (bar 7.7 ff.). Here again the composer makes much use of threes, both in crotchets (in the tune) and quavers (in the accompaniment derived from the 'light music'

Example 8.8 Symphony No. 6, I, bb. 8.1–4

theme). Threes are somewhat less prominent here than earlier, however, and the current direction of the rhythmic struggle is suggested by the increasing significance of duplets, for some instruments are playing in 2/2 at the same time as others are playing in 6/4 (see Example 8.8). Here crotchets and quavers are both grouped into threes, while a steady underlying duple organization is maintained. During the development section the B minor theme is recalled in G minor (Figure 11); here the groups of three crotchets and the groups of three quavers that are counterpointed against them virtually eliminate any feeling of duple rhythm.

It is at the repeat of the material shown in Example 8.8 – now in E major – that duplet rhythms and triple groupings are held in the most precise balance, a (temporary) reconciliation highlighted by the glorious melodic line and glowing orchestral sound. The result is like some stately galliard left over from the music for the Sons of the Morning in the composer's 'Masque for Dancing', *Job* (first performed 1930). Vaughan Williams enlivens the slow duple pulse by giving each beat three crotchets (see Example 8.9): the triplet quavers of the 'light music' theme have now vanished. Only at the end of the tune does a hemiola (bar 17.7) attempt to break the flow – and even that is in a bar of three duplet minims, so that elements of both two and three are present.

The conflict between rhythmic elements grouped in threes and those in twos is sustained in the later movements. Three repeated notes ♪♪♩ albeit not of equal length, are a characteristic feature of the second movement (though at first without upsetting the prevailing 4/4), and the series of central fanfares contains triplets. Vaughan Williams turns the repeated-

Example 8.9 Symphony No. 6, I, bb. 15.1–4

note rhythm into a terrifying element towards the end, where it batters its way into the mind of the listener as if it will never cease. From bar 10.8 onwards the repeated-note rhythm becomes ♩♩ ♩ followed by quaver rest: here the figure takes up the space of three quavers before being immediately repeated. The resulting syncopation affects the surrounding music at times (see Example 8.10), as the repeated-note rhythm clearly attempts to over-whelm all duple elements.

If for any reason it has up to now escaped the listener that a conflict is taking place, Vaughan Williams dramatizes the point by scoring the ♩♩ ♩ pattern for trumpets and drums, instruments that had for centuries been the harbingers of battle and the means of communicating within it. For many bars a group of four descending semiquavers is pitted against the three-quaver pattern, but the triple rhythm forces this into submission. For large stretches the bar-lines become irrelevant to the music, the 4/4 metre no longer having any kind of hold over it. The rhythmic conflict between three and two finally generates a massive climax, the parallel chords shown in Example 8.10 being augmented at its height. The trumpets and drums cease and the movement dies away to a mutter, as if in exhaustion at the end of battle; duple and triple elements are both evident at the end, though very subdued.

The fugue which opens the scherzo uses triplets only incidentally at first (see bars 5.3–15, and 7.10–9.10, for example), and Vaughan Williams reinforces the solid duple motion of the subject very soon after the begin-ning, when he turns to a march episode that evokes the wind-band style of which he was so fond. The grim humour, the march mocking in brutish

Example 8.10 Symphony No. 6, II, bb. 10.8–10

fashion the scholarly fugue, masks a more serious musical purpose, as Vaughan Williams uses the shift from fugue to march to reinforce the duple rhythmic element. The triplets that sound during this episode – in bars 1.6–8, for instance – do nothing to upset the march's onward progress, but seem instead to be strait-jacketed by the duple rhythm. The influence of triplets grows later, when at Figure 8 a series of hemiola figures using minim triplets forces the rest of the music into three-note segments; but it is the duple march rhythm that wins the day at the end of the first part of the scherzo.

Vaughan Williams uses a mixture of 2/4 and 3/4 in the trio, and phrases of three-quaver lengths frequently introduce syncopation. The texture of the trio is basically three part, although the bass is doubled in fifths. The recapitulation of the scherzo is markedly different from the opening of the movement: an inversion of the fugue subject gives a new prominence to triplets (see Example 8.11). There is considerable conflict between these crotchet and quaver triplets and the duplets that character-ized the opening of the scherzo, and it is here that battle is most obviously joined between the two elements. Vaughan Williams delays the reprise of the march element, allowing time for the triplets to gain the upper hand. Elements of the march attempt to push themselves forward from time to time; elements governed by multiples of three oppose them, as when the recall of the march at Figure 36 is accompanied by a series of detached chords that generate attacks every third quaver. But duple elements eventu-ally overcome the triplets, celebrating their triumph in an enhanced return of the trio material (Figure 39), now *ff*, entirely in 2/4, and almost free of

Example 8.11 Symphony No. 6, III, bb. 21.1–7

Example 8.12 Symphony No. 6, III, bb. 39.1–7

triplets (see Example 8.12). Moreover, just as Vaughan Williams had in the trio adopted what was basically a three-part texture, now he emphasizes the dupleness of this triumphant coda by organizing it into two main strands (with doubling of the principal element at the major third). A few final mutterings allude to a sequence of figures of three quavers' duration, recalling the earlier syncopation – but it is clear that duplets have eventually triumphed in this movement.

Despite its allusions to the three-note figure with which the symphony began, the finale almost entirely eschews triple elements. The 'life' that they give to music is thus not to be found in the finale, and the utter desolation and deadness of the movement are at least in some measure due to the Pyrrhic victory gained over them. In the Sixth Symphony Vaughan Williams's rhythmic argument forms a vital part of the logic of the work as a whole; so fundamental is it to the construction that it is difficult to isolate it from the other elements of composition. Vaughan Williams could scarcely have gone further in producing a symphony which is a total unity, and it would be fair to say that the composer's last three symphonies do not use rhythm as part of the overall armoury of unifying devices in nearly such a thoroughgoing way. Nevertheless, the

Scherzo alla Marcia of Symphony No. 8 (composed 1953–5) raises points of great rhythmic interest.[8]

Symphony No. 8: *Scherzo alla Marcia* (*per stromenti a fiato*)

The culmination of much that Vaughan Williams had learned about the handling of rhythm is to be found in this movement.[9] Ostensibly a march for wind band, it builds on the experience gained in the scherzo of the Sixth Symphony, and contains many subtleties that place it far beyond the norms of the march genre. Vaughan Williams's procedures can be compared with those of the great composers of classical minuets: because the minuet is a dance, Haydn, Mozart, and Beethoven knew that their listeners would have a preconceived notion of the form, expecting it to have a regular phrase structure, with an overall AABA shape each segment of which would consist of two four-bar phrases. Given this well-defined background, Haydn, Mozart, and Beethoven (respectively in the String Quartet Op. 64 No. 5 in D, the 'Jupiter' Symphony, and the second of the 'Rasumovsky' quartets, for example) could play with the form by frustrating the audience's expectations in various ways. For twentieth-century listeners, more familiar than the minuet is the march. By its very nature the march requires a regular duple background and matching phrases; as we have seen, these features made march-like material the ideal foil for triple elements in the scherzo of the Sixth Symphony. In Symphony No. 8 Vaughan Williams brings the march centre-stage and plays with its associated expectations as his classical forebears had done with the minuet.

Two works by earlier composers will help our understanding of Vaughan Williams's specific procedures in this movement. One of them is

---

[8] See also Alain Frogley, 'The Genesis of Vaughan Williams's Ninth Symphony: A Study of the Sketches, Drafts and Autograph Scores', D.Phil. (University of Oxford, 1989), vol. I, pp. 69 ff., for an analysis of Vaughan Williams's subtle manipulation of duplets and triplets as part of a gradual acceleration and deceleration across the first movement of the work.

[9] A comparison of this movement with the march from the finale of *A London Symphony*, discussed in n. 3 above, shows how vastly more sophisticated Vaughan Williams's compositional technique had become in the intervening years.

Example 8.13 J. S. Bach, Two-part Invention in E minor, opening

J. S. Bach's Two-part Invention in E minor. Rhythmically, the whole invention is a study in upbeats, which are also a central concern in Vaughan Williams's movement. Upbeats of different lengths produce various levels of strong and weak beats, so that a strong element on one level can be weak on another (see Example 8.13: stressed beats are marked –, unstressed ∪). The *Scherzo alla Marcia* also shares features with a movement by Mozart (even Vaughan Williams's opening flourish has its counterpart there). The first movement of the Piano Sonata in A minor, K. 310, is another piece in which the interaction of upbeats and downbeats creates much fascination. Mozart's first subject begins on a strong beat; but the performer is immediately faced with the problem of deciding whether the appoggiatura D♯ placed before the initial E of the tune is to be played on the beat or before it. Moreover, the status of the whole first bar as a strong beat of the macrorhythm is questioned when bar 2 provides a 2–4–5–7 chord which, because of its pungent nature, sounds much stronger than the opening chord (see Example 8.14). In a sense, then, bar 1 can sound like an upbeat to bar 2; but the provision of an upbeat to the revised statement of the opening two bars (that is, the D and B in the right hand at the end of bar 2) contradicts this impression by its preparation of bar 3. Mozart provides patterns that all listeners will recognize as iambic, 'upbeat' figures in bars 5–7; but he does so in such a way as to develop the ambiguity already suggested, for these figures are given, as it were, in stretto, so that the two hands play *per arsin et thesin*. These rhythmic tensions are developed as the movement proceeds. Mozart's second subject makes a much more obvious use of the

Example 8.14 W. A. Mozart, Piano Sonata in A minor, K. 310, I, opening

iambic formulae; the effect is to thrust the music temporarily into segments of a single bar, the two-bar segments and larger multiples only returning later in the section. The upbeat character can be found at its most extended at the retransition, which acts as a large-scale upbeat to the recall of the first subject: the D♯ – an appoggiatura in the exposition – is continually foreshadowed during the retransition, and the effect is to make the first subject in the recapitulation start as if with an upbeat.

Subtle and shifting relationships between upbeat and downbeat are vital to the life of the second movement of Vaughan Williams's Eighth Symphony. These upbeats and downbeats need to be appreciated on the very lowest level – within a single bar – as well as on the highest level: the feeling that a whole section is either more weighty or less weighty than those surrounding it. It is clear that any listener who is aware that the piece has the word 'marcia' in the title – even those hearing it for the first time and without a score – will expect regular two-bar or four-bar phrases. Such an expectation is mildly frustrated at the very opening (see Example 8.15), for one imagines that the initial two-bar segment will be followed immediately by a matching one, a strong beat being felt at the start of bar 5. Instead the first four-and-a-half bars prove to be merely an upbeat to a tune that begins in the middle of bar 5. In turn, the opening of the tune sounds initially like an upbeat to bar 6 (an interpretation aided by the presence of an isolated

Example 8.15 Symphony No. 8, II, bb. 1–7

chord in the lower instruments at the start of bar 6), so forcing the listener to reinterpret the opening 'till-ready' bars as an asymmetrical five-bar segment. But such is the nature of the theme that one could equally well place the first structural downbeat at the beginning of the upward scale in bar 7; this interpretation of the accentuation has the advantage that the preceding bars can be mentally organized into three two-bar segments, thus preserving the regularity expected of a march.

In both of these interpretations the tune begins with an upbeat, but the very nature of the upbeat itself poses interesting problems. It leads from dominant to tonic; yet it does so by descending a fifth, where in a melody line an ascent by a fourth, throwing the weight firmly on to the higher tonic, would be more normal. The parallel with Mozart's A minor Sonata is obvious. In Vaughan Williams the higher note – the one that naturally feels as if it ought to have more weight – is in fact the upbeat, not the main accent. The opening of the tune is a version of the flute-and-piccolo flourish with which the movement starts; this flourish rises from tonic to dominant, and here too Vaughan Williams places the lower note at a stronger point of the bar than the higher one. As a result, this flourish can also be heard in two ways, either as a trochee with a strong pulse on the first note, or as an iamb

Example 8.16 Symphony No. 8, II, bb. 4.1–6

with upbeat figure leading to the longest note, the G on the second quaver of
the bar.

The opening theme is an exploration of upbeats: so it is hardly surprising that the second subject (the trumpet solo beginning at Figure 3,
introduced by its own 'till-ready' bars) is the exact opposite, exploring
trochaic, downbeat rhythms. (Indeed, the use of a more obviously 'tuneful'
melody for the second subject, along with the scoring for solo trumpet,
make the first thirty-five bars feel in retrospect like a prolonged upbeat to
bar 3.5.) Ambiguity is again evident, as Vaughan Williams's woodwind
extension of the second subject (beginning at Figure 4) has a three-beat
rhythmic accompaniment – of an iambic, upbeat nature – that necessarily
shifts its position in the bar when repeated (see Example 8.16). The composer explores the ambivalence further in the following passage, for clarinets and solo trumpet use a figure that has all the hallmarks of a strongly
iambic pattern – indeed, it is clearly derived from the accompaniment of
bars 4.1–6 (and perhaps bars 5–6), where the figure is used as an upbeat
element – but all the imagined 'upbeats' are in fact now placed on the strong
beats.

The figure in clarinets and trumpets at bar 4.7 forms the basis of a
fugue that begins five bars before Figure 7. There is a further ambiguity
here. The traditionally cerebral nature of fugue might make this section
feel 'stressed' when set in the lighter context of a march, but Vaughan
Williams counters the tendency by using soft dynamics and generally
underplaying the section, as if to shrug off its natural weightiness. The
subject begins with the iambic figure of bars 4.1–6, though this is first of
all used on a downbeat; and it continues by referring to the three-beat

Example 8.17 Symphony No. 8, II, bb. 6.7–12

accompaniment of bars 4.1 ff., stating it in diminution. Similarly, as in bars 6.9–11, a syncopated crotchet–quaver figure (with several repetitions) might be mentally organized into either an iambic or a trochaic pattern (see Example 8.17), although the slurs tilt the balance in favour of the trochaic interpretation. Vaughan Williams compounds the confusion surrounding upbeats and downbeats generated by the fugue subject by having the answer enter on the second beat of the bar rather than the first, and by using augmentation later in the fugue. The augmentation makes clear the derivation of the ♩ ♪ segments from the accompaniment of bars 4.1 ff. by returning to a three-crotchet rhythm played against the prevailing duple time.

As the listener expects, the march contains a central trio section; this begins two bars before Figure 11, and transforms the opening theme of the movement into a much gentler line. (Clearly on the very largest scale this is not a downbeat section, for its very understatement makes it seem like an upbeat.) The descent from dominant to tonic recurs, the higher note again being in the unstressed position. The nature of the theme, in which groups of quavers at the end of a bar frequently lead to a crotchet on the first beat of the following bar, serves to convince the listener that the alternation of crotchet and quaver in the accompaniment should be heard as a trochaic rather than an iambic rhythm. That accompanying rhythm – clearly derived from the version at bars 6.9–11, where it is syncopated across the prevailing simple duple rhythm – can now be felt as a settled pattern, without ambiguity. Vaughan Williams evokes this feeling by changing the basic metre from simple duple to compound duple (6/8): the tensions of the opening section are relieved by breaking away from its march background.

The listener expects that there will be a recapitulation of the march, and Vaughan Williams certainly provides a recapitulation of sorts; but most of this section – which is much more condensed than the first part of the movement – is concerned with a stretto on the fugue subject, and a final reference to the ♩ ♪ figure (with many repetitions) that recalls the ambiguity experienced in the opening section. There is clearly a sense that, on the largest scale, this section is a 'stressed' one, prepared by the understated and upbeat nature of the trio. But Vaughan Williams pulls one last rhythmic trick by, in turn, underplaying this recapitulation, albeit via a different technique from that used in the trio: here radical telescoping does the job. The 'underplaying' is, however, countered at another level by concentrating on new contrapuntal artifice in the recall of the fugue, in particular, on the climactic use of augmentation combined with stretto. The final demi-semiquaver flourish, which on paper looks as if it is placed on a strong beat, is actually ambiguous because the preceding syncopations have very largely destroyed any feeling about where the strong and weak beats lie. Rhythmically, then, Vaughan Williams ends the movement with a question mark.

*

Rhythm has been a Cinderella among the elements discussed by writers on the development of the symphony, and in analyses of Vaughan Williams's contributions to the genre in particular; yet until a serious investigation of its contribution to symphonic logic is undertaken, we cannot pretend that analysts have adequately understood the works involved. Furthermore, it is time to jettison the idea that triplets represent a facile kind of folksiness in Vaughan Williams: an appreciation of his use of conflict between rhythmic manifestations of the prime numbers two and three is in fact basic to an understanding of the Fifth and Sixth symphonies. The composer is quoted as denying that the Sixth Symphony had a programme: he observed that people did not seem to believe that a composer might simply have set out to write a piece of music, with no extraneous events or pictures in mind.[10] Even if – as I believe – there *is* a programme behind No. 6, the composer's comment is understandable, for the first critics of the work were inclined to take the easy approach offered by a story-line, ignoring the more rigorous discipline of attempting to discover what intrinsically musical logic lay behind the symphony. Rhythm plays a large part in that logic: so important a part, indeed – its manifestations have

---

[10] Kennedy, *Works*, p. 302.

185

only barely been touched on in this chapter – that it requires further detailed study. Yet this should in turn be grounded in a comprehensive investigation of Vaughan Williams's approach to rhythm across his music as a whole. I hope this preliminary study will lead others to explore the matter further.

9 'Symphony in D major': models and mutations

ARNOLD WHITTALL

I

The question-master on a rather highbrow quiz-show might stimulate a lively discussion with the following poser: 'Of which composition was it said, in a book published in 1954, that it was "the most successful attempt since Beethoven to use music as a direct penetration of the mystery of life. It is perhaps a more successful attempt than Beethoven's to deal with metaphysical issues in the language of sound"?'[1] Plausible answers might include Wagner's *Tristan* and *Parsifal*, Bruckner's Eighth or Ninth symphonies, or several by Mahler or Sibelius. What are in fact comments on Vaughan Williams's Fifth Symphony, by Frank Howes, might now be judged as exactly the kind of exaggerated, blinkered adulation that says more about the insularity and eccentricity of a certain generation of English music critics than about artistic realities, and which helped to make a determined, prolonged backlash inevitable.

The force of that backlash is vividly encapsulated in Donald Mitchell's magisterial put-down of Vaughan Williams in 1965: 'His *art*, I think, though it made history, was also defeated by it, and will, if I have to hazard a guess, prove to be minor'.[2] Yet this reaction (stemming as it does from Constant Lambert's *Music Ho!* of 1934)[3] has never succeeded in

---

[1] Frank Howes, *The Music of Ralph Vaughan Williams* (London: Oxford University Press, 1954), pp. 42–3.

[2] Donald Mitchell, 'Vaughan Williams', in *Cradles of the New: Writings on Music, 1951–1991*, sel. Christopher Palmer, ed. Mervyn Cooke (London: Faber and Faber, 1995), p. 96; originally a talk broadcast on the BBC Third Programme, 25 April 1965.

[3] *Music Ho! A Study of Music in Decline* (London: Hogarth Press, 1934), see in particular pp. 106–10.

sweeping all before it. Even in the 1960s, when cosmopolitanism was in and nationalism out, and Tippett's rejection of what he perceived as 'aimless rhapsody'[4] set the standard for most younger British composers, an intensifying cultural pluralism enabled Vaughan Williams's admirers to continue to make their presence felt, and also to make strong claims on behalf of the Fifth Symphony. For Michael Kennedy it is perhaps 'the greatest' of all his works.[5] For Wilfrid Mellers it is 'Vaughan Williams's greatest work because it is a quest that *attains* its goal'. As Mellers argues, 'we know that the New Jerusalem does not, cannot, exist in solid reality: whereas in the Symphony the validity of art for a moment makes the vision true'.[6] Mellers evidently endorses Howes's view that the work deals with 'metaphysical issues in the language of sound', though he does not presume to contend that it is more successful in the task than anything by Beethoven. Indeed, for most more recent critics, especially when they are aware of Tippett's aspiration towards a vision of the transcendent that acknowledges the greatness of Beethoven's achievement while challenging its relevance to the late twentieth century,[7] the assumption that any direct comparisons can usefully be made between Beethoven and a twentieth-century English composer is far more dubious than Howes's particular claim about Vaughan Williams's ability 'to use music as a direct penetration of the mystery of life'. In that respect, Vaughan Williams may even be felt to have something in common with the pronouncedly anti-modern, spiritual stylistics of Górecki, Pärt, and Tavener, through which, their devotees might well argue, a (musical) New Jerusalem has at last been created.

Present-day interpretative musicology likes nothing better than a Problem Piece, where one of the Problems is the interaction between the 'purely musical' and the 'extra-musical' – preferably such an intimate interaction that the debate concerning whether any genuine aspects of a work's meaning may properly be deemed 'extra-musical' can be sharply intensified. In these terms, the Fifth Symphony's 'problems' range from

---

[4]   Ian Kemp, *Tippett: The Composer and his Music* (London: Eulenburg Books, 1984), p. 70.   [5] See Kennedy, *Works*, p. 283.

[6]   Wilfrid Mellers, *Vaughan Williams and the Vision of Albion* (London: Barrie & Jenkins, 1989), p. 186.

[7]   See Arnold Whittall, 'Resisting Tonality: Tippett, Beethoven and the Sarabande', *Music Analysis*, 9 (1990), pp. 267–86.

questions about the quality of its musico-metaphysical thought, and its handling – blending? – of modality and tonality, to the basic topic of its generic integrity as a symphony (closely associated as it is with Vaughan Williams's stage work *The Pilgrim's Progress*) and, particularly, the issue of connections between traditional formal models and the musical genres implied by the four movement titles. For example, there has been some unease at the composer's decision to call the third movement 'Romanza'. Howes declares bluntly that it is 'ill-named',[8] and while Mellers notes the generic validity of the title for the movement, 'because it tells a tale',[9] the suspicion remains that the profound associations with the Crucifixion that the original, deleted inscription indicated[10] are left casually in limbo – an optional extra to be remembered while the mind plays with the more conventional, yet also incongruous and even distasteful, associations of 'romance' as wholeheartedly secular.

It seems to be generally accepted that the Fifth Symphony's greatness, if not exactly conditioned by such ambiguities, is not diminished by them. Perhaps, indeed, the strangeness of genre and association in connection with the Romanza is a necessary price to pay if, as in Mellers's reading, a work which begins 'in doubleness and ambiguity' does not merely end with the rediscovery of 'cadential resolution' but a rediscovery in which the composer finds 'a gateway to Paradise'.[11] This 'Symphony of the Celestial City', as Kennedy calls it,[12] would seem to offer a definitive example of that Sibelian process, so admired by Vaughan Williams, of a pilgrimage beyond doubt and instability to fulfilment and resolution – the transcendence, not simply the setting-aside, of ambiguity. It is not my intention here to deconstruct this proposition, reminding readers of 'the ability of the pastoral style to convey genuine pain'[13] as a prelude to arguing that there is an idealized unreality at the end of this wartime

---

[8] *Ralph Vaughan Williams*, p. 48.
[9] Mellers, *Vaughan Williams and the Vision of Albion*, p. 181.
[10] See Howes, *Ralph Vaughan Williams*, p. 48.
[11] Mellers, *Vaughan Williams and the Vision of Albion*, pp. 177 and 186.
[12] Kennedy, *Works*, p. 283.
[13] Paul Harrington, 'Holst and Vaughan Williams: Radical Pastoral', in Christopher Norris, ed., *Music and the Politics of Culture* (London: Lawrence & Wishart, 1989), p. 115.

Example 9. 1 Hypothetical opening of Symphony No. 5

fantasy about the achievement of peace that functions as its own decon-struction.[14] Rather, by examining more closely than is usual the 'double-ness and ambiguity' of the work's earlier stages, I want to consider some of its processes in the light of alternative but not contradictory models of resolution: those which absorb the enriching elements of ambiguity, and those which positively exclude – declare redundant – the very forces that serve to delay their own earlier emergence.

II

Example 9.1 shows one of the ways in which Vaughan Williams did not begin his Fifth Symphony. Had he done so the technical question of whether or not the work is 'in D major', rather than only reaching an unequivocal D in the finale, would have to be approached differently – and all the more so if we were to imagine a continuation of my fictitious opening which does not totally exclude D from any further role as a bass note in the remainder of the movement.

The title 'Preludio' itself offers its familiar musical ambiguity. Is this complete movement in some sense preliminary, and, if so, to what? Vaughan Williams may have used the title out of self-deprecation, so that the listener would not expect a large-scale symphonic allegro; yet in view of the fact that the whole technical point of the movement lies in the way that the symphony's declared tonic is never used as a sustained harmonic root in the bass, there is indeed something preliminary about this 'prelude', if only

---

[14] See U. Vaughan Williams, *R.V.W.*, p. 254. At the first performance, which the composer conducted, 'the music seemed to many people to bring the peace and blessing for which they longed'.

because this degree of distance from harmonic and tonal explicitness is not sustained in the rest of the work.

As a discipline with pretensions to intellectual sophistication as well as aesthetic pertinence, musical analysis is often least comfortable when it finds itself obliged to adjudicate between literal and implied presences, or cope with a musical ethos in which the inferred presence of something fundamentally important cannot be ruled out – an ethos, in other words, in which techniques of substitution may be involved. In this context, the concept of 'fact' as used in the previous paragraph must be handled with especial care. As will be seen, the 'fact' that the tonic D is used in the Preludio in the way it is has complex consequences in respect of such features as the role of the bass line, the nature of the consonance/dissonance relation, and other matters pertaining to voice-leading. Vaughan Williams's particular procedures in the Preludio create a musical atmosphere which has consistently impressed listeners, even though ways of describing it vary. The horn calls, with their initial whole-tonal context,[15] seem to signify an unearthly, veiled kind of pastoral, and whether or not the unearthliness is the result of connections with *The Pilgrim's Progress*, a work which occupied the composer at intervals during the 1930s and 1940s, the symphony's pastoral connotations seem to link into that metaphysical dimension acknowledged by most commentators.

One of the earliest attempts to interpret the work in this way remains one of the most challenging. In 1950 Wilfrid Mellers was not simply content to declare that the symphony 'offers a profound religious conviction which is paralleled in no other English music of today except possibly the later symphonies of Rubbra'. He also declared it to be 'impregnated with that Christian Puritanism which ultimately played its part in producing the chaos of the modern world. But it is that Puritanism as full of beauty, humanism, charity and hope for the future as it was in the eyes of Bunyan and Lilburne, before it soured into commercialism and industry.' In other words, 'in the pervasively rural and religious Fifth Vaughan Williams is

---

[15] It has long struck me that this opening gesture may be Vaughan Williams's not-so-covert tribute to Sibelius, whose Symphony No. 4 begins by presenting a C – F♯ tritone and an F♯ – E oscillation, and in a whole-tone context that creates initial tonal ambiguity. This is just one of many possible Sibelian angles on the work.

turning his back on the more immediate issues of the modern world'.[16] Thirty years later Mellers would refine that judgement with his claim that a great work of art can make 'true' that vision of the New Jerusalem which 'cannot exist in social reality'. It is a bold, perhaps unnecessarily concrete, interpretation of the work's undoubted spiritual dimension.

As an alternative, it might be proposed that the symphony's first movement suggests something of the mystery of the human condition, as a response to the number of unanswerable questions that even humanists must acknowledge. The work then moves from mystery to morality, the correct mode of behaviour, according to Vaughan Williams, and one of whose possible musical embodiments is the manifestation of the tonic in its most stable position. If the unsolved mysteries of the universe and human existence require humans to lead a moral life (whether or not they also commit themselves to particular religious or political creeds), the power of the Fifth Symphony is not so much in its mirroring of Bunyanesque imagery (the Celestial City) as in its focus on this deep impulse to counter mystery with confidence. That may seem easy enough, given that the mystery in question appears to be peaceful, not warlike: even its darker shades are not seriously menacing. Yet this interpretation also raises the possibility that the mystery to which Vaughan Williams is responding is not simply that of human behaviour, but of nature in general: the Preludio is perhaps his most penetrating expression of the pastoral as transcendent.

It may appear glib to claim that this focus on the topic of 'mystery' has precise technical equivalents. But to resist the claim is to imply a disjunction between musical atmosphere and musical technique which is wholly unjustified. Musical character resides in the conjunction of methods and materials, process and product. At the same time, however, it must be admitted that the rather special, unusual attributes of the Preludio make it more difficult than usual with Vaughan Williams to define the nature of the materials, even in elementary terms.

A favoured approach has been to acknowledge an ambiguity of tonality, and to ascribe this to varieties of scale or mode, which are present singly or interact with others. Such identifications, as in the writings of Hugh

---

[16] *Music and Society: England and the European Tradition*, 2nd edn. (London: Dennis Dobson, 1950), pp. 170–1.

Ottaway,[17] have their place, but only as a preliminary to the much more essential topic of how these scales or collections are actually used. There is a world of difference between, on the one hand, deployments of the 'Mixolydian major' or 'Dorian minor', which suggest inflected forms of diatonic major or minor, and can lead to the assignment of scale-step functions to chords in relation to a Fundamental Bass, and, on the other, usages which might imply some kind of post-tonal context. My proposal here is not that pitch-class set analysis would succeed in explaining procedures in Vaughan Williams when functional harmonic analysis has failed. Rather, it is to observe that the music moves between different orientations; it is, in a sense, purposefully non-committal, and to interpret it in terms of a single strategy, such as degrees of concealment of an all-pervading D tonic, is excessively reductive. Study of the voice-leading (provided this is not confused with subjective assumptions about the composer's actual decision-making) serves to counter such reductiveness by highlighting the music's flexibility, and to confirm that the Fifth is indeed a virtuoso exercise in sustained symphonic thought.

III

Although there is no evidence that Vaughan Williams knew anything of Schenker, or that he harboured a covert concern with matters theoretical, his music is usually tonal enough to suggest associations with the kind of basic generative structures represented by Schenker's concept of the *Ursatz*. The importance of Schenkerian theory is that it can illuminate truly tonal procedures of many kinds, and even (despite Schenker's own blinkered, nationalistic ideology) procedures which challenge tonality at the same time as they depend on it. Schenker's theories are particularly likely to prove germane when a tonal composer's thinking is strongly

---

[17] 'VW5 – A New Analysis', *The Musical Times*, 105 (1964), p. 354; *Vaughan Williams Symphonies*, BBC Music Guides (London: British Broadcasting Corporation, 1972). On the BBC Music Guide, see also Ottaway's letter in *The Musical Times*, 114 (1973), p. 897, in which he disclaims and deplores 'certain changes ... made in the text without consultation, after I had corrected and returned page proofs'; these affected in particular his 'careful distinction between modes, keys and modally-inflected keys' in his analysis of the first movement of the Fifth Symphony.

linear, polyphonic, as Vaughan Williams's most certainly was. They tend, on the other hand, to seem most limited and even redundant when composers begin to think not only in terms of new kinds of counterpoint but of new kinds of cadences also: when they acknowledge the emancipation not only of the dissonance but also of chromaticism, and thereby engage with the kind of techniques which Mellers associates with 'doubleness and ambiguity'.

A brief indication of the dangers inherent in imposing inflexibly unified models on Vaughan Williams can be found in Felix Salzer's interpretation of three bars from the Fifth Symphony's first movement (Example 9.2). For the neo-Schenkerian Salzer, this passage demonstrates 'harmonic-prolonging chords with contrapuntal implications'; the 'descending fifths in support of a melodic sequence combine to prolong either the progression between two chords or harmonies or to prolong a single chord'.[18] Salzer therefore interprets the three-fold sequence, with descending fifths in the bass, with which the passage begins, as a prolonged E minor tonic progressing to the next chord of similar structural significance, the II (or 'CS' (contrapuntal-structural) chord in Salzer's terminology). In the case of music which is tonally more stable than this Vaughan Williams movement, it might be argued that Salzer's reading of such sequential progressions is preferable to a 'Roman numeral plus modulation' analysis that breaks up the musical surface into a series of tiny, separate vertical events, an approach that deems the brief 'tonicization' of G major no less important to the effect of the passage than those chords which belong even more essentially to E minor. Yet it is significant that the other examples Salzer offers of this technique, from works by Handel and Schubert, already demonstrate the difference (on which Salzer does not comment) between sequences which remain within the prevailing key (Handel) and those which effect local modulation (Schubert). All the hard-won subtlety of Vaughan Williams's 'doubleness' – in this instance, the interplay of tonality and modality, of monotonality and modulation, by way of highlighted third-relations which are the more significant given the absence of E minor's

[18] Felix Salzer, *Structural Hearing: Tonal Coherence in Music*, 2 vols. (New York: Charles Boni, 1952), vol. I, pp. 164–5; vol. II, p. 123 (Example 331).

Example 9.2 Felix Salzer's analysis of Symphony No. 5, Preludio, bb. 6.3–5

'correct' leading note – is lost in Salzer's dogmatically single-minded hierarchization of the music. He is perfectly right to observe that one way in which this passage functions is as an expansion of a cadential progression, but, for Vaughan Williams, to expand is to enrich, and even to undermine, as much as to reinforce.

My purpose here is not lightly to overturn all the hard-won rewards which analysis in terms of structural levels has brought to the study of tonal music, but to move that analysis forwards towards that 'reconciliation' between 'hierarchical unity and plural unities' which is increasingly canvassed in the theoretical community. We can begin to develop the exploration of Vaughan Williams's emancipation of dissonance and chromaticism by way of voice-leading models which, in their simplest form, embody a basic cadential motion, but whose juxtaposition challenges tonal continuity. The basic transpositional relation present in Example 9.3a is not in itself literally employed by Vaughan Williams in the first movement of the Fifth Symphony. Rather, his way of relating the two tonally distinct motions is to present a C in both (Example 9.3b). At the same time, he eliminates the upper voice of the F major version in Example 9.3a altogether, and this serves to strengthen the chromatic shift from F♯ to F♮. On the one hand, the C is a link; on the other, the change from F♯ to F♮ is an emphatic one.

The relationship so far discussed is, of course, that which is composed out in the first movement's coda, the beginning of which is shown in Example 9.3c; here, according to Hugh Ottaway, 'the sense of alternating between two conflicting tonal centres, D and F, heightens the indeterminacy of the ending'.[19] Yet 'indeterminacy' is scarcely an appropriate term for the remarkable precision with which Vaughan Williams preserves, juxtaposes, and superimposes these elements at the end. It is the principle that closure can function as summary (of the prevailing structural characteristics) rather than as resolution (on to one 'determinate', unambiguous tonic) that is of the essence here. In addition, what is being summarized is not simply the possibility of alternating related but distinct types of material, a model and its derivation: Vaughan Williams is reinforcing a resistance to tonal harmony as it conventionally operates, and a post-tonal reading of this coda would indicate an alternation between pitch-class sets (0,2,6) and (0,2,5) (Example 9.3d) which ends with a simple, sustained (0,2) – the cello C and viola D (Example 9.3e). The alternation process brings out the one interval-type which is missing from each of the two trichords as independent entities – the semitone between F♯ and F♮ – whose 'harmonization' by C and F cannot fail to dramatize the non-functionality of that 'V-I' in the bass, even if it can be rationalized in terms of a modal interpretation of the two-flat key signature (see, again, Example 9.3c). Generalized, this summary seems to tell us that 'V – I's – full closes like the motion from C to F – are illusory, that semitone steps cannot be presumed to represent 'proper' scale degrees (3–4, 7–8), and that, in consequence, tritones and major seconds

---

[19] 'VW5 – A New Analysis', p. 356.

Example 9.3 Tonal ambiguity in Symphony No. 5, Preludio

a)

b)

c)

d)

e)

can be held to be more stable than their conventionally more consonant fellow intervals. At the same time, however, that apparent stability, especially of the major second, is countered by the more 'traditional' role it plays in those neighbour-note relations which are crucial to the movement's evolving linear structure.

197

IV

After these preliminary observations in respect of technical fundamentals, a closer reading of the Preludio is offered as a development of these procedural topics. Such narratives are notoriously resistant to literary elegance, and the object here is not to 'translate' the score into words, but rather to provide a parallel text, interpreting certain elements which can be inferred from the score's notation – and thereby, of course, raising the possibility of alternative readings and responses. (This narrative will assume a sonata-form model for the movement.)

The first of the three principal paragraphs of the first-subject exposition – that is, the music up to the return of the horn calls at Figure 2 – will seem to most listeners to be primarily concerned with the shift from a D major to a D minor triad over a persistent C♮ bass note. Linearly and motivically, however, it is the emphasis on the high D against the C at Figure 1 which seems most salient, not least because it reinforces the destabilizing contrast between the bass C and the role of C in the upper line, which is that of a neighbour to D. The music from bar 1.1 is itself heard in the context of the upper-line progressions from C to D in bars 3 and 7, where the structural functions of the two notes – which is subordinate to which? – are more ambiguous (Example 9.4). So what is clarified before Figure 2 is – paradoxically – the stability of a tension; and this effect is reinforced by the varied repetition of Paragraph 1 provided in Paragraph 2 (bars 2.1–3.7), in which the equality of C and D is only gradually re-established after the lighter bass presentation of C between Figures 2 and 3.

On the largest scale, the third, developmental paragraph of this first-subject exposition (from bar 3.8 to Figure 5) 'resolves' the structural dissonance by settling (from Figure 4) on a two-voice outline of C over C. Resolution may seem an even more appropriate term, given that, at Figure 4, the bass C at last becomes the root of a 'root position' C minor chord. Meanwhile the upper line has descended on to C from the F that is required if it is to continue the motivic preoccupation with the linear fourth.

The first-subject exposition, then, invites the ear to allot to C the function of the most stable harmonic entity, and, given that the C over C with which it closes is balanced in the recapitulation by F over F, we might feel obliged to confront the startling prospect of a first movement of a

198

Example 9.4

(a) Preludio, bb. 3–4, D as neighbour to C

(b) Preludio, bb. 5–8 subordination of D to C is reinforced

(c) Preludio, bb. 10–1.3, C as neighbour to D (upper parts)

'Symphony in D major' that displays a strong desire to revert to the key of the composer's preceding symphony, No. 4. All the more reason to acknowledge that 'C' and 'F' in the Fifth Symphony cannot, in the end, be separated from relationships that involve the still more fundamental D.

The second-subject sections of the exposition and the recapitulation provide the first movement with its main passages of contrast, and the Alleluia-like opening phrase with its strong bass roots underlines the contrast in voice-leading types with the first-subject material. Vaughan

Example 9.5

(a) Preludio, bb. 3.11–4.1 (selected string parts only)

(b) Preludio, bb. 6a.15–17 (strings only)

Williams skilfully contrives one parallel, in the basic shift within the second subject from the major to the minor mode, and despite the element of 'doubleness' already discussed in relation to Salzer's 'singular' analysis, it might be felt that the bass E is a relatively unequivocal tonic, with linear descents from the fifth and octave evident in the upper voice, and no doubts about the orthodox voice-leading function of neighbour notes. If this is the music of the Celestial City, then it is indeed confidently distant from the more earthly, questing concerns of the first subject, and Vaughan Williams might be felt to dramatize the 'return to earth' between Figures 6a and 7, not just with an obvious darkening of the harmony – the shift from E to the E♭ which will feature prominently in the development – but by returning to the C over C cadence (Allegro, bar 6a.16) – the structural point reached by the first subject at Figure 4, before the interruption of the Celestial City theme (Example 9.5).

It could be argued that the movement's exposition is founded on a symmetry: the gradual discovery of C as a relatively stable tonal centre (first subject) is inversely paralleled by the second subject's immediate assertion and later undermining of E as a tonal centre. The tension created between these two complementary strategies (the centres either side of D) might then be felt to provoke the 'explosion' that is the development section, at a faster tempo and increasingly high dynamic levels. If the principal, background motions of the exposition are, first, the progression from ninth to octave (first subject) and, second, the reinforcement of the octave as essential cadential goal (second subject), the development explores that reinforcement rather than questioning it: indeed, questioning on that level is not renewed until the recapitulation. The development itself seems more concerned with the tension that can be created between constant cadencing, where the outer structural voices converge on the same goal tone, and that shifting and ambiguity of key that arises when the music explores various modal collections rather than committing itself to tonal 'scale steps'. Moreover, on a rhetorical level, the development seems to allow the anxiety which is more or less suppressed in the first-subject music to rise unambiguously to the surface and boil over, the release itself becoming a reason for the sense of triumph which attends the climax, from Figure 10.

The development could also be regarded as referring to a traditional harmonic background, since a path can be traced through tonal centres from C, E♭, and F♯ to A, this last being reached (bar 9.12) and sustained through the movement's main climax, as if embracing its proper role as the dominant of the movement's real tonic, and preparing for the return of the tonic in the recapitulation. Such structuring by thirds (*Terzverwandschaft*) has an honourable romantic pedigree (e.g. the first movement of Tchaikovsky's Fourth Symphony), but in Vaughan Williams's hands it is a proposition to be interrogated rather than a blueprint to be realized. Even to say that it makes good sense to regard the C which ends the exposition as a substitute for the real dominant of D (A), and the crisis of the development as the dramatic search for that real dominant, culminating in the turbulent excitement of its discovery, is to read the reality of an orthodox background to the movement in a rather more explicit way than is ultimately convincing.

From another perspective, the narrative of the development involves first testing the stability of C as centre – it is, after all, reinforced by movement on to its diatonic dominant (bar 7.4) in a way which does not conflict

201

Example 9.6 Preludio, bb. 10.14–11.1

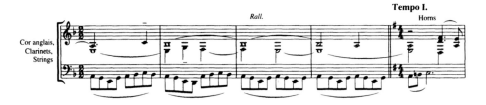

markedly with the Phrygian orientation of the harmony. But the shift to E♭ (bar 8.9) signals an equation between change of centre and loss of relative stability, and with the move up another minor third (bar 9.3) the likely identity of the most important modal final (C♯, F♯?) is less obvious. The arrival on A (bar 9.12) is notable for the persistent Phrygian colouring which leaves no doubt as to the neighbour-note, dissonant status of B♭. It is this modal consistency which helps to promote the smooth return to C♯ in the bass at Figure 11 as the recapitulation begins (Example 9.6), and offers the strongest evidence of the sense in which this music is not concerned with a traditional kind of tonality: it deals with voice-leading around centres which acknowledge the constraints of the consonance/dissonance relation, but not the scale-step logic of conventional tonality. As Ottaway in particular has observed,[20] we cannot completely avoid hearing the end of the development as a dominant preparation, but what it actually prepares is the return of a structure in which, so far, C has been the most stable and persistent point of melodic and harmonic focus.

The element of dominant preparation for D at the end of the development means that as the recapitulation begins there is another opportunity to establish D-based harmony and reveal the work's designated tonic. To the contrary, however, Vaughan Williams's reshaping of the first-subject section, reduced to twenty-one bars from the exposition's fifty-nine, strengthens the 'D over C' sonority. It is true that in the very last bar (12.6) of the first-subject section of the recapitulation, this D over C resolves out on to an octave D, with the bass rising from C by way of a cadential motion which leaves the D modally divided between tonic and dominant tendencies. Then, in another manifestation of late romantic, third-related pro-

---

[20] Ottaway, *Vaughan Williams Symphonies*, p. 38.

202

Example 9.7 Preludio, bb. 14.12–15.1

gression, the music moves from the D to B♭ for the second subject (parallel-ing the exposition's move from C to E). Again there is compression, but more important than that is the additional shift of a third (minor this time) from B♭ to G at Figure 13, which is reinforced by two local full closes (at bar 13.5 and at Figure 14). On the other hand, what seems initially to be a pure G major is gradually infiltrated by interactions with elements of B♭, and neither of those 'full closes' has the sharpened leading note to confirm the function of its bass dominant. Simply because the voice-leading of this second-subject section is again relatively orthodox, however, the effect is of an interruption of, or even escape from, the main symphonic argument, which resumes with the establishment of G over G at Figure 14.

The final stages of the movement use material from the end of the exposition (the 'codetta' theme and the recall of the horn call) but in a radi-cally different tonal context. On its own, the bass line traces a motion from G through F and E♭ on to D (bar 14.10) which turns out to be the last oppor-tunity to treat D as decisively closural. Instead, it is treated as the pivotal point of a potentially symmetrical progression, since the bass moves back through E♭ on to F (bar 14.13) as the upper line also focuses on F at Figure 15 (Example 9.7). This represents yet another possible point of closure. Overall, the tonality of the movement has had such a floating effect that a little elaboration of F over F to stabilize it conclusively could make this a perfectly satisfying ending to the structure, with echoes of the Fourth Symphony winning out after all. However, in his boldest gesture so far, Vaughan Williams denies the closural force of the octave, and, as illustrated earlier in Example 9.3e, brings the opening and closing of the movement into juxtaposition around the bass note C. In the end the initial D over C is also, as an echo, the final sound. Symmetry replaces resolution, and we have to wait until the closing stages of the finale for the D over C to resolve on to and into a D major tonic (see Example 9.10).

V

The expressive power and technical interest of the Preludio derive in large part from the movement's exploitation of a basic interaction between dependency on associations with the sonata-form model and a simultaneous countering of that model in the sphere of tonal and harmonic structure. Therein lies the essential 'doubleness and ambiguity', and the organicizing analyst is bound to consider the degree to which the succeeding three movements of the symphony are similar to the first.

If we are justified in characterizing the Preludio as an acknowledgement of the fact that a triumphant assertion of faith and confidence (the recapitulation of the second subject) can provoke, not calm acquiescence, but a redoubled insecurity and doubt (the coda), none of the remaining movements cover the same ground or offer the same kind of harmonic framework. With respect to D major, the Preludio might be regarded as a clear case of Schoenbergian 'schwebende Tonalität' ('fluctuating: suspended, not yet decided' tonality).[21] The Scherzo and the Romanza differ from the Preludio in that both end in tonal areas which can be regarded as 'tonic' for the entire movement, even if the whole point is that those areas are not delineated before the ending, if at all, with the kind of explicitness common to the classic and romantic traditions. Thus the Scherzo ends on a quiet, understated A which can be interpreted as retrospectively conferring 'A as tonic' status on the movement's early stages, where emphasis shifts between E, A, and D. Similarly, the Romanza's final A major cadences contextualize the movement's opening, where the A major chords sound more like dominants to an unstated D minor than like tonics, and even this dominant quality is weakened by the presence of C major chords. On the one hand, both these movements progress towards final presentations of their goal-tonics; on the other, both can be regarded as exemplifying the

---

[21] See Roy E. Carter's note on the translation of Schoenberg's term in Arnold Schoenberg, *Theory of Harmony*, trans. Roy E. Carter (London: Faber and Faber, 1978), p. 383.

Schoenbergian concept of 'extended tonality', in which 'remote transformations and successions of harmonies' are 'understood as remaining
within the tonality'.[22] 'Extended tonality' in this sense could also apply to
the Passacaglia, not least because the tonality which 'remote transformations and successions' remain within is stated at the beginning with less
ambiguity than in the preceding movements of the work.

These features of difference between the Preludio and what follows
are reinforced if we attempt a hermeneutic interpretation. In the Scherzo
Vaughan Williams builds a structure in which the initially subordinate,
more earth-bound theme (first heard at bar 3.18) gains its greatest independence on its final appearance (from Figure 17) in a structure notable for
what Hugh Ottaway felicitously terms 'organic waywardness'.[23] This
episode involves the interactive development of the movement's two main
thematic types in a tonal context referring to centres (C and E♭) which are
third-related to the ultimately explicit A, and the crisis of the movement is
encapsulated in the way that the aggressive, earth-bound material gains
strength while the otherworldly, meditative polyphony is increasingly submerged. Then, at Figure 21, the tables are suddenly turned as the string
counterpoint rises out of the final splutters of the earth-bound material.
What Mellers calls 'a song of infinite longing'[24] establishes a mood of quiet
rapture within which the Scherzo's soft, dance-like coda is heard. Within
the Fifth Symphony as a whole, the passage marks a decisive turning-point:
a texture more expressive of seraphic calm than grandly confident conviction emerges for the first time, and introduces the expressive state that will
end the work (Example 9.8).

The basic association between C and A which the Scherzo explores is
radically rethought in the Romanza, and from the very start, when the first
two chords present C major and A major as richly spaced major triads.
Once again the composer works with two types of material, the symphony's
earlier dialogues (doubt/confidence in the Preludio, secular/spiritual in
the Scherzo) replaced by a more evenly balanced exploration of what, in
their fundamental manifestations, seem like sorrowing and serene forms of

---

[22] Arnold Schoenberg, *Structural Functions of Harmony*, ed. Leonard Stein, rev.
edn. (London: Ernest Benn, 1969), p. 76.

[23] Ottaway, *Vaughan Williams Symphonies*, p. 61.

[24] Mellers, *Vaughan Williams and the Vision of Albion*, p. 180.

Example 9.8 Scherzo, bb. 21.1–14

metaphysical reflection: that is, the cor anglais melody (bars 7–1.1) and the string polyphony (bars 1.1–1.17) respectively. The disparity between these states provokes a crisis, as if doubt is redoubled when the true nature of the transcendent cannot be agreed upon. There may even be something a little artificial about this crisis, with its tremolandos and rhetorical repetitions

Example 9.9 Romanza, bb. 11.1–12.4

which prefigure the opening of the Sixth Symphony. The outcome is strikingly convincing, however, in that the fully developed, 'serene' material is expanded (from bar 9.6) to embrace what survives of the 'sorrowing' alternative. A basic technical point here – that a contrapuntal texture has more potential for expressive development than 'pure' solo melody – is perhaps more crucial than the harmonic strategy which ends the movement by confirming its ultimate, unambiguous allegiance to A-based harmony (Example 9.9). The final cadences are dangerously saccharine, and could even be interpreted as embodying the kind of spiritual balance and confidence which, in terms of this symphonic design, is premature. Such a form of spirituality can only be confirmed unambiguously after the crisis represented by the first movement has been explicitly confronted and resolved.

A reading of the Passacaglia which remains faithful to this hermeneutic account of the first three movements might comment on the way it builds first to an assertive, triumphalist projection of D major, in which contrasts, seeking to establish a more earthly tone, are kept subordinate. The spiritual crisis, and technical turning-point, are then to be found at bar 8.10, focused in the simple device of switching directly from D major to D minor. It is here that the concern of the Passacaglia to grapple again with the issues of the Preludio is first made clear (compare with bars 15.9–10 of the first movement). The consequence for the Passacaglia is a continuation framed by 'darkening' progressions from F to C (bars 9.6 and 10.10, then bars 13.1 and 13.8), which explicitly oppose subsequent attempts to move by thirds through E♭ (bar 11.10) and F♯ (bar 11.12) to the dominant (bar 12.2). The ultimate consequence of the shift from D major to D minor at bar 8.10 is the literal return of the Preludio's music at bar 13.10, in its most challenging 'D over C' format, within which the shift from F♯ to F♮ is again enacted. The fact that the Preludio material is not unaffected by more recent events – the Passacaglia bass clings on – does not in itself provide conclusive musical grounds for not ending the symphony, like its first movement, in doubt and insecurity. Such an ending, soon to be found in the Sixth Symphony, was no doubt psychologically impossible in wartime. And so the work's most extreme crisis ensures the positive, serene outcome. The point at which the bass moves from C via G to D (bars 15.1–3) and the upper lines change F♮ back into F♯ (Example 9.10) is not in itself at all stable, however, and, simply because there is no return to triumphalism, there may still be some reservations about accepting the ending, unreservedly, as one of 'pure blessedness' in which 'every tension is resolved'.[25]

VI

In eloquent phrases about Vaughan Williams's *Sancta Civitas*, leading to the conclusion that the composer's approach to religious and social experience as 'a necessary duality' had much in common with William Blake's, Wilfrid Mellers observes that 'the piece confronts head-on the issues of private and public responsibility in the modern world, offers no answers, ends on a question mark, and tempers hope with strength'.[26] Mellers similarly interprets *The Pilgrim's Progress* as 'open to be taken in several ways. Fundamentally, it describes a psychological pilgrimage such as we all may, perhaps must, embark on; we may also take it, if so inclined, as a Christian journey to an after-life.' And because the ending of the stage-work can be interpreted, in part, as a 'question mark',

> the ultimate apotheosis of the vision is not here but at the end of the Fifth Symphony. It is as though Vaughan Williams needed the abstraction of instrumental music to realize a vision theatrically inapprehensible. In the opera itself ... Bunyan himself emerges, in front of the curtain, to sing the epilogue: which is noble and heroic, but no longer visionary.[27]

While it might appear from this that the ultimate, paradoxical duality is to 'realize a vision' by way of 'abstraction', Mellers is sure that the ending of the Fifth Symphony 'is not ambivalent'. Bringing Blake and Bunyan together,

---

[25] Ottaway, *Vaughan Williams Symphonies*, p. 40.
[26] Mellers, *Vaughan Williams and the Vision of Albion*, p. 141.
[27] *Ibid.*, p. 130.

Example 9.10 Passacaglia, bb. 14.14–15.3

he refers to Vaughan Williams's 'rediscovery of cadential resolution', and his finding in it 'a gateway to Paradise'.[28] Mellers struggles determinedly to synthesize his response to the music, and the use the composer made of it in the opera, with his belief that 'the New Jerusalem does not, cannot exist, in social reality'. The result is, perhaps intentionally, another paradox, and although Mellers does not make the connection, Vaughan Williams's vision of unreality might be compared with Beethoven's at the end of the Ninth Symphony, a work on which Vaughan Williams's views are well known, and which involved a crucial comparison with Bach.

> It is admittedly harder to write good music which is joyful than that which is sad. It is comparatively easy to be mildly dismal with success. But to my mind, two composers and two only, and they but seldom, have been able to write music which is at the same time serious, profound, and cheerful – Bach in the 'Cum Sancto' of the B minor Mass and Beethoven in the finale of the Choral Symphony. Incidentally, both these movements are in D major.[29]

Feeling obliged to pursue his comparison of Bach and Beethoven, Vaughan Williams concluded that 'Beethoven when he looks into eternity sees clearer and further than Bach; but Bach when he thinks of his very human deity has the richer and warmer consciousness. So on the human side Bach has Beethoven completely beaten.'[30]

On the whole – though exceptions can be proposed – by temperament Vaughan Williams was evidently attracted more by the humanity of a 'richer and warmer consciousness' than by the possibility of using music to see 'clearer and further' into eternity. He would, I suspect, have had little

---

[28] *Ibid.*, p. 186.

[29] R. Vaughan Williams, 'Some Thoughts on Beethoven's Choral Symphony', in *National Music*, p. 88.   [30] *Ibid.*, p. 90.

interest in a music like that of Messiaen, whose *Quartet for the End of Time* (a work roughly contemporary with the Fifth Symphony) ends with a remarkable 'look into eternity' in the movement called 'Louange à l'immortalité de Jésus'. Vaughan Williams, closer to Charles Ives in this respect if no other, is more at home in the real world of the hymn-tune, and never to greater effect than when he recalls the ones he wrote himself, like *Sine nomine* ('For all the saints') in the Preludio's second theme.

The case made against Vaughan Williams in the years since his death has been supported to some extent by convictions that he remained too close to established religion (as well as to folk music) for the good of his work. Michael Tippett, pre-eminently, has shown how to exploit mystical, spiritual states as well as political moralities in ways which owe more to Blake than to Bunyan, and which indeed evoke the latter only to mark out a very different claim. For example, picking up the composer's own acknowledgement that the final spiritual in *A Child of Our Time*, 'Deep River', suggests the river which Christian and Hopeful (in *The Pilgrim's Progress*) have to cross before entering the Celestial City, Ian Kemp observes that 'in this ordeal Christian is encouraged by Hopeful's exhortation: "Be of good cheer. Jesus Christ maketh thee whole." With Tippett the inference is that Jesus Christ can accomplish nothing of the kind.'[31]

Such vigorous secularism was not Vaughan Williams's way, and yet his clear preference for Bach over Beethoven, for the 'human side' rather than the far-seeing look 'into eternity', acts as a warning against simply conflating morality and metaphysics. From a more human perspective, therefore, the peaceful coda of the Fifth Symphony might best be regarded as a representation of satisfying human repose and tranquillity – a Keatsian 'soothest Sleep'. In sleep, the symphony's protagonist dreams up echoes of *Sine nomine*'s Alleluias, and these suggest the sense of security which established religion and practical morality can provide, rather than a deeply mystical vision of the immortality of Jesus, or of some divine purpose operating mysteriously throughout the universe. The result is serious, profound, and – if not exactly cheerful – expressive of deep contentment and fulfilment. If it is still ambiguous, it is because something of the Beethovenian vision coexists with the Bachian humanity – a coexistence

[31] Kemp, *Tippett*, p. 157.

Example 9.11

(a) Beethoven, Symphony No. 9, IV, 'Ode to Joy' theme

(b) Beethoven, Symphony No. 9, II, Trio

(c) Vaughan Williams, Symphony No. 5, counter-theme to Passacaglia bass

the more plausible if we accept Nicholas Cook's reading of the Choral Symphony as 'profoundly ambivalent', not least because it 'proclaims the ideals of universal brotherhood and joy ... but at the same time ... casts doubts upon them'.[32] Cook clearly has a deeper ambivalence in mind than that resulting from the fact that Beethoven was, in Vaughan Williams's phrase, 'a truly religious man, and was therefore not ashamed to place earthly jollity cheek by jowl with deep adoration',[33] and on the face of it it might seem improbable that the English composer should have sought any parallels whatever between his own Symphony in D major and a work about which he had such mixed feelings. Yet when he cites the melody of the Ninth Symphony's 'Trio', describing it as an 'Elysian vision' – 'Did not Gluck use this same type of melody for his Elysian fields?'[34] – it is impossible not to be struck by the degree to which the Fifth Symphony's Passacaglia counter-theme echoes and elaborates the Beethoven (Example 9.11).

In the Fifth Symphony Vaughan Williams may have temporarily

[32] Nicholas Cook, *Beethoven: Symphony No. 9*, Cambridge Music Handbooks (Cambridge: Cambridge University Press, 1993), p. 104.

[33] R. Vaughan Williams, 'Beethoven's Choral Symphony', p. 114.

[34] *Ibid.*, p. 107.

turned his back 'on the more immediate issues of the modern world', as Mellers observed, but, as the technical sections of this essay have aimed to show, his symphonic technique is one which engages modernity with sophistication and resource. It is for this very reason that, despite the 'abstraction of instrumental music' to which Mellers refers, the ending of the work is an 'ultimate apotheosis' from which all traces of a question mark cannot be entirely erased – at least as far as the possible metaphysical connotations of morality are concerned. If not 'profoundly ambivalent' to the extent of Beethoven's Ninth or Tippett's Third (a later twentieth-century work explicitly indebted to the Beethoven), Vaughan Williams's Fifth uses its 'human side' to raise questions about 'eternity' which are by definition unanswerable in terms of human experience. The work can also be appreciated as a structure which takes its flexibly evolving melodies and modally formulated counterpoint and places them in the context of the four-movement symphonic model, not excluding the sonata-form design. The result is the more powerful for not offering a seamless synthesis between its various facets of meaning and form – for observing Elysium with both feet firmly on the ground.

10 The place of the Eighth among Vaughan Williams's symphonies

OLIVER NEIGHBOUR

'On the main point, however, I am not taking your advice. I feel the thing *is* a symphony and it is going to remain one.' Vaughan Williams was writing to Frank Howes,[1] who had attended an early run-through of the Eighth Symphony on the piano in April 1955 and had evidently questioned its symphonic status. Doubts of that kind have more often been raised about its immediate predecessor, the *Sinfonia Antartica*, and Vaughan Williams was probably teasing Howes when he wrote in his programme note for the first performance of the Eighth, 'I understand that some hearers may have their withers wrung by a work being called a symphony whose first movement does not correspond to the usual symphonic form'.[2] Nevertheless, the Eighth clearly differs from the other symphonies in important respects.

It is widely agreed that most of them explore some extra-musical idea. Vague talk of philosophical or spiritual statements is easier to dismiss than the abiding impression that they are in some way present. There is naturally plenty of room for argument about the composer's intentions in any one case: if they could be precisely spelt out there would be no need for the symphony. He himself left a few clues, but they are hard to interpret, no doubt deliberately so. They may take the form of a picturesque title that obscures rather more than it explains, an association with some other work that deals with a specified extra-musical subject, or merely a remark made to a friend. In the Eighth Symphony, however, he could scarcely have made it plainer that no wider conception was intended. Although the four movements most certainly belong together they are so sharply set apart from one another, especially by their instrumentation, that in aggregate they appear

---

[1] Quoted in U. Vaughan Williams, *R.V.W.* , p. 358.
[2] See Kennedy, *Catalogue*, p. 237; Kennedy reproduces the entire programme note, as he does notes by the composer to all the symphonies except the Fifth.

213

to imply nothing beyond themselves. This, for once, is a symphony concerned above all simply with the making of music. Even so, there are signs that it shares underlying affinities with its companions which the composer was not inclined to go into in his few decisive words to Howes. It was typical of him to let simple comprehensive pronouncements cover much that he preferred to leave unspoken.

It would be a mistake to approach Vaughan Williams's symphonies as though he had planned them consciously as a sequence of works with special significance. He did everything he could to counter any such idea in others, and probably in himself too. At first the enormous prestige with which the genre had been invested by the end of the nineteenth century made him hesitate to assay it at all. Not that he lacked ambition. After the successful launch of *Toward the Unknown Region* in 1907 he commented dismissively, 'After all it's only a step and I've got to do something really big sometime'. Two years later he delivered something big in the form of *A Sea Symphony*, 'my best work I believe up to the present'.[3] Whether it was a symphony or not did not trouble him. In a programme note of 1913 he found it convenient to emphasize its symphonic qualities.[4] On the other hand some two years earlier George Butterworth had given the initial impetus for *A London Symphony* by remarking to Vaughan Williams that he ought to write 'a symphony', and 'from that moment the idea of a symphony – a thing which I had always declared I would never attempt – dominated my mind'.[5] One reason for adopting the town and country epithets for the first two orchestral symphonies was no doubt to avoid association with the pretensions that he felt the unadorned symphonic title might imply.

From the composer's point of view the use of keys rather than numbers to distinguish the later symphonies had the same advantages. It continued to leave the ultimately trivial question of the status of *A Sea Symphony* in the air, and to discourage any notion that one work might have

---

[3] Both these quotations are from letters to his cousin Ralph ('Randolph') Wedgwood; see Kennedy, *Works*, p. 400.

[4] Kennedy, *Catalogue*, pp. 53–4.

[5] A.K.B. [Sir Alexander Kaye Butterworth], ed., *George Butterworth 1885–1916* (York, private publication, 1918), pp. 92–3. For a slightly different but not contradictory account of 1950, mentioning very early symphonic essays long since destroyed, see 'A Musical Autobiography', *National Music*, p. 193.

a bearing on another: each spoke only for itself. But the musical world would have none of it, numbering the symphonies from the Fourth onwards as resolutely as the composer refused to do so – at least in public. In private he soon found the numbers handier, like everyone else. By 1951 he could refer to his symphonies up to then as 'my family of 6'.[6] The doubtful legitimacy of the seventh child, the *Sinfonia Antartica*, set up a new stumbling block for his audience. When Gerald Finzi asked him why he had called it a symphony he replied that if he had not, no one would have played it,[7] a shrewd answer that nicely side-stepped every issue. But like *A Sea Symphony* it was undeniably something big, and that may have weighed with him when sometime between the early performances of the Eighth and its publication he was finally, and very reluctantly, persuaded to sanction the numbering.

Yet however obstinately Vaughan Williams resisted the establishment of a set, ordered canon for his symphonic output, by the end of his life his own view of it had changed considerably, as he must have realized. He had always been a composer for whom the thoughts, feelings, and experiences that most deeply concerned him imperatively demanded absorption into music. In early years he looked for texts that reflected them, but as time went on he began to find words inadequate for the purpose, even though he continued to compose important vocal works. Thus the symphonies became the province of certain themes to which he returned with increasing frequency from different points of view and with different emphases, and a group of works which had seemed disparate in the extreme gradually acquired a loose coherence from the enduring preoccupations that inspired them.

To try to give a name to such preoccupations is a dangerous venture, one of which the composer disapproved sharply and with good reason, for the tendency is always to equate or confuse the point of departure with the work to which it gave rise. But while in the nature of things there can never be complete answers, something in the music impels those who write about Vaughan Williams to make the attempt.

---

[6] In a letter to John Barbirolli quoted in Michael Kennedy, *Barbirolli: Conductor Laureate* (London: MacGibbon and Kee, 1971), p. 243.
[7] Information from Howard Ferguson, who had it from Finzi.

Certainly any discussion of the symphonies' underlying kinship must accept the risks. The argument presented here[8] involves all the symphonies: the place of the Eighth obviously cannot be determined without a framework in which to place it. Much of this essay, indeed the greater part of it, will thus be devoted to tracing various recurrent ideas through the other eight symphonies. Only after that will it be possible to turn to the Eighth and consider it in more detail.

*

Through its sheer size and scope *A Sea Symphony* dominates the works of Vaughan Williams's thirties. With its precursor *Toward the Unknown Region* it might be supposed to epitomize his most deeply held beliefs up to that time. It is true that spiritual aspiration in an agnostic context was a fundamental preoccupation not only then but permanently. However, Whitman's unfocused optimism, though it clearly fired his imagination and held it during the long haul of the symphony's composition, had no deep root in his outlook on life. The euphoria was never to return, nor indeed was hope itself with the same ring of conviction. In his long support for the ideal of international federalism[9] he hoped steadfastly to see 'a pennant universal' hoisted above the 'separate flags of nations'; but in his music hope, the cardinal virtue that he found most elusive, answered his calls to service at best diffidently: at the end of *Dona nobis pacem* the assertion that 'Nation shall not lift up a sword against nation' subsides into hesitant prayer, and the last of the six wartime Choral Songs to words by Shelley closes almost disconcertingly, with hope in any positive form bowing out.

A poet who stood closer than Whitman[10] to Vaughan Williams was Matthew Arnold. As early as April 1899 the composer completed a setting of

---

8   It will inevitably entail overlap with previous writings on the composer, for instance those of Michael Kennedy and Hugh Ottaway.

9   U. Vaughan Williams, *R.V.W.*, pp. 234, 317, 361; Kennedy, *Works*, p. 324; R. Vaughan Williams, *National Music*, pp. 71, 155.

10   When Michael Kennedy asked Vaughan Williams in the last month of his life what he felt about Whitman, he replied 'I've never got over him, I'm glad to say' (*Works*, p. 100). But his words imply that he understood well enough how one might get over him, and he complained to Ursula Vaughan Williams that Whitman 'was too fond of the smell of his own armpits'.

Dover Beach. It did not satisfy him and has not survived.[11] Whether he shared all Arnold's concerns may be doubted: he probably viewed the retreat of the 'Sea of Faith' with greater equanimity, and did not find the world quite so joyless as Arnold claims to in his famous conclusion. But the last three lines strike a note that was to echo powerfully through Vaughan Williams's music to the end:

> Ah, love, let us be true
> To one another! for the world ...
> Hath ... neither joy, nor love, nor light,
> Nor certitude, nor peace, nor help for pain;
> And we are here as on a darkling plain
> Swept with confused alarms of struggle and flight,
> Where ignorant armies clash by night.

What can only be felt as anguish at human conflict and confusion erupts violently at key points in *A London Symphony* and increases its hold right through to the equivocal resolution of the Epilogue. As a pervasive component in the sum of experience explored in Vaughan Williams's symphonies it has arrived to stay. The meaning that the dissonant outburst at the beginning of the first-movement allegro will eventually acquire for the listener is not clear at first. It is at odds with much else in the movement, which was for Albert Coates,[12] along with 'something fiercer, something inexorable', 'full of that mixture of good humour, animal spirits, and sentimentality that is so characteristic of London'. Vaughan Williams embraces these things

[11] The existence of the work is recorded in a contemporary letter of Adeline Vaughan Williams, quoted in U. Vaughan Williams, *R.V.W.*, p. 57. The forces used are unknown. On more oblique connections between Arnold and Vaughan Williams, and the development of the composer's spiritual outlook, see Byron Adams's essay in the present volume.

[12] In a programme note of which the composer commented in a letter, now in the New York Public Library, to Ray Henderson of 30 March 1923: 'Mr Coates' notes on my "London Symphony" were unauthorized &, to my view, misleading'. However, at the end of his life he seems to have remembered it more favourably. Michael Kennedy wrote to the present writer on 7 January 1994: 'My recollection of VW's sanction of the Coates note is that when I was writing one myself in 1957 (?) he referred me to the Coates as a good one, so I presume he approved it'. The note is printed in L. Biancolli and W. S. Mann, eds., *The Analytical Concert Guide* (London: Cassell & Co., 1957), pp. 706–10.

without irony. In an essay written in 1912,[13] during the composition of the symphony, he described his own work in progress when he advised young English composers to find the raw material of their works in the varied forms of popular music that they heard all about them. He does not say how the raw material should be treated. In his programme notes to the symphony[14] he emphasizes that the occasional descriptive touches are incidental to the music, which is 'self-expressive'. But when in the first movement the swash-buckling band music at the end of the exposition stops in its tracks as the first subject returns with redoubled vehemence, questions impose themselves. Is the composer repudiating vulgarity? No, he goes along with it. Does he regret the limitations it may entail? Possibly, but the reaction here is out of all proportion to a qualification of that kind. Does he fear that the stability that permits a sense of well-being may all too easily crumble? Yes, for it is already happening: after the carefree mouth-organ in the trio of the scherzo has receded again into the sounds of the night, sighs in the orchestra prepare for the *appassionato* opening of the finale, a movement in which the listener cannot miss the pain and turmoil, or their significance for the work as a whole.[15]

The composer's remark 'For actual coda see end of Wells' *Tono-Bungay*' has attracted a good deal of comment. It has been shown that the connections between the larger concerns of the novel and the symphony encompass much more than what may be inferred from their endings.[16] Yet

---

[13] 'Who Wants the English Composer?' *The RCM Magazine*, 9/1 (1912), pp. 13–14; also in Hubert Foss, *Ralph Vaughan Williams: A Study* (London: Harrap, 1950), p. 200.

[14] He wrote two programme notes, in 1920 and 1925. Both are given in Kennedy, *Catalogue*, pp. 76–7.

[15] One of a number of passages in which Albert Coates (see n. 12) heard a reflection of the darker side of London life occurs in the middle section of the slow movement, before the *largamente* climax. There is a detail here that appears to support him. At three points mysterious detached chords are heard on harp and lower strings; the harmony on the third occasion may be described as the notes of the whole-tone scale lacking the third and sixth degrees. In the *Sinfonia Antartica* the death knell that sounds in the first, fourth, and fifth movements is accompanied by a transposition of the same harmony, given out by detached chords similarly, if more heavily, orchestrated.

[16] Kennedy, *Works*, pp. 139–40; Anthony Arblaster, '"A London Symphony" and "Tono-Bungay"', *Tempo*, 163 (1987), pp. 21–5; Alain Frogley, 'H. G. Wells and Vaughan Williams's *A London Symphony*: Politics and Culture in Fin-de-siècle England', in C. Banks, A. Searle, and M. Turner, eds., *Sundry Sorts of Music Books* (London: British Library, 1993), pp. 299–308.

Wells's concluding image of the river leaving behind the life and history lived upon land, and merging with the open sea, had a special importance for Vaughan Williams, for it draws on an established literary tradition to which he had long been attracted. He had completed in the same year as his *Dover Beach* (1899) a setting of Swinburne's *The Garden of Proserpine*, a dozen scarcely heart-felt stanzas about the land of the dead ending with 'sleep eternal in an eternal night'.[17] The penultimate stanza uses the river image:

> From too much love of living,
> > From hope and fear set free,
> We thank with brief thanksgiving
> > Whatever gods may be
> That no life lives for ever;
> That dead men rise up never;
> That even the weariest river
> > Winds somewhere safe to sea.

About 1908 Vaughan Williams drafted a setting of Arnold's poem *The Future*.[18] 'Man', which through most of the poem means the individual, is born at some point on the river of Time. This flows from the mountains, where primitive tribes knew it, down to the plain of the present time, where it is bordered by cities, and out to the sea of the future; here 'man' seems to become mankind. The poem steers a course between the pessimism of Swinburne and the optimism of Whitman's exhortation 'O farther sail' at the end of *A Sea Symphony*, and avoids the glibness of either. Excerpts will show its bearing on *Tono-Bungay* and *A London Symphony*:

> This tract which the river of Time
> Now flows through with us, is the plain.
> Gone is the calm of its earlier shore.
> Border'd by cities and hoarse
> With a thousand cries is its stream ...

[17] Kennedy, *Catalogue*, pp. 8–9. The Swinburne poem comes from the notorious first series of *Poems and Ballads* (1866).

[18] The date is Michael Kennedy's suggestion (*Catalogue*, p. 45). The manuscript takes the form of a continuity draft. It was originally in two books, but the second is lost. Vaughan Williams omitted the fifth and sixth sections of the poem ('What girl' and 'What bard'). Book 1 ends at 'In a blacker, incessanter line'.

> And we say that repose has fled
> For ever the course of the river of Time.
> That cities will crowd to its edge
> In a blacker, incessanter line;
> That the din will be more on its banks ...

Then, near the end:

> And the width of the waters, the hush
> Of the grey expanse where he floats,
> Freshening its current and spotted with foam
> As it draws to the Ocean, may strike
> Peace to the soul of the man on its breast ...

In both Arnold and Wells night falls as the shores widen. Wells's loquacious chief protagonist too steers his destroyer 'into the great spaces of the future', though he hopes for more than Arnold's 'peace to the soul'. Wells is probably only partly ironic in the stumbling and repetitious phrases he gives him as peroration:

> This is the note I have tried to emphasize ... a note of crumbling and confusion ... But through the confusion sounds another note ... Sometimes I call this reality Science, sometimes I call it Truth. But it is something we draw by pain and effort out of the heart of life, that we disentangle and make clear. Other men serve it, I know, in art, in literature, in social invention ... I see it always as austerity, as beauty ... I do not know what it is, this something, except that it is supreme.

And so on. Vaughan Williams would not have wished to reject such a quest, but his symphony ends differently, reaching out towards Arnold's peace yet haunted by the echo of unresolved conflicts.

What Victorian poets and their heirs shared in their river and ocean symbolism was the desire to distance themselves from the confusions of the new industrial world and their own confusion in the face of it. Escapist or reformist, each in his own way needed an agnostic stand-point from which to regain perspective. After social unrest had been temporarily submerged in the almost unimaginably greater conflict of 1914–18, the need to stand back in order to reach any sort of comprehension or acceptance of events increased proportionately. Distancing is at the heart of Vaughan Williams's *A Pastoral Symphony*, completed in 1921. The composer begins his brief programme note for the first performance with a necessary word of

220

warning to the unprepared listener: 'The mood of the Symphony is, as its title suggests, almost entirely quiet and contemplative'. About the object or the mood of the contemplation he says nothing, nor does he take the precaution of adding, as he had in describing *A London Symphony*, that apparently descriptive elements should not be mistaken for the principal matter in hand. Unannotated, the essence of the work seems to lie in a vision of eternity, not, of course, the fancied eternal values of some lost pastoral age, but an impassive eternity which takes no account of the presence or passing of landscapes with figures. In 1938, however, Vaughan Williams did supply some annotation, though privately:[19] 'It's really war-time music – a great deal of it incubated when I used to go up night after night with the ambulance waggon at Ecoives and we went up a steep hill and there was a wonderful Corot-like landscape in the sunset – it's not really lambkins frisking at all as most people take for granted'. That is both under- and overstated: understated because Vaughan Williams, like the vast majority of those who returned from France, never spoke of his experiences of war[20] and here leaves the contrast between the landscape and what awaited the nightly waggon at its destination to be imagined; overstated because at this early stage his only possible musical response to war was to distance its reality to the point where all human life dissolves and leaves not a rack behind. He could only hope with Whitman, in words that he set in 1936[21] when war was once again threatening, 'that war and all its deeds of carnage must in time be utterly lost, That the hands of the sisters Death and Night incessantly, softly, wash again and ever again this soiled world'.

Between 1918 and 1920, while working on *A Pastoral Symphony*, Vaughan Williams made extensive cuts and revisions in *A London*

---

[19] Quoted in U. Vaughan Williams, *R.V.W.*, p. 121.
[20] Information from Ursula Vaughan Williams.
[21] In 'Reconciliation', the third movement of *Dona nobis pacem*. Whitman's poem anticipates the theme of Wilfred Owen's 'Strange Meeting', which Britten included in his *War Requiem* just before the 'In paradisum'. Britten had always disliked Vaughan Williams's music, but when the older composer died he wrote movingly of their shared beliefs (Kennedy, *Works*, p. 346). That the 'In paradisum' may be felt, perhaps uniquely in Britten's mature music, to carry a suggestion of Vaughan Williams about it may be due to one of those (often short-lived) reconciliations that death is apt to induce in the mind of the survivor.

Symphony, much to its advantage. In the process the scherzo lost a dissonant second trio and a more elaborate preparation for the anguished first
subject of the finale, while this was itself shortened by a couple of bars and a
big development of it (nearly twenty bars) cut entirely. His success in
increasing the impact of the work by severely pruning and reshaping some
of its most dramatic material must surely owe something to his post-war
aversion to overt protest and tragic gesture as inadequate to the untold
suffering that war had brought. Yet the stoicism that kept the dark under-
currents of *A Pastoral Symphony* for the most part a little below the surface
could not hold indefinitely. The reaction came in the Fourth Symphony,
begun a decade later. The violent opening might appear to derive from the
finale of *A London Symphony* by way of Holst's *Mars*. However, the composer claimed to have cribbed it deliberately from Beethoven's Ninth,[22] an
association that underlines the bleakness of his conception. For whereas
Beethoven is able to dismiss his cacophony and turn to a vision of the brotherhood of man, Vaughan Williams's own symphony ends where it began.
Moreover the transition from the scherzo to the finale, which recalls that in
Beethoven's Fifth, bursts into a parodistic instead of a triumphal march.

  More than once in the next few years Vaughan Williams professed
some coolness towards this bitter work.[23] One reason appears in his essay on
Beethoven's Ninth Symphony,[24] written in 1939–40 when his own Fifth
Symphony was under way: 'Tovey describes the first movement as tragedy,
the second – scherzo – as satiric drama. To my mind these movements transcend the human limitations of tragedy, satire, or drama and are direct
visions of what lies beyond them.' The last thing he had tried to do in the
Fourth was to transcend tragedy or satire. But now, for the moment disen-

---

[22] 'A Musical Autobiography', *National Music*, p. 190. Tippett too composed a
  symphony in response to Beethoven's Ninth: his Third. He may have had the
  Vaughan Williams in mind as well. Both finales contain a soft *lento* episode for
  muted strings sharply contrasted with its surroundings. Tippett's follows the
  first of his three direct quotations of the opening outburst from Beethoven's
  finale (and also the third, but overlaid with a voice part). The Vaughan Williams
  passage forms part of the symphonic structure, but the Tippett, which is slightly
  reminiscent of it, seems to function purely as a dramatic contrast, reinforcing
  the impression of a perhaps conscious reference comparable to the Beethoven
  quotation.   [23] Kennedy, *Works*, pp. 247, 402.

[24] 'Some Thoughts on Beethoven's Choral Symphony', *National Music*, p. 90.

chanted with a mode of expression perhaps too near to despair for his own approval, he fixed his sights on 'what lies beyond them'. Such language is far from untypical. In an essay of 1920, for instance, he writes:

> Before going any further may we take it that the object of art is to obtain a partial revelation of that which is beyond human senses and human faculties – of that, in fact, which is spiritual? And that the means which we employ to induce this revelation are those very senses and faculties themselves? The human, visible, audible and intelligible media which artists (of all kinds) use, are symbols not of other visible and audible things but of what lies beyond sense and knowledge.[25]

Here Vaughan Williams makes a general statement about the nature of art according to which the Fourth and Fifth Symphonies would have equal claims to be considered revelatory, and as an agnostic he leaves it open whether human faculties apprehend or project spirituality. But when taking issue with Tovey he uses the phrase 'what lies beyond' more narrowly.

The Fifth Symphony embodies his most sustained and single-minded attempt to express what he found it natural to call spirituality in this narrower sense. Shadows there most certainly are, for all his more important works contain tensions between light and dark, but he admits no major distractions. Naturally the character of this spirituality cannot be precisely defined. There is no close link with Christianity, although Vaughan Williams often used Christian symbolism because it was to hand and well understood by his audience. At times, perhaps, he hoped for the existence of some independent higher reality: the quotation from Plato's *Phaedo* that prefaces *Sancta Civitas* allows doubt about the soul's future state but not about its survival (though he often seems to hold the contrary belief, and more firmly). But in the then unfinished opera *The Pilgrim's Progress*, from which some of the material of the Fifth Symphony derives, Bunyan's Christian becomes an undenominational Pilgrim, and any progress present in the symphony is not Pilgrim's: in his contemporary Beethoven essay[26] the composer remarks that abstract music can 'portray the very depth of the soul, but it does not do so on the lines of a story, but

---

[25] 'The Letter and the Spirit', *Music and Letters*, 1 (1920), p. 88; also *National Music*, p. 122 (slightly revised).

[26] *National Music*, p. 97. For a more detailed discussion of the nature of meaning in the Fifth see Arnold Whittall's essay in the present volume.

rather on those of a building'. The symphony does not depict a journey to the Celestial City, but bravely attempts to 'stretch out to the ultimate realities'.[27] Insight into these may derive from many things. The style of the symphony is most extensively prefigured in the last section of *Flos Campi*. The composer may well have been aware of the connection, for in a letter of 1951[28] he wrote: 'Human love has always been taken as a symbol of man's relationship to divine things. *The Song of Solomon* has been treated in all the churches as a symbol of the relationship of God to man'.

In each symphony up to this point Vaughan Williams arrives at a quite different perception of the human condition, though his concentration on a deeply felt interpretation is never too closely circumscribed. In the later symphonies, however, there is a marked change. The emphasis becomes less unified: viewpoints shift between one movement and the next. There is no precedent for the extreme contrast in the Sixth Symphony between the turbulence of the first three movements and the protracted *pianissimo* Epilogue. Early commentators who angered the composer by reading into this work, composed in 1944–7, an image of war and its devastation were not entirely wrong, as a conversation remembered by Howard Ferguson shows.[29] 'The occasion was at one of those run-throughs at Maida Vale No. 1 ... I said to him at the end of No. 6, "That's a pretty grim piece"; to which he replied, "*I* call it The Big Three." And that was the end of that.' It was a typically oblique statement in which the federalist was made to stand in for the composer. Vaughan Williams's dismay at the great powers' division of the post-war world into zones of influence as a solution to its troubles was certainly not the subject of his symphony. To hint otherwise was to admit by substitution that war was at least involved in it. But it was no more a depiction of war than was *A Pastoral Symphony*. In fact the Pastoral and Sixth symphonies resemble each other closely in their shared response to the wars they followed (in the case of the Sixth no doubt to both wars). The conflicts of the earlier movements of the Sixth are those of the Fourth and of

---

[27] 'A Musical Autobiography', *National Music*, p. 189.

[28] Kennedy, *Works*, p. 316.

[29] Letter of 4 January 1994 to the present writer. Studio No. 1 at Maida Vale, London, was where the BBC Symphony Orchestra rehearsed and regularly broadcast. The Big Three were Churchill, Roosevelt, and Stalin, who met at the Yalta Conference in February 1945 to plan the final stages of the war and the occupation of Germany after her surrender.

Beethoven's Ninth; the Epilogue represents not the aftermath of the atomic bomb but the oblivion that ultimately receives all humanity. As the composer himself wrote in 1956,[30] 'I think we can get in words nearest to the substance of my last movement in "We are such stuff as dreams are made on, and our little life is rounded by a sleep"'.

If Vaughan Williams had been born half a century later he might have advertised his *Sinfonia Antartica* as an anti-symphony. In refashioning his music for the film *Scott of the Antarctic* so as to turn story into building he largely rejected symphonic development in favour of blocks of material which might relate to one another in various ways: through near-identity, thematic transformation, or more general characteristics. Such correspondences occur as often between movements as within them, so that the central idea of man's will to challenge the immutability of his lot, here symbolized by nature, and his inevitable defeat, is implicit throughout, even though the opposition comes to the fore only at certain points. The human and the inanimate are sharply distinguished in the music, and for that reason there are limits to the obvious affinities between its desolate conclusion and that of the Sixth Symphony.

It is the Ninth Symphony to which the Sixth may be more usefully compared. This work contains programmatic elements which the composer was reluctant to disclose, no doubt because of his habitual fear that cause would be mistaken for effect. There is enough annotation in the manuscripts for the general shape of the underlying plan to be glimpsed,[31] and some knowledge of it is helpful to the listener. The first movement was originally called 'Wessex Prelude', a phrase clearly intended to suggest Hardy's view of human destiny rather than a mere locality. The second movement is modelled rather closely on the arrest and execution of the heroine of *Tess of the D'Urbervilles*. Although it bears no musical relation to its opposite number in the Sixth Symphony, both evoke the working of blind, hostile forces. Whereas heavy brass succeed in exorcizing the persistent, capering

---

[30] Kennedy, *Works*, p. 302; the slip 'by a sleep' instead of 'with a sleep' is in the original letter.

[31] Complete list in Alain Frogley, 'Vaughan Williams and Thomas Hardy: "Tess" and the Slow Movement of the Ninth Symphony', *Music and Letters*, 68 (1987), pp. 42–59. This essay is the source for the programme of the slow movement given here.

dance rhythms in the first movement of the Sixth, in the second movement the full orchestra is powerless to destroy the menace of the reiterated trumpet B♭s.[32] In the second movement of the Ninth the mercilessness of the gods who kill Tess for sport is represented by sonorities of unyielding harshness. The big phantasmagoric scherzos that follow resemble one another not only in character but in their dramatic placing. For the listener conscious of the parallel this makes the decisive divergence of the finales all the more striking. It is the direction taken by the Sixth that stays closer to Hardy: it has been said that 'after the end of the first movement the only human positives are endurance and acceptance'.[33]

The genesis of the finale of the Ninth may go back as far as July 1938. After a fallow period Vaughan Williams had begun work on the Fifth Symphony. Needing solitude for reflection he spent a few days walking on the Wiltshire downs and one day reached Salisbury.

> He arrived hot and dusty and had dinner, then about nine he went to the Close and found Walter Alcock at home. ... It was quite late when he asked if Ralph would like to hear the organ in the cathedral. He played Bach while Ralph listened in the dark empty building.[34]

The sense of closeness across the centuries with builders and a musician who had stretched out to the ultimate realities would have appealed to him particularly strongly at the time of the Fifth, but the experience is reflected more closely still in the Ninth. The first part of the finale, more relaxed but scarcely less sombre than the opening movement, is entitled 'Landscape' in one manuscript.[35] At the end a 'steeple tune' comes into view and marks the transition to the second part, the main theme of which is labelled 'Introibo

---

[32] The composer wanted their 'fierce quality' brought out; see Kennedy, *Barbirolli: Conductor Laureate*, pp. 240–1.

[33] Hugh Ottaway, *Vaughan Williams Symphonies*, BBC Music Guides (London: British Broadcasting Corporation, 1972), p. 46.

[34] U. Vaughan Williams, *R.V.W.*, pp. 222–3. See also p. 396 for a repetition of the experience in Westminster Abbey in the summer of 1958, after the symphony had been completed and performed.

[35] The title 'Landscape' is found four times on drafts or scores of the slow movement, in two cases replaced by 'Pastoral'. Neither title is remotely appropriate to the real programme of the movement, which they seem designed to conceal; they were very sensibly dropped. On the other hand the finale must surely open in a landscape through which the cathedral is gradually approached.

ad altare Dei'. A few paces inside the cathedral a suggestion that the 'beyond' of the Fifth Symphony may be in store quickly evaporates. Bach the contrapuntist is present, though scarcely more so than in the troubled first movement,[36] echoes of which soon invade the church and extend through to the impressive close. This, unlike its first movement model, is in the major and throws at least a shaft of light. The world may be Hardy's world, but the human capacity to aspire belongs there too, whatever it may betoken.

*

In the interpretation of Vaughan Williams's symphonies offered here three themes predominate: near-despair at the human condition,[37] the search for stoicism in its contemplation (in contrast to the wish once expressed by Hardy – and Britten – for the reaffirmation of nescience), and a counterbalancing belief in things of the spirit. Such a pared-down formulation of the symphonies' essential content may seem to bypass much of their richness, but it may also help to define the quality most often attributed to them, their humanity. Vaughan Williams's starting-point is in life itself. His experience of it leads him on to ultimate questions of existence and humanity's place in it, but outer space for its own sake does not interest him. In the *Sinfonia Antartica*, where insensate nature dwarfs human thought and feeling almost to the point of insignificance, the opening and penultimate paragraphs of the whole work occupy a special place. Though the source for much of the heroic music, they stand outside the struggle. They appear to ponder the essence of heroism: 'der Dichter spricht'. In other symphonies, however, the composer speaks with the same intensity from the heart of the conflict as from beyond it. This breadth of human reference is all the more telling because the focus is never on himself.

Such largeness of vision is absent from the Eighth Symphony taken as a whole. Yet in general character it stands nearer to the composer's usual

---

[36] In his programme note for the first performance Vaughan Williams said that the first theme 'occurred to the composer after playing some of the organ part of the opening of Bach's St Matthew Passion'.

[37] 'Yet will I not despair: Despair I will not.' Vaughan Williams placed Arnold's words (from *Thyrsis*) near the end of his *Oxford Elegy*. They refer to the struggle to keep faith with long-held ideals, but the composer may be expressing a more general determination too. (The work ends with one of his special cadences: compare 'this soiled world' in *Dona nobis pacem*, or 'hoping it might be so' in *Hodie*.)

symphonic manner than to his instrumental works in other genres, and despite its reputation as a lighter piece its tone is on balance decidedly serious. In itself it does not require elucidation as the Ninth perhaps does: questions arise only when it is compared with the rest of the canon. Such questions are none the less interesting, and certain musical details suggest possible answers to them.

For a start, the composer remarks in his programme note for the first performance that the first seven bars of the final Toccata constitute 'a short, rather sinister exordium'.[38] The movement is in 3/4 and D major, which together invariably signal one of his pieces in the heroic mould, such as the Galliard to which the Sons of the Morning in *Job* eject Satan from heaven, or Bunyan's hymn 'Who would true valour see' in Act II of *The Pilgrim's Progress*. In neither of these is D major seriously challenged, indeed in musical terms the Sons of the Morning may be felt to have rather an easy ride. But throughout the clangorous course of the Toccata the Neapolitan implications of the exordium are at war with the tonic. A slight anticipation of this is heard in the B♭s punctuating the Bunyan hymn and warning of dangers to come. However, it is to the Galliard that the ritornello of the Toccata is related. Example 10.1, which gives only melodies and basses, shows the main connections; Example 10.1a represents the Galliard and Example 10.1b the Toccata. In addition, the high F#–E–D descent in Example 10.1a occurs, though with altered rhythm, in the expanded version of Example 10.1b that follows a few bars later. Figure x is used in the bass of the ritornello only in this first fully harmonized statement, almost as though the composer wanted to include it for his private satisfaction.

At the first American performance Paul Henry Lang noticed something else. In his first impressions, printed next morning,[39] he wrote of the Cavatina, 'As the cellos started it was hard to be sure whether the composer was meditating or pulling our leg: the opening phrase is an exact copy –

---

[38] He also describes the symphony as ending with a reference to 'the sinister exordium'. But when the note was reprinted, 'by his kind permission' and almost unchanged, for the first London performance twelve days later, the word 'sinister' had vanished from both passages. It looks as though he had argued that it was no good telling people that something was sinister if they did not hear it like that, and had rather typically regretted saying too much.

[39] *New York Herald Tribune*, 9 October 1956.

228

Example 10.1 Comparison of themes from Galliard in *Job* and the final Toccata in Symphony No. 8

though rhythmically disguised – of the famous Passion chorale "O sacred Head"'. This elicited the following letter from the composer:[40]

> I have been sent your notice of my eighth symphony in which you suggest that the opening of the slow movement was taken from the Passion Chorale. This is to a certain extent true: I was thinking about the slow movement and how I wanted a cello tune, an[d] it suddenly occur[r]ed to me how lovely that chorale would sound on the cellos, so, as far as I can remember, without deliberately adopting it, the two themes got mixed up in my mind, with the result you know. I am quite unrepentant!

Example 10.2a shows the opening of the chorale with that of the Cavatina, Example 10.2b its close with a phrase used several times in the middle section of the Cavatina and again at the very end. Thus the last two movements of the symphony suggest respectively an elegy, rather than a cavatina, and the idea of courage in the face of adversity. It seems reasonable to ask whether they might point to a train of thought running right through the work.

---

[40] Dated 18 October 1956. The letter is now in the Butler Library, Columbia University, New York.

Example 10.2 Comparison of Cavatina from Symphony No. 8 and the
Passion chorale 'O Sacred Head'

At the beginning of the first movement the flute melody and the use
of vibraphone and celesta in the accompaniment recall features of two passages in the *Sinfonia Antartica*. In the Prelude of the earlier work vibraphone and celesta combine in an ensemble depicting the shimmer and
glitter of the frozen landscape. The lonely flute melody makes a similar
effect to the woodwind solos in the antarctic Intermezzo. This fragile movement bears an inscription about love, and is based on music for the film
associated with the wives of Wilson and Scott and the death of Oates. Its
position in the shadow of massive evocations of the glacial wilderness
seems to deny any permanence to human love and altruism. In the Eighth
nothing threatens to overwhelm the flute tune or the brief main motif that
anticipates it, but the accompaniment places them in a cold climate. Had
they any special significance for the composer? A brief digression may
throw light on the matter.

Few who attended Remembrance Sunday services between the wars
are likely to forget those dreadful occasions. The various organizations
concerned, each in their uniforms and behind their own banners, would
assemble at the local war memorial and march in procession to the church.
At one point during the service the Last Post would be sounded outside. In

any community with a sedentary population the toll taken of each family had often been appalling. Memories of the dead were still fresh for the women and the surviving male relations who came to hear the long lists of names read out from the roll of honour. It was a deeply emotional ritual and a necessary one for the bereaved, who included almost everyone present. One hymn had become a fixture. Though published in 1917 with the title *The Supreme Sacrifice* it is better known by its first line, 'O valiant hearts, who to your glory came'.[41] The original tune, late Victorian in flavour and undeniably memorable, appealed strongly to the taste of the congregations, who made the most of it with heavy vibrato and portamentos. It was torture because the usual relief from embarrassment, inner laughter, was out of the question. When in 1925 the hymn book *Songs of Praise* appeared, the editors knew that the hymn must be included. It was re-christened 'Commemoration', and two verses were judiciously marked as candidates for omission. Vaughan Williams rejected the tune outright, and asked Holst to write a new one. This he did, providing four-part and unison versions under the title 'Valiant Hearts'. Vaughan Williams adapted a traditional melody as a simpler alternative, calling it 'Valor'.[42] Predictably neither tune supplanted the original. Holst's is given in Example 10.3a.

It will be seen that the very important opening motif of the symphony (Example 10.3b) coincides with Holst's main idea;[43] the difference of mode is defined solely by the harmony. The phrase occurs at Holst's pitch only once in the symphony, at the beginning of the flute tune that first develops it (bar 9). As with the single bass reference to the Galliard in the Toccata (Example 10.1b), it looks as though Vaughan Williams worked it in simply because he wanted to include it; that, at least, is how it may appear if it is accepted that four notes in the same rhythm can establish a connection at all. In fact the circumstantial evidence for this seems strong. Holst's phrase is associated with self-sacrifice and, like the Toccata, with valour. It is hard

---

[41] John S. Arkwright wrote the words, Charles Harris the music.

[42] The hymn was No. 163 in the 1925 edition of *Songs of Praise*. It became No. 293 in the revised and enlarged edition of 1932; no changes were made in words or music.

[43] After this article had been submitted Alan Beechey drew attention to the correspondence between these two phrases in the *Journal of the RVW Society*, 2 (1995), p. 7.

Example 10.3 Comparison of Holst's 'Valiant hearts' and opening motif of Symphony No. 8

to believe that its appearance in an antarctic environment that Vaughan Williams had previously set in opposition to these very qualities can be fortuitous. His mind evidently continued to run on the same virtues, but now particularly as he had known them in the still undispelled horror of the 1914–18 war. The origins of Holst's tune make this connection clear enough; the passionate outburst that follows the chilly first paragraph, the cheerful swagger and hard-bitten humour of the minor-key Scherzo alla marcia, and the elegy and strife of the later movements all fit in with it and help to confirm it.

Since the background to the symphony is decipherable only with the aid of external evidence, its contribution to the finished work cannot be pinned down at all closely. Moreover, such evidence is unlikely to give a complete picture: other human attributes may have played their part, for instance the wider range of love fleetingly alluded to in the *Sinfonia Antartica*. Yet it seems permissible to hear the Eighth Symphony as placing at the centre the human sphere which its predecessor had quite exceptionally separated from the rest of existence. And this gives the key to its own position. Humanity is not seen here in its relation to some wider theme: to the confusion and conflict that it brings upon itself (as in the *London*, Fourth, Sixth, and Ninth symphonies), or to eternity (the *Pastoral*, Sixth and, in simpler terms, *Antartica*), or to its spiritual potential (the *Sea*, Fifth, Ninth). No doubt all these things are present in some measure, but they remain subsidiary. The Eighth presents only one half of the kind of equation found in the other symphonies, even though it is the half common to all. The shift of emphasis affects the character of the music itself. Invoking now extinct representatives of the human race, Vaughan Williams once wrote:[44]

> The wildest howl of the savage, or the most careless whistling of the errand boy is nothing else than an attempt to reach into the infinite, which attempt we call art. And it seems to me that for this reason music is able to grow out of our ordinary life in a way that no other art can.

For him music was inseparable from its human source, and from human aspiration; in staying close to the source the Eighth Symphony reflects the spontaneity of humanity's music-making and takes on a rather different aspect from its siblings in the family of nine. But its ties with them could scarcely be stronger.

[44] *National Music,* p. 63.

Index of Vaughan Williams's works cited

Categories are based on those used in Kennedy, *Catalogue*, Index of Works.
U = unpublished.

Index of names

Printed in the United States
124781LV00001B/209/P